HAU

MERIDIAN

Crossing Aesthetics

Werner Hamacher

Editor

Stanford
University
Press

—————————

Stanford
California
2017

HAUNTING HISTORY

For a Deconstructive Approach to the Past

Ethan Kleinberg

Stanford University Press
Stanford, California

© 2017 by the Board of Trustees of the
Leland Stanford Junior University. All rights reserved.

Printed in the United States of America
on acid-free, archival-quality paper

Library of Congress Cataloging-in-Publication Data

Names: Kleinberg, Ethan, 1967– author.
Title: Haunting history : for a deconstructive
approach to the past / Ethan Kleinberg.
Other titles: Meridian (Stanford, Calif.)
Description: Stanford, California :
Stanford University Press, 2017. |
Series: Meridian: crossing aesthetics |
Includes bibliographical references and index.
Identifiers: LCCN 2016057432|
ISBN 9781503602373 (cloth : alk. paper) |
ISBN 9781503603387 (pbk. : alk. paper) |
ISBN 9781503603424 (e-book)
Subjects: LCSH: History—Philosophy. |
History—Methodology. | Historiography. | Deconstruction.
Classification: LCC D16.8 .K495 2017 | DDC 901—dc23
LC record available at https://lccn.loc.gov/2016057432

Contents

Acknowledgments

The completion of this manuscript was facilitated by grants from the Colonel Return Jonathan Meigs Fund, the École des hautes études en sciences sociales, and support from Wesleyan University. I also want to thank Berber Bevernage and the International Network for the Theory of History for inviting me to present a plenary address that eventually became Chapter 4. I benefited enormously from conversations and support from my colleagues in the College of Letters and the History Department at Wesleyan, as well as the faculty, students, and postdoctoral fellows at our Center for the Humanities. I couldn't have completed the book without the help of Erinn Savage. I owe a special debt to my colleagues at *History and Theory*: Brian Fay, Philip Pomper, William Vijay Pinch, Richard Vann, Laura Stark, Matthew Specter, Julie Perkins, and especially David Gary Shaw. Carolyn Dean, Peter Gordon, Nitzan Lebovic, Jeffery Andrew Barash, Adam Tooze, Judith Surkis, Sandrine Sanos, Martin Hägglund, Hans-Ulrich Gumbrecht, Berel Lang, Frank Ankersmit, Jörn Rüsen, Eelco Runia, Allan Megill, Gabrielle Spiegel, and Michael Roth all offered excellent counsel, challenges, and advice. Special thanks are in order to Dominick LaCapra and Hayden White for their inspiration and guidance. Werner Hamacher challenged me to think more carefully and more adventurously throughout this project, and I cannot thank him enough for the time and care he gave to the manuscript. I also owe a huge debt of gratitude to Emily-Jane Cohen and the editorial staff at Stanford University Press, as well as the anonymous readers.

Last, I want to express my love and gratitude to my friends and family. My daughters Lili and Noa give me inspiration every day and the love of my life, Tracy, fills me with energy and joy. I dedicate this book to my mother and father, Irene and Marvin Kleinberg. They instilled in me a love of learning and intellectual curiosity for which I am forever grateful. This book is for both of you.

HAUNTING HISTORY

§ Introduction

Like the ghost, this book is an interruption, a provocation, an unsettling of the orderly boundaries and lines by which we conventionally think about the relation between past and present and thus the way we "do" history. In it I conjure the specter of deconstruction to advocate for a reevaluation of these boundaries and our strategies for thinking and writing about the past. Deconstruction is a spirit that has haunted and frightened the historical profession, as we will see in Chapter 1, but, practically speaking, very few historians have attempted a serious engagement with Derrida or deconstruction for the practice of history. To my mind there are two main reasons for this: one that is inherent to current dominant historical practices and another that is announced explicitly as the reason deconstruction is inappropriate for the practice and writing of history.

The first reason is that most conventional historians are what I refer to as "ontological realists." I define ontological realism as a commitment to history as an endeavor concerned with events assigned to a specific location in space and time that are in principle observable and as such are regarded as fixed and immutable. Here the historian accepts that there is a possibility for epistemological uncertainty about our understanding of a past event, but this is mitigated by the ontological certainty that the event happened in a certain way at a certain time. Central to this position is a commitment to empirical data that serve as something of a false floor to hold it. In the end, getting the past "right" is a question of historical method. We will explore the workings and repercussions of ontological realism in Chapter 3, but for the moment I want to point to a stronger and weaker variant of this position. The stronger variant adheres to the position that there is a past and we can have full access to it. To my mind, this is a position that no, or very few, working historians currently hold. Instead, it is the weaker variant that I wish to target, wherein the past is said to have an ontological reality that we can only approach from limited perspective and incompletely from our position in the present and thus with epistemological uncertainty about that which is ontologically certain. This latter, weaker variant, I argue, is the position that most conventional historians hold, but I also want to suggest that the stronger version is always at work unannounced in the weaker one.

The error of ontological realism is that it fails to recognize the limitations of our own historical horizons, the extent to which our personal perspective is determined and directed by our past. The current epistemological understanding of the past is taken to be the ontological reality of the past. It is this indifference to the epistemological understanding that allows one to take our historically contingent mode of understanding as indicative of a method that is universally valid for all time. And it is here that we can see the ways that the current attempted rapprochement between our historical methods and our historical condition is predicated on a misunderstanding of our current practices as contained within a permanently enduring present that fosters a similarly misconceived representation of a permanently enduring past.

But what holds the ontological certainty of the past event given the possibility of epistemological uncertainty in recounting that event? Most conventional historians either avoid or defer this question, working purely on the assumption that method is sufficient to bring the past into the present. But the past itself has no ontological properties, or if it does, it has a latent ontology; thus, the past event cannot be made present. Any reappearance is the untimely visitation of a ghost. This leads to a more troubling question about the category of ontology itself and specifically the ontology or hauntology of the past. *Hauntology* is a Derridean term that relies on the sonic affinity between *ontology* and *hauntology* that the concept of hauntology haunts by replacing (when spoken, *ontologie* and *hontologie* are indistinguishable in French). History, too, is a replacing of this sort where the past event or figure is silently determined by the telling that replaces it. But the telling in the present is haunted by the ghost of the past, which is neither present nor absent, neither here nor gone. This disjunction or disruption at the core of "history" exposes the ways that origins and grounds are always posited to determine the beginning from the point of view of the end, thus smuggling both a teleology and rigidity into the account. Conventional historians give the past event the ontological reality of a fixed and permanent object silently replacing the spectral status with a fleshly one, but the ontological properties of the past event are constructed by the historian in the present.

Here I want to make clear that I am not advocating for an understanding of history or the past as constructed whole cloth by the historian in the present. In this regard I am sympathetic to traditional disciplinary historical methods and to recent work by philosophers of history such as Frank Ankersmit, Hans Ulrich Gumbrecht, Eelco Runia, and other proponents of the "presence" paradigm—especially regarding the latter's investigation into the forceful way that the past presses on the present and touches us even if we cannot touch it. But I am also deeply critical of the presence model, as will become apparent in Chapter 2. Ironically, given that the thinkers of presence provide a forceful critique of conventional historical scholarship, their emphasis on the material presence of the past in the here and now is strangely similar to that of the ontological realist approach insofar as both are predicated on a logic of presence. To be sure, the ontological approach of these philosophers of history is a focus on our historical mode of being in the present, while the epistemological approach of those historians who emphasize the importance of method is a focus on ascertaining the reality of the past; each emphasizes what is present and not what is absent. Runia, Gumbrecht, and Ankersmit do so by arguing for the presence of the past in the present. Conventional historians do so by arguing for the enduring and recoverable presence of the past as past.

In what follows, I embrace Hayden White's emphasis on language and the place of constructivism in the historical endeavor to critique such approaches, but I also cultivate aspects of the presence model as well. In this way the deconstructive approach to the past for which I advocate is neither a "realism" nor a "constructivism." Instead, it operates with elements of the latter without giving up the claims of the former to insistently engage with the real. I do not mean this in the sense offered by proponents of speculative materialism, the "real" of the natural sciences, or the "real" of sense data. Instead, I look to Derrida to engage with and make explicit the perturbations that the past returned convokes. This opening onto the relation of presence and absence through a hauntological approach to history accounts for the entangled and unstable relation of presence and absence without privileging one over the other.

This leads me to the second reason for the conventional historian's disdain or fear of deconstruction. Rather than confront the radical instability that deconstruction exposes, historians have typically dismissed it as counterproductive to, or incompatible with, the historical endeavor. For the historians Joyce Appleby, Lynn Hunt, and Margaret Jacob deconstruction denies "our ability to represent reality in any objectively true fashion"; thus, "in the final analysis there can be no postmodern history."[1] Other historians such as Richard Evans, Jerrold Seigel, Georg Iggers, and Keith Windschuttle concur.[2] Joshua Kates argues that the justification for such a dismissal is a reading of Derrida and his project, exemplified by the 2001 *Norton Anthology of Literary Theory and Criticism*, which takes deconstruction's "focus to be language, and sees it as arriving at what is essentially a new, more radical form of skepticism."[3] On this reading, the problem with "deconstruction" for the conventional historian is the overemphasis on language and the gap between words and the things they reference. If the signifier can never really reach the signified, so this logic goes, then there can be no meaning, and we descend into relativism. Following this reading, Jane Caplan concludes that "while deconstructive method may be borrowed by the historian for the interpretation of single texts, deconstruction as an epistemology is virtually incompatible with the historian's enterprise."[4]

But this is not the only reading of Derrida's project and works. Kates and scholars such as Geoffrey Bennington, Peter Fenves, Rodolph Gasché, Dana Hollander, Michael Naas, and Edward Baring have each contested this understanding of Derrida and the project of deconstruction, pointing to Derrida's sustained interest and engagement with the problem of "history" since his earliest work.[5] This can be seen in Derrida's published work such as his introduction to *L'origine de la géométrie*, by Edmund Husserl, of 1962; "Violence et métaphysique: Essai sur la pensée d'Emmanuel Levinas," from 1964; "De la grammatologie" (I and II), from 1965 and 1966; and "Cogito et histoire de la folie," from 1967.[6] It can also be seen in his seminars, first at the Sorbonne in 1963–64, when, as an assistant, he taught the course "Histoire et vérité" (History and Truth) using his own syllabus and then as an instructor at the École normale supérieure in 1964–65, where he taught the course "Heidegger: La question de l'être et l'histoire" as part of the *aggregation* curriculum.[7] The latter was recently published first in French in 2013 and then in English in 2016, leading Derrida scholars to revisit his early focus on history in relation to his later work.

But it is important to distinguish Derrida's interest in the problem and understanding of history from the concerns of practicing historians. For the most part, Derrida's interest in history was focused on the history of philosophy or the ways we operate as beings for whom our past, history, or traditions are part of our makeup. In the 1963–64 "Histoire et vérité" lectures he follows Hegel, using the term *Geschichte* to designate our historical condition as opposed to *Historie*, which designates the science of history.[8] In his course "Heidegger: The Question of Being and History" of the following year he phrases the distinction following the language of *Being and Time*: "since there would be no historical science without the historicity of *Dasein* (no *Historie* without *Geschichte*), the hermeneutics that gives us to read or think the historicity of *Dasein* is the condition of possibility of hermeneutics as the method of historical science."[9] Here Derrida is clear to assert that the concerns of historians are of a derivative nature and predicated on our historical mode of being in the world. Derrida's own concern is with the "history of being," and he states, again working through Heidegger, "it is pointless to go to the historian *qua* historian and ask him what historicity [*Geschichtlichkeit*] is. The historian is the scholar who is already dealing with a delimited scientific field that is, precisely, called historical reality . . . , and the historian has an object he deals with and that he calls the historical object. But as to the origin and the condition of possibility of this field of objectivity, the historian *qua* historian, in his historical practice, can tell us nothing."[10] For Derrida it is pointless to turn to the historian to ask about the question of history because while the historian understands the field in which she or he works, she or he has not thought deeply about the grounds on which that field is constituted. Derrida indicts the ways that "history and the epistemology of history deal with the objective thematic face of science but they do not think to go definitively searching for the pre-scientific origin of science."[11] Thus, Derrida looks toward Heidegger to investigate the moment prior to the constitution of history as a field of scientific objectivity, and here one can see how the target of Derrida's investigation expands beyond the realm of history as practiced by historians to the larger question of the prescientific origin of science. The point I want to emphasize is that while I think there is much to glean from Derrida's critique of historians and historical practice, it is not the focus of his engagement, nor does he offer direct guidance about how his project might apply to the practice of history. This will be my task.

Philosophers of history of the nineteenth-century variety do not fare much better in Derrida's early analysis because to his mind "the level of *Weltgeschichte* and the philosophy of history is that of the greatest naiveté since they both rely or at least claim to rely on a *historical truth* delivered by science. They are both certain that something like *historical truth* is possible, that an opening that gives us access to the historical past is possible, whatever the critical work one then proceeds to carry out on documents, signs, monuments, archives, and so on. The critical work presupposes the very thing it is trying to protect: namely, the possibility of historical truth."[12] These are the philosophical or theoretical coordinates that are employed by conventional historians to justify the ontological realist position, and we will confront these in Chapter 3. But earlier, Derrida identified a tension in the coordinates by which we conventionally designate the "truth" of "history" insofar as that if history is defined as the realm of change, and truth as the realm of the eternally same (as in Plato), then truth could not originate in history. Truth would have to preexist the world.[13] The formulation is phrased as a philosophical exercise, and Derrida seeks to apply it to case studies such as mathematics, where something like geometry can be said to be "true" in the eternal sense, but also to have a historical origin even if the truth of geometry can be said to preexist it. But when this logic is cast back on more conventional subjects of history, it is also one that draws attention to the internal contradiction at work in ontological realism, where the instability of history as the realm of change is replaced by a sense of fixity as historical truth: the past event as it "really happened." The danger of such a position is that it ascribes ideal ontological properties to the past that are silently assigned from the position of the present and then determined to be the criteria by which to adjudicate the fidelity of the historical account to the past event. This is why Derrida says that the critical work presupposes the very thing it is trying to protect.

Thus, Derrida advocates for a radical critique of history that takes issue with the suppositions of philosophers of history and historians alike and questions the very possibility of objective history and a stable past. Peter Fenves argues that "nothing is perhaps more daring in Derrida's early writings than this reluctance to affirm that history is possible and that the philosophy of history—true to the tradition of transcendental argumentation inaugurated by Kant—need only ask about the conditions of its possibility."[14] For Derrida this limited question is insufficient because it leads to an understanding of history as a closed system insofar as the on-tological realist presumes that the past is ontologically singular, clear, and recoverable so long as one has the right epistemological tools and meth-ods at one's disposal. This understanding of the past as singularly true restricts the possibilities of what we might understand the past to be or to have been. Instead, Derrida looks to reoccupy "the word 'history' in order to reinscribe its force and in order to produce another concept or concep-tual chain of 'history': in effect a 'monumental stratified, contradictory' history; a history that also implies a new logic of *repetition* and the *trace*, for it is difficult to see how there could be history without it."[15] I will explore how such a contradictory history can be applied in Chapter 5, but, in brief, Derrida is asking us to rethink "history" in order to account for the ways that *Historie* (the historical sciences) presuppose *Geschichte* (our ways of taking up the past) and the resultant entanglement of past, present, and future. When history is written, it is made repeatable, but the repetition itself can become a part of another conceptual chain pulled out of the initial context. Geoffrey Bennington, argues that for Derrida "'ideas' always escape any given context, and in a way that breaks or bursts any semantic or hermeneutic horizon," and that this should "unsettle our very understanding of what a library, an archive, archival research, or in-tellectual history might be."[16] Bennington provides the evocative example of an escaped tiger that needs to be put back in its cage before "mayhem ensues" as akin to the historian's "stern or panic-stricken injunction to 'put it back in its context' without having the means to ask the question of how it got out" or what it was doing in a cage in the first place?[17] It is the moment prior to the "putting in context" or "putting in the cage" that interests Derrida; therefore, rather than beginning with an orginary moment constructed in the present and based on the material assumption of a past "as it really happened," he looks to a logic of the ghostly *trace*. But this interest and engagement in what one might call arche-history is a concern with a moment prior to what Derrida refers to as the science of history.[18]

As I have noted, this concern led Derrida to a sustained engagement with the history of philosophy and thinkers such as Hegel, Husserl, Hei-degger, Foucault, and Levinas but rarely to one with practicing historians or specifically on the topic of history in that sense. For the most part historians serve the purpose of foil as in *Aporias*, where Phillipe Ariès, author of *Western Attitudes Towards Death*, is put forward to demon-

strate the axiomatic nature of the historical endeavor.[19] Derrida is concerned with the ways that Ariès, as a historian working on the topic of
death, "knows, thinks he knows, or grants to himself the unquestioned
knowledge of what death is, of what being-dead means; consequently,
he grants to himself all the criteriology that will allow him to identify,
recognize, or delimit the objects of his inquiry or the thematic field of
his anthropological-historical knowledge. The question of the meaning
of death and the word 'death' . . . and of knowing if death 'is'—and what
death 'is'—all remain radically absent as *questions*."[20] We can see the critical engagement with what Derrida sees as the limitations of conventional
history but also how the questions he asks, and seeks to answer, lead him
away from an engagement with history in that sense.

One notable exception is Derrida's *Archive Fever*.[21] This book takes Sigmund Freud, the legacies of Judaism and psychoanalysis, and the status of
the archive as its central focus, but what interests me here is the way this
book is also a sustained engagement with the historian Yosef Yerushalmi
and his own book, *Freud's Moses: Judaism Terminable and Interminable*.[22]
It is worth noting that Derrida's most substantive interaction with disciplinary historians revolves around those historians' explicit references to
the dead, as we saw with Phillipe Ariès. In the case of Yerushalmi, what
draws Derrida's attention is the historian's encounter with the ghost of
Freud, for this is the place in Yerushalmi's work where the norms, proce-
dures, and boundaries of traditional historical practices break down. In
this portion of the book, Yerushalmi the historian breaks with scholarly
convention to engage in an exchange with Freud by means of a letter addressed to the dead father of psychoanalysis, "in truth Freud's ghost."[23]
Derrida notes that "these thirty-odd pages" are to be classed as fiction,
"which would already be a break with the language that has dominated
up to this point in the book, that is, the discourse of scholarship, the
discourse of a historian, of a philologist, of an expert on the history of
Judaism, of a biblical scholar, as they say, claiming to speak in all objectivity."[24] But the fictional quality of this intervention has another originality:
"the apostrophe is addressed to a dead person, to the historian's object
become spectral subject, the virtual addressee or interlocutor of a sort of
open letter."[25] It is this blurring of the lines between "fact" and "fiction,"
between the living and the dead, between past and present, between presence and absence that interests Derrida and that I will take up in the
chapters that follow.

Derrida sees Yerushalmi's rhetorical move, the apostrophe to Freud, as a "gesture incompatible in principle with the norms of classical scientific scholarship, in particular with those of history or of philology which had presided over the same book up to this point."[26] Derrida later elaborates:

> Up to this point, in any case up to the fictive monologue, Yerushalmi had measured his discourse—for the bulk of what, in theory, was shown and demonstrated—on the classical norms of knowledge, of scholarship, and of epistemology which dominate in every scientific community: here, the objectivity of the historian, of the archivist, of the sociologist, of the philologist, the reference to stable themes and concepts, the relative exteriority in relation to the object, particularly in relation to an archive determined as *already given, in the past* or in any case only *incomplete*, determinable and thus terminable in a future itself determinable as future present, domination of the constative over the performative, etc.[27]

There are several issues to be taken up here and that I will address over the course of this book. First, the place where conventional or scientific history breaks down is the place of the ghost—of haunting and of hauntology. Second, the openness and incompleteness of the archive leaves open to the future the determination of the past as "history." Every archive is necessarily incomplete, and any addition to it in the future changes the past. Third, and in response to the second, conventional historians tend to operate as if the archive were already complete or in the realm of a future completeness to come that sanctions the archive's authority even as they acknowledge its incompleteness in the present. "Yes, we know there is more to come that may change our understanding of the past; nevertheless, we operate as if it is complete and thus can scientifically verify what we know of the past in the present."

Past events are brought "back" to the present through the work of the historian, but other aspects of the past haunt us, our archives, and the very history to which we cling. These are the ghosts of things forgotten, buried, or erased from the record being rigorously researched by traditional historians and that so often support dominant ideologies. But, to modify a question Derrida asks, how does one prove in general an absence of archive, if not relying on classical norms (presence/absence of literal and explicit reference to this or to that, to a this or a that which one supposes to be identical to themselves, and simply absent, *actually* absent, if they are not simply present, *actually* present, how can one not, and why not, take into account the radically absent archives of a past unaccounted for but nevertheless ~~there~~)?[28] How can we account for the missing portions of the past without simply assuming them to be the missing part of a larger whole whose properties and scope we have already determined? On my account, the haunting or the ghost allows for the presence of this absence without predetermining the "what" of what the ghost or haunting is, without supposing it to be something known and determinable but simply absent. This is what I will refer to as the past that ~~is~~ (present and absent). I develop this concept in Chapter 5, but here I want to note that I place a bar across the "~~is~~," both striking it out and indicating an obstruction that restricts access.

In Yerushalmi's work the insertion of the ghost of Freud comes after the historical work has been done and the record has been shown. The case is closed and Yerushalmi has provided all the historical evidence to reach some conclusion regarding Freud and his relationship to his Jewish identity. Even so, Yerushalmi conjures the ghost to seek answers to the questions that continue to haunt him and disturb the historical account previously presented. The excess or surplus of the past that had been restricted or excised from the historical account returns in Yerushalmi's book in ways that suspend "all the axiomatic assurances, norms, and rules which had served him until now in organizing the scientific work, notably historiographic criticism, and in particular its relationship to the known and unknown archive."[29] All archives are haunted this way because their structure is spectral, "spectral *a priori*: neither present nor absent 'in the flesh,' neither visible nor invisible, a trace always referring to another whose eyes can never be met, no more than those of Hamlet's father, thanks to the possibility of a visor."[30] The visor can be read as the bar that blocks and restricts access to the past event: to the past that ~~is~~. Try as the historian might, even the ontological realist acknowledges that one cannot lock eyes with the past.

Thus when confronted with this haunting, Yerushalmi the historian dares "to cross a limit before which 'ordinary historians' have always been intimidated."[31] Yerushalmi is uncomfortable with this transgression that at first glance appears to come at the joint between truth and fiction, but as Derrida tells us, "The last chapter, the most fictive, is certainly not the least true."[32] I will explore the relations between "truth" and "fiction," between "evidence" and "imagination" throughout this book, but for the moment I want to focus on the transgression of borders, limits, and disciplines at work here. In his book Yerushalmi reveals the limits of conventional history and the ontological realist understanding of the past. These are limits before which "ordinary historians" have always been intimidated but that a deconstructive approach to the past can cross and transgress to locate fractures, disturb remains, and promote alternative arrangements.

In Chapter 1, "Haunting History," I provide an intellectual history of the reception of deconstruction in the American historical profession by means of a ghost story. I see deconstruction as akin to the ghost because while it has been repeatedly targeted in attacks against the dangers of postmodernism, poststructuralism, or the "linguistic turn," very few historians actively use deconstruction as a historical methodology; in this regard the target has always been a phantom. But it is also akin to the ghost because of the ways that deconstruction itself haunts disciplinary history, exposing the axiomatic assumptions of conventional historians and revealing the complex nature of our relationship with the past. In Chapter 2, "Presence in *Absentia*," I deploy the Ghost of Christmas Present from Charles Dickens's *A Christmas Carol* to explore the recent trend in philosophy of history known as "presence." Here I work through texts by Eelco Runia, Hans-Ulrich Gumbrecht, and Frank Ankersmit to show the limitations of this model and its affinities to conventional ontological realist history. In Chapter 3, "Chladenius, Droysen, and Dilthey: Back to Where We've Never Been," I look to the German historicist tradition and the figures of Johann Martin Chladenius (1710–59), Johann Gustav Droysen (1808–84), and Wilhelm Dilthey (1833–1911) to determine its relation to "ontological realism" and to expose the limitations of that model in our current intellectual milieu. But I also suggest that a closer look at these three thinkers sheds light on the utility of deconstruction for the project of history as well as the possibility of a hauntological historical approach to the past that is guided by, though not beholden to, Derrida. In Chapter 4, "The Analog Ceiling," I build on the previous three chapters to argue that the dominance of ontological realism in the historical profession is no longer justifiable based on our current understanding of the past but is supported by our current scholarly publishing practices, what I refer to as the "analog ceiling." The ceiling metaphor functions because it allows one to argue that even though the past may not really correlate to the narrative reconstructions of ontological realism, this form is nevertheless the best analogy to make the past intelligible, understandable, and comprehensible. To counter this model, I look to current innovations in digital scholarship and the ways that a deconstructive approach to the past enables us to innovate and reimagine how history can be done. In this regard my book is a gamble that academic research and publishing as we know it are changing and will continue to change in ways that will alter how we think about the past, how we write about the past, and as a result the discipline of history. In my final chapter, "The Past That ɪs," I conclude by offering my deconstructive approach to the past as a theory of and practice for history. Using Washington Irving's *Legend of Sleepy Hollow*, I explicate how a hauntological approach to history that embraces the past that ɪs (present and absent) rather than a fixed and static snapshot of a moment in time is able to account for the enigma of a past that is both here and gone. The past, like the ghost, does not properly belong to the present, but neither does it remain entirely in the past; it begins by coming back.

In his discussion of Yerushalmi and the ghost of Freud, Derrida is careful to articulate that "Freud did everything possible not to neglect the experience of haunting, spectrality, phantoms, ghosts. He tried to account for them. Courageously, in as scientific, critical, and positive a fashion as possible. But by doing that, he also tried to conjure them."[33] I would argue that this is also an apt description of the historian's attempt to account for the past in as scientific, critical, and positive fashion as possible. But just as Freud and Yerushalmi ended up conjuring ghosts they ultimately could not control, so, too, does the historian. What is more, I would suggest that this scientific conjuring is an attempt to restrict and limit the unruly past, and in this sense it is another attempt to put the "tiger back in the cage." In this book I want to let the ghosts out.

§ 1   Haunting History

We begin with a ghost story or rather a *Geist* story. It is both a *Geist-geschichte* (intellectual history) and a *Geistergeschichte* (ghost story) of the specter of deconstruction that has been haunting historians since it first began appearing and disappearing in the late 1960s. Like most ghost stories, this one involves a phenomenon that is hard to explain and has engendered varying responses. A small cadre of historians have welcomed this spirit as a benevolent guide to reveal aspects of the past and the future hitherto undetected. A larger and more vocal group takes this spirit to be a malevolent *Poltergeist* hell-bent on causing mischief and ultimately destroying the historical profession. Yet others see deconstruction as a conjuring trick performed with smoke and mirrors by disingenuous charlatans. But the vast majority of historians view deconstruction as they do most ghost stories, with bemused skepticism and guilty fascination. Most have read or heard about it secondhand in the works of the historians aforementioned or perhaps in works by other historians who have cited them, and as with most ghost stories, this has led to exaggerations, inaccuracies, conflations, recastings, and revisions. The ghost is at times a monster or a demon. Furthermore, deconstruction is but one spirit among many that have haunted the historical profession since the early 1980s under the general terms of *postmodernism, poststructuralism,* or the *linguistic turn.* "Archaeology," "genealogy," "emplotment," and "deconstruction" are often lumped together, as are figures as diverse as Jacques Derrida, Michel Foucault, Hans-Georg Gadamer, Clifford Geertz, Richard Rorty, and Hayden White.

13

But in terms of the practice and production of history, I would suggest that the term *specter* is more appropriate for deconstruction and the figure of Jacques Derrida than for the other figures and methods mentioned. This is because while deconstruction, invariably linked to the person of Derrida, is repeatedly invoked in attacks against the dangers of postmodernism, poststructuralism, and the linguistic turn, it has seldom been applied in the historical profession. Practically speaking, there are very few historians who actively use deconstruction as a historical methodology; thus, this target has always been a phantom. The death of Jacques Derrida in 2004 and the pronounced death of postmodernism and the linguistic turn in works such as Victoria E. Bonnell and Lynn Hunt's *Beyond the Cultural Turn* (1999), Ernst Breisach's *On the Future of History: The Postmodern Challenge and Its Aftermath* (2003), Gabrielle Spiegel's *Practicing History: New Directions in Historical Writing After the Linguistic Turn* (2005), Michael Roth's "Ebb Tide" (2007), and Nancy Partner's "Narrative Persistence" (2009) appear to have put the final nails in the coffin.[1] Twenty-first-century trends in historical writing and the theory of history emphasize the return of agency, the primacy of experience, memory, testimony, and, most recently, the importance of "presence" for the project of history. Even stalwart proponents of the deconstructive project for history turned their gaze toward a more critical encounter with the work of Derrida, as in the case of Dominick LaCapra or Joan Scott. All indications seem to be that the postmodern moment has passed, the linguistic turn has moved to the great beyond, the subject has returned as the solid empirical ground for historical investigation, and the poltergeist has been exorcised from the historical profession. All that is left is to inter the remains of deconstruction.

But as this is a ghost story, it is precisely after death that the plot thickens and the deeper and perhaps darker purpose is revealed. After all, one cannot kill a ghost. This is certainly the lesson to be learned from Derrida's *Specters of Marx*. With the "death" of deconstruction, facilitated by the death of Derrida, one can now revisit its historical life. It is a past artifact to be reconstituted so as to reconstruct its impact and emplot the narrative of its influence or lack thereof. But by disturbing the remains, by revisiting deconstruction, we also raise it from the dead and bring back the past, and this act, implicit in all historical work, reveals a key aspect of the relation between deconstruction and history. To push this further, I will argue for a deconstructive approach to the past that makes explicit the links between *différance*, history, and what I call the latent ontology of the past that is.

In broad strokes the deconstructive strategy is to approach a text (historical or otherwise) as a site of contestation and struggle, where one tendency in that text asserts itself as the source of order and thus establishes a hierarchy of meaning. The hierarchy is constructed in an oppositional binary that is presented as neutral and thus conceals the organizing principle (good and evil is a simple one). The intention of the author is rendered irrelevant for the deconstruction because the construction of the text may very well lie on unconscious, unquestioned, or implicit assumptions that are at work in the ordering process. The deconstruction exposes the binary construct and arbitrary nature of the hierarchy by revealing an exchange of properties between the two tendencies. Furthermore, much can be gleaned by what is left out of the text, and this, too, can be used to unsettle authoritative pronouncements.

In the case of this chapter, one could point to the privileging of "presence" over "absence" as provoked by the specter/ *Geist*/ghost or in the implicit assumption that because most historians do not "do" deconstruction, it is not of practical use for the writing of history. As it turns out, most historians don't employ deconstruction (an absence) that is the prime motor of this chapter despite the fact that this exploration of deconstruction is justified by drawing attention to the disproportionate number of articles attacking it (a presence or event) as dangerous for the practice of history. Here the binary is exposed and the hierarchy unsettled by the exchange of properties (absence is at work in presence, and presence is at work in absence). In general, the writing of history is concerned with the construction of narratives highlighting events that occurred in an attempt to make them present to the reader or listener. Historians are much less concerned with what didn't happen although that certainly plays into the analysis as well. One could argue that it is precisely the constructive nature of the project of history (the assembly of information, the architecture of the argument, the presentation of a comprehensible narrative) that makes deconstruction such an inappropriate strategy. The historian is building something, and the end result would be a cumbersome two-step if one were to deconstruct each part along the way.

In one of the earliest critiques of deconstruction (1976), Hayden White, who in most cases haunts the postmodern mansion hand in hand with Jacques Derrida, warned against the dangers of Derrida's "absurdist criti-

cism" because with Derrida "there is no 'meaning,' only the ghostly ballet
of alternative 'meanings' which various modes of figuration provide."[2] Here
again, the historian, and not just the historian, is warned to keep clear of
the "ghostly ballet" unleashed by deconstruction and the damage it is capable of inflicting. In response to this threat, White dismisses Derrida with
this question: "When the world is denied all substance and perception is
blind, who is to say who are the chosen and who are the damned? On what
grounds can we assert that the insane, the criminal, and the barbarian are
wrong?"[3] The diagnosis of deconstruction's incompatibility with the project
of history on the grounds that it disallows the possibility of concrete statements and opens the door to moral relativism is certainly to be expected
among those "proper historians" who, White contends, "seek to explain
what happened in the past by providing a precise and accurate reconstruction of the events reported in their documents." This is because these historians construct their narrative by "suppressing as far as possible the impulse
to interpret the data, or at least by indicating in the narrative where one is
merely representing the facts and where one is interpreting them."[4] But this
diagnosis of deconstruction is somewhat surprising coming from White,
given his subsequent claim that "in metahistory, by contrast [to proper his-
tory], the explanatory and the interpretative aspects of the narrative tend to
be run together and to be confused in such a way as to dissolve its authority
as either a representation of 'what happened' in the past or a valid explanation of why it happened as it did."[5]

Deconstruction can certainly serve the purpose of metahistory by dissolving authority but, according to White, does not serve the greater
claim that "there can be no proper history without the presupposition of
a full blown metahistory by which to justify those interpretative strategies
necessary for the representation of a given segment of the historical process."[6] Ostensibly, deconstruction goes too far because it does not allow
a space for critical judgment and justification but only endless critique,
and here again we encounter the understandable argument that at some
point history must build something while deconstruction is ceaselessly
"unbuilding." But White also reveals his desire to find an Archimedean
point, a moral ground from which one can make judgment. The desire
for an Archimedean point to ground history is prevalent to many conventional historians as we will see.

The question is, why did White see deconstruction as the point of no
return, where the ballet turns ghostly and all judgment, discrimination,

and perspective are lost?[7] In his 1978 review of White's book, Dominick LaCapra suggests that "one way to see White's reaction is as a turn toward secure 'sanity' and conventional irony in the face of the 'other,' who actually articulates things that are 'inside' White himself—but an 'other' whose articulation is perhaps too disconcerting or at least too alien in formulation to be recognizable."[8] In deconstruction White saw the ghostly reflection of himself and recoiled with dislike, much as Freud had done when he saw his own reflection in the window of his sleeping compartment on the train.[9] Freud notes that, as with White, rather than being "*frightened* by [our] 'doubles,' [we] simply failed to recognize them as such." Freud goes on to ask, "Is it not possible, though, that our dislike of them [the reflection] was a vestigial trace of the archaic reaction which feels the 'double' to be something uncanny?"[10] Here Freud is referring to the archaic reaction of fear and anxiety produced by what he terms the *unheimlich* (uncanny). The uncanny itself seems to be produced by a slippage or inversion in which the "other" turns out to be the "same" (as in the case of Freud's reflection), but it is also produced when established orders break down (thus the ghost story also produces an *unheimlich* sensation). The "other" posited by LaCapra turns out to be White himself because "the things Derrida discusses *are* inside White." White's initial rejection and distrust of Derrida can thus be read as the repression of those tendencies inherent in White that are made explicit by Derrida.

To take this a step further and gain some separation from the figures of White and Derrida, let us be so bold as to state that deconstruction reveals history's darkest secret and in doing so provokes the fear and anxiety of the uncanny, which is met by repression. The fear, rejection, and repression of deconstruction are linked to another tendency inherent in the historical profession. The reconstruction of a historical event requires imagination in constructing a compelling argument and narrative. Deconstruction exposes the ordering of the events or argument, laying bare the authorial choices that also become apparent in the work of Hayden White. But the relation of imagination and reality are also brought into question in such a move. It is true that one can discern this interplay without recourse to deconstruction, for instance, in Robert Finlay's critique of Natalie Davis's *The Return of Martin Guerre*.[11] But this critique was posited from the position of a historian who was out to set the record straight and get to the available facts. In response Davis put on her historian's robe to present the full complement of footnotes, archival data, and source material that served to legitimate her imaginative narrative. A key issue in the exchange was whether Davis's historical monograph was simply too literary, and both Davis and Finlay seem to agree that being overly "literary" or imaginative is a bad thing for historians; thus, each privileged the real over the imaginary. I would argue that the deconstructive critique is more radical because it does not begin from a position that assumes facts serve as the foundation of historical investigation or writing but seeks to unsettle the hierarchical order that assumes facts take priority over imagination. Indeed, it questions the assumptions about the workings of time on space that underpin the ontological realist understanding of the past and history. In doing so it announces the possibility that imagination is equally crucial to the historical endeavor, whatever its relation to "reality," which is quite an unsettling proposition for the working historian. In relation to the project of history, the point is not to force the historian into a position of total relativism, White's "ghostly ballet," but to bring to light the conditions surrounding the construction of a historical narrative both in terms of content and form. The proposition that imagination plays so active a role in the writing of history is unpalatable to a discipline that models itself as a science. In response to the "uncanny effect [that] is often and easily produced when the distinction between imagination and reality is effaced," the historian does not engage this possibility but denies it.[12]

The "Linguistic Turn" and the Metaphysical Concept of History

Given the demarcation between the imaginary and the real, it is of interest that the exchange between Hayden White and Dominick LaCapra, both historians by training, did not take place in journals devoted to the historical profession but in journals dedicated to literature and literary theory. White's piece was first published in 1976 in *Contemporary Literature* and became of historical interest when it was included in his *Tropics of Discourse* in 1978. Similarly, LaCapra's review article, which engaged *Tropics of Discourse* and thus pushed the issue into a historical framework, was first published in *Modern Language Notes* (1978). It was the later republication of this review as a chapter in *Rethinking Intellectual History: Texts, Contexts, Language* in 1983 that coincided with the entrance of Derrida and deconstruction into historical discourse in the United States.

LaCapra was instrumental in bridging the gap between literary criticism and the writing of history through the aforementioned work but also through his article "Rethinking Intellectual History and Reading Texts," published in *History and Theory* in 1980 and, more important, republished in the 1982 volume *Modern European Intellectual History: Reappraisals and New Perspectives.*[13]

This volume was based on the proceedings of a conference held at Cornell University in 1980 that brought together a group of "younger older (or older younger) scholars" such as Roger Chartier, Martin Jay, Hans Kellner, Mark Poster, E. M. Henning, Keith Baker, Peter Jelavich, David Fisher, and Hayden White.[14] In the introduction Kaplan and LaCapra asserted that "for at least a decade, intellectual historians have had a growing belief that their field is undergoing a far-reaching change. The change in direction is still difficult to discern. But the recent invasion of new theoretical perspectives and research practices from Europe has agitated the whole realm of historical studies." In response to this belief, Kaplan and LaCapra sought to discern the relevance of "Critical Theory, hermeneutics, structuralism, and poststructuralism" to "research in intellectual history" by exploring "one of the more significant claims of figures who belong to these 'schools' (for example, Jürgen Habermas, Hans-Georg Gadamer, Michel Foucault, and Jacques Derrida)" that "their reconceptualization of problems has important implications for the understanding and for the writing of history itself."[15] Thus, this volume brought the recent trends in theory to bear on the practice and writing of history, but it did so in a way that led to two unforeseeable repercussions.

While the article by LaCapra articulated the positive possibilities that deconstruction offered the practice of history, as did the article by E. M. Henning, the volume itself presented a number of possibilities for the practice of history as articulated by the group of intellectual historians. The goal was to present a cross section of the recent innovations and various possibilities, but the volume also created the impression that all of these theories and theorists were related if only as alternatives to conventional theories of history. Henning's article, "Archeology, Deconstruction, and Intellectual History," does an excellent job of presenting the differences between these two methodologies, as well as the ways that they can be integrated into the practice of history; but it also creates the impression that Foucault's "archaeology" and Derrida's "deconstruction" are part and parcel of the same trend, which in some ways they are. Thus it is not surprising that subsequent discussions of the theorists included in the volume would fall under the common umbrella of "postmodernism," "poststructuralism," or the "linguistic turn." This is the first consequence.

Martin Jay's contribution, "Should Intellectual History Take a Linguistic Turn?," broached this question by providing a lucid intellectual history of the rise of the interest in "language" in the twentieth century and the ways that "the linguistic turn in philosophy affected many other disciplines and came in many forms." With his characteristic clarity, Jay describes the many variants of this "linguistic turn," whether the French variants descended from Saussure, which include Foucault and Derrida; the English tradition descended from Wittgenstein, J. L. Austin, and Gilbert Ryle; or the German tradition in its Heideggerian form as articulated by Hans-Georg Gadamer or descended from the Frankfurt school as in the work of Habermas. Jay highlights those thinkers whose work and methodology "threaten to penetrate the defenses of that most conservative of cultural enterprises, the study of history, through the opening provided by intellectual historians who have allowed what they examine to influence how they examine it."[16] The essay is cautious, as the title suggests, and it is clear that Jay finds some approaches, Habermas's for instance, more palatable than others. For our purposes it is important to note that Jay, guided by White's essay, finds the Derridean variant to be one of the least palatable, even demonic.[17] This is the second consequence.

Although Jay is careful to differentiate between more and less useful theories for history, the overall tone of the essay is one of skepticism and even admonishment for those historians who "have allowed what they examine to influence how they examine it." Jay's essay combines all of the various strands under the rubric of the "linguistic turn" but also reveals anxiety about following such an example, especially in its Derridean incarnation.[18] Jay's was not the only "anxious" contribution to the volume. For the reasons articulated by White and then revisited by Jay, deconstruction was initially the cause of this anxiety, but as we will see, other postmodern specters, especially Foucault, were later tarred with the same brush.

But before we turn to these critics, let us turn to France. It was not until the early 1980s that deconstruction entered into historical discourse in the United States, at least among intellectual historians, but in France Jacques Derrida had been drawn into this discussion much earlier and for different reasons. In 1972 Derrida published a collection of three interviews under the title of *Positions*.[19] It is the third interview with Jean-Louis Houbedine and Guy Scarpetta, "Positions," that is of interest for our story both because of Derrida's statements about the relation of deconstruction to history and because of the context surrounding the interview. This interview took place in June of 1971 and came on the heels of a conflict involving Derrida, the journal *Tel Quel*, and the newspaper of the French Communist Party, *L'Humanité*. In 1969 Jean Pierre Faye, who had been one of the editors of *Tel Quel* before he broke with the journal on ideological grounds, published an article entitled "Le camarade Mallarmé," in which he attacked *Tel Quel* as an enemy of the French left. The brunt of the attack was the allegation that *Tel Quel* had facilitated the introduction of a "language derived from Germany's extreme-right," which had been "displaced, unknown to all, and introduced into the Parisian left." Derrida had published a number of articles in *Tel Quel*, and although he was not mentioned by name in Faye's article, it was clear that he was the target. For Faye, Derrida was indicative of "le malheur heideggérien" (the Heideggerian misfortune), which is the appropriation of a right-wing and ultimately National Socialist philosophy by an ostensibly left-wing philosopher. Thus, according to Faye, despite its pronounced support for and affiliation with the French Communist Party, *Tel Quel* was surreptitiously leading the French youth away from communism and toward right-wing extremism.[20] Phillipe Sollers, the editor of *Tel Quel*, responded to Faye's attack and accused him of defaming Derrida. Faye published a counterresponse in *Tel Quel*, and this provoked a final response by the entire editorial board of *Tel Quel*. The upshot of this sequence of events was that in June of 1971, *Tel Quel* broke with the French Communist Party and declared itself Maoist. This was the moment of Derrida's interview with Scarpetta and Houbedine, who had been members of the French Communist Party but had come over to join *Tel Quel*.[21] Thus, this particular interview is politically charged, specifically about what Derrida's position on Marxism was, as well as on the relation of deconstruction to dialectical and historical materialism.

Derrida was not evasive but clearly did not want to commit to a position for or against Marxism. In response to a question by Houbedine asking about his reluctance to address the intersections of deconstruction and dialectical materialism in his work, Derrida responded: "Do me the credit of believing that the 'lacunae' to which you alluded are explicitly calculated to mark the sites of a theoretical elaboration which remains, *for me*, at least, *still to come.* And they are lacunae not objections."[22] To Derrida's credit this theoretical elaboration did come twenty years later in the form of his lecture, and then publication, *Specters of Marx.*[23] Derrida's statements about "history" are in response to questions about the specifically Marxist variant of history although often couched in the structuralist language of Althusser. In this light Derrida's statements are clearer and his criticism of "history" more precise: "What we must be wary of, I repeat, is the *metaphysical* concept of history. This is the concept of history as the history of meaning: the history of meaning developing itself, fulfilling itself."[24] The speculative variant of history in the Hegelian or Marxist form proffers a linear teleology that both produces itself and recounts its production in the same breath. This "metaphysical concept of history is not only linked to linearity, but to an entire *system* of implications (teleology, eschatology, elevating and interiorizing accumulation of meaning, a certain type of traditionality, a certain concept of continuity, of truth, etc.)."[25] Here the critique expands, but its origins are based in this "metaphysical" concept of history that provides an ideological scaffold on which "history" organizes itself but then presents itself as "historical truth." But the expansion of the critique also demonstrates Derrida's reservations about "history" and the possibility of conceptualizing "history" without smuggling in the metaphysical baggage. "Therefore it is not an accidental predicate [*metaphysical concept* of history] which could be removed by a kind of local ablation, without a general displacement of the organization, without setting the entire system to work." Removing the term *metaphysical concept* or, to take it a step further, ignoring the ways that the project of history fits into, and may be directed by, a larger understanding of metaphysics only serves to ignore the problems detected by Derrida. In 1972 these problems were closely related to his critique of logocentrism as presented in *Of Grammatology.* "Logocentrism is *also*, fundamentally, an idealism. It is the matrix of idealism. Idealism is its most direct representation." Furthermore, this idealism "can always be found in the philosophies that *call themselves* nonidealist, that is, antiidealist."[26] And here, Marxism (but not only Marxism) should come to mind given the context of the interview.

Despite the critique, Derrida is not seeking to dismiss or discredit "history" entirely; furthermore, "history" serves an important extratextual function for Derrida:

I have never believed that there were *metaphysical* concepts *in and of them-*

selves. No concept is by itself, and consequently in and of itself, metaphysical, outside all the textual work in which it is inscribed. This explains why, although I have formulated many reservations about the "metaphysical" concept of history, I very *often* use the word "history" in order to reinscribe its force and in order to produce another concept or conceptual chain of "history": in effect a "monumental stratified, contradictory" history; a history that also implies a new logic of *repetition* and the *trace*, for it is difficult to see how there could be history without it.[27]

For Derrida there is a use and application for history that attempts to disrupt the assumptions of surety and continuity that are implied in the "metaphysical" variants. To be sure, this is done through strategies of contradiction and repetition that privilege the search and research for a ghostly trace over the decidedly more material assumption of a past "as it really happened" or an ideologically driven telos that determines a historical scaffold. But this use of history is no ghostly ballet either because, according to Derrida, "there is a powerful historical unity that must be determined first if one is not to take dross for gold every time that an emergence, rupture, break, mutation is allegedly delineated."[28] Thus, the history Derrida advocates is not a "free-for-all" where perspective and judgment are suspended but instead a call to understand how every context can itself be contextualized that is ever wary of the ways that the historical project is always in danger of being "reappropriated by metaphysics."[29] I want to suggest that Derrida's statements hold differing meaning depending on context. And one might take dross for gold if one were to ignore this.

If one reads Derrida's statements on history unaware that they are a critique of the Hegelian/Marxist variant, the criticism of history seems far-reaching and unwieldly. If the context and specifics of the critique are retained, however, it is more discrete and unfolds on possible usages of history that rely on deconstruction as a beginning and end, as it were, but do not continuously unravel. This is a history that asserts the spectral nature of the past and troubles the metaphysical tendencies that are surreptitiously enfolded into the historical project but are exposed by the historian's emphasis on "presence" and "reality."[30] These are issues we will explore in Chapters 2, 3, and 4.

In both cases, the more and less discrete critique, it is clear that Derrida has grave reservations about Marxist history. Indeed, *Tel Quel* and Derrida severed relations on precisely this issue soon after the interview was published. But more important, this provides us with a clue to one of the sources of the later conflicts. Derrida's work, and specifically deconstruction, is at odds with historical materialism and by extension with the Marxist variants of social and intellectual history. This is significant because the 1970s marked the apex of a steady rise in social history in the United States "fostered by the influence of two dominant paradigms of explanation: Marxism on the one hand and the 'Annales' school on the other."[31] Furthermore, the edited volume by LaCapra and Kaplan explicitly positioned itself in response to the rise of social history: "Within the profession, it is social history that has posed the greatest challenge to intellectual history—a challenge that can be seen in a variety of ways. Statistical research may reveal that the number of courses under the label 'intellectual history' has remained constant in the recent past. But the relative growth and the absolute excitement often seem to have passed to social history."[32] In his earlier piece for *History and Theory* LaCapra described this challenge as a "crisis significant enough to open the question of the field's nature and objectives," and in response to this crisis he proposed "to define and to defend in relatively theoretical terms the approach to the field and specifically, to modern European intellectual history, that I have come to find most fruitful."[33] With Derrida as his ally, LaCapra critically explored the current trends in intellectual history and offered alternative approaches to the study of the past. Although the focus of the article is intellectual history, it is clear that the challenge of "social history" is a key pressure:

> The more recent elaboration of a social history of ideas has seemed to offer an answer . . . , for in its rigor and methodological sophistication it goes beyond the older forms of contextualization, and it promises to give intellectual history access to the remarkable achievements of modern social history. . . . But intellectual history should not be seen as a mere function of social history. It has other questions to explore, requiring different techniques, and their development may permit a better articulation of its relationship to social history. It may even suggest areas in which the formulations of social history stand in need of further refinement.[34]

LaCapra thus sought to revitalize intellectual history by drawing it away from trends in social history and instead offering new paths based largely on the work of Derrida. This drew the ire of, and responses from, intellectual and social historians alike.

But LaCapra's confident assertions about the possibilities of decon-struction and the limitations of more conventional strategies coincided with other trends that made his call to rethink historiography appear more hostile and threatening than he had intended.[35] This is the rise of subaltern studies following the publication of Edward Said's *Orientalism* in 1978 and the emergence of New Historicism through the publication of Stephen Greenblatt's *Renaissance Self-Fashioning* in 1980 and the found-ing of the journal *Representations* in 1983 that established the movement as a school of thought.[36] Both of these movements originated from figures associated with comparative literature and literary studies. It would be a stretch to say that there is a direct connection between the methodology espoused by LaCapra and that of either Said or the New Historicists but given that (1) deconstruction and the work of Jacques Derrida had had its greatest impact in the field of literary criticism, (2) the work of LaCapra was closely linked to literary theory, and (3) Said himself and many of the New Historicists were scholars of literature who had now embarked on projects that encroached on the discipline of history, there was a growing sense among historians that a storm was gathering.[37] Something wicked this way comes. The discipline of history feared the threat from literary scholars who wanted to bring their techniques to the project of history.

J. G. A. Pocock took umbrage at the unwelcome visitor in the pages of the *Intellectual History Newsletter*, a key site of correspondence and exchange for intellectual historians in the United States.[38] In 1980 E. M. Henning had reported on Kaplan and LaCapra's conference at Cornell University in the *Newsletter*, bringing the various issues and methodolo-gies to the attention of European and American intellectual historians. In 1985 LaCapra, Kaplan, and Henning wrote a letter to the editor, and in 1986 Pocock published an article entitled "A New Bark Up an Old Tree." Here, Pocock reveals anxieties about the recent trends in intellectual his-tory quite different from and much more acute than those described by Hans Kellner.[39] The Charybdis that Pocock asks intellectual historians to avoid is the criticism of "failing to relate (they mean subordinate) 'ideas' to 'realities.'" While this seems to emphasize the same forces that led LaCapra and Kaplan to produce their volume in the first place, it is also clear that Pocock wants to assuage these critics: "You can reply that the relations of theory to practice and speech to action may be very many and various, that you have no general theory of what these relations are, and merely wanted to know what happened in various recorded instances."[40]

Unlike the contributors to LaCapra and Kaplan's volume, Pocock's emphasis is on the criticism that intellectual history is a less "real" form of history because he sees it as indicative of a greater danger facing intellectual history. The Scylla that Pocock sees rising before him is precisely the intellectual historian who has embraced the recent trends; thus, Pocock is compelled to distinguish two types of intellectual historians. The first sounds suspiciously like a mélange of Dominick LaCapra and Hayden White:

> It is possible to define "intellectual history" as the pursuit by the "intellectual" of an attitude towards "history," and to write it as a series of dialogues between the historian himself, as intellectual, and his probably French or German predecessors, in the attempt to arrive at a "philosophy of history" or something to take the place of one. Such "intellectual history" will be a metahistory, meaning that it will be [a] reflection about "history" itself.[41]

This is the historian who has lost sight of the historian's mission to "know what happened in various recorded instances" and instead has embarked on the grandiose but misguided mission of metahistory, where reflection on history replaces the simpler goals of history itself. The danger of this Scylla seems more acute than that of Charybdis—especially for those intellectual historians, like Pocock, who do not subscribe to the reflective methodology and are in danger of being swallowed up by it, or at least, seen as part of that same monster by other historians. In response, Pocock provides an account of another sort of intellectual historian:

> But it is also possible to imagine a "working historian" who desires to be a historian but not (in this sense) an intellectual, who desires to practice the writing of history but not to arrive at an attitude towards it, and who does not look beyond the construction of those narrative histories of various kinds of intellectual activity which he or she knows how to write.[42]

The assumption is that our first type of intellectual historian (LaCapra, White) does not desire to be a historian and instead seeks to be something else, perhaps a literary critic, a French philosopher, or some other sort of "intellectual." The second sort of intellectual historian is, however, a historian's historian. This is a historian who is not concerned with theory or reflection but with the writing of history via the construction of narratives about intellectual activity that he or she knows how to write. And here we return to the ghost story. Pocock feels compelled to reclaim intellectual history for "working historians," and to do so, he must exorcise the evil spirits from the house of history. It is clear that the danger has come from without, from those historians who do not desire to act like historians and instead take their cues from other sources, perhaps literary criticism, New Historicism, or continental philosophy? But it is a danger, none-theless, that threatens to ruin intellectual history for the conventional or "working" intellectual historians. Even worse in the eyes of traditional historians, it threatens to do so by shifting the focus from the reconstruc-tion of the past through narrative history to the critical reflection about the ways that historical discourses work. Thus while Pocock's target is exceedingly large, here, too, deconstruction seems to constitute the major threat to a tradition built on the confident and nonreflective construction of narrative.

Given its timing, Pocock's piece seems to smack of nostalgia for a sim-pler time when history was history and the discipline was self-contained. John Toews's review article, "Intellectual History After the Linguistic Turn: The Autonomy of Meaning and the Irreducibility of Experience," published in the *American Historical Review* in 1987, confirmed that the historical ground was shifting under Pocock's feet.[43] Toews's review is sig-nificant for several reasons. First and foremost, it was published in the *AHR*, the representative journal of the largest professional historical asso-ciation in the United States. The title announced that a "linguistic turn" had occurred leading to important changes in the field of intellectual his-tory, and the fact that the journal decided to publish this article signaled that the historical profession thought these changes were significant for the profession as a whole. Pocock may have wished away this trend in intellectual history, but now it was presented front and center for all his-torians to see.

The scope of Toews's review also reified the sense that there was a school of thought or body of texts that all fall under the umbrella of the linguistic turn (as in the volume edited by LaCapra and Kaplan).[44] Toews discussed twelve books published between 1982 and 1986, some of which were clearly indicative of the infiltration of the linguistic turn as critical theory or philosophy into the writing of history (David Hollinger, LaCapra, Richard Rorty), others that were about theorists or philosophers in this tradition (Alan Megill, Mark Poster), some that used the study of discourse as their methodological scaffold (Jean-Christophe Agnew, Martin Jay, Peter Jelavich), and some that indicated the way this trend in-

formed more conventional historians (Pocock, Quentin Skinner).[45] Toews
is careful to distinguish between these works, but he is also eager to point
out that they all share a common cause: "It is striking the extent to which
they [the twelve books] virtually all assume, however, the validity of [the]
general claim that intellectual history is an integral part of the interdisciplinary study of the history of meaning and that the pursuit of this study
involves a focused concern on the ways meaning is constituted in and
through language."

But beyond the shared assumptions about language that one could de-
tect in earlier pieces, Toews's article reveals a decidedly different tone and
presentation. He continues: "A new self-confidence is clearly evident. The
fears of being conquered and colonized by the perspectives and methods
of social historians, so prevalent among intellectual historians just a few
years ago, have diminished considerably, and one can even find warn-
ings about the dangers of overconfidence and intellectual imperialism."[46]
Toews presents intellectual history as a revitalized leader whose turn toward language is now in a position to dictate the terms of historical methodology. It is no longer a beleaguered subdiscipline facing obsolescence;
to use Toews's language, the colonized had become the colonizer. The
language is significant given the growing interest in postcolonialism and
subaltern studies and the connections between these fields, deconstruction, and the work of Derrida and Foucault. But this imperial tone also
created the impression that these historians were poised to assert their
will and methodologies on the profession as a whole, and this played into
the fears articulated by Pocock. It is not clear whether this development
should be seen as innovation or threat.

In the section on LaCapra's *Rethinking Intellectual History* Toews articulates what he perceives to be LaCapra's contribution to this revitalization
of intellectual history, but in so doing he also provokes, or echoes, some
of the chief criticisms.[47] A further development is that in many parts of
his article, Toews presented deconstruction uncoupled from Jacques Derrida, or rather, he suggested that deconstruction assumes a wider definition than that articulated by either Derrida or LaCapra. In his discussion
of Roger Chartier's essay "Intellectual History or Sociocultural History?
The French Trajectories," Toews describes Chartier's argument in these
terms: "deconstructing the opposition of elite and popular entails a reconsideration of the oppositions of creation-reception and production-
consumption as well. . . . Meanings are never simply inscribed on the

minds and bodies of those to whom they are directed or on whom they are 'imposed' but are always reinscribed in the act of reception."[48] Whether or not Chartier's work is best described as "deconstruction," this is the term that Toews uses, and in so doing he releases the spirit of deconstruction from the body of Jacques Derrida. To be sure, when Toews expands his discussion to include LaCapra, he is quick to state that "LaCapra develops this point into a general theory, often formulated in the terminology of Derrida, about the reading and interpretation of texts."[49] Nevertheless, discussion of the use of deconstruction for historical investigation is present throughout the text in the sections on Chartier and LaCapra but also in those on Jelavich, Megill, and Skinner, and in the latter deconstruction often takes on a pejorative meaning. Toews ends his article on an optimistic but cautionary note. He tells us that "the history of meaning has successfully asserted the reality and autonomy of its object. At the same time, however, a new form of reductionism has become evident, the reduction of experience to the meanings that shape it. Along with this possibility, a new form of intellectual hubris has emerged, the hubris of wordmakers who claim to be makers of reality."[50] Toews does not tell us who these "wordmakers" are exactly, but the assertion about the "reality and autonomy" of the historical object is fundamentally at odds with the deconstructive critique of history. Furthermore, the claim to the primacy of experience and the need to "rethink the relationship between experience and meaning with the same critical intensity and sophistication that has been devoted to exploring the ways in which meaning is constituted in language" implies that the emphasis on language is offtrack or at least out of balance. The main point is that deconstruction as presented in the article appears to be the chief offender and thus directly susceptible to Toews's cautionary criticism.

It is true that Toews's article presents one of the least scary stories about the *arrivant* deconstruction and is indicative of an optimistic, albeit critical, survey of the potential benefits of the "linguistic turn." But it is important to note that deconstruction was not the central focus of the article, and in some respects it was the least well received of all the linguistic theories under review. Thus, as in the earlier discussion, it provided a bull's eye for criticism of the entire phenomenon despite the fact that it was not the center of the article. Instead, the central focus of the article was the ways that culture could be read as a text and thus interpreted using the various models of linguistic theory presented in the review.[51] It would be the cultural historian who would reap the benefits of the "linguistic turn" in the late 1980s and throughout the 1990s.

The Cultural Turn

In 1987 a conference titled "French History: Texts and Culture" took place at UC Berkeley. The event was planned on the occasion of a month-long visit by Roger Chartier, and Natalie Zemon Davis served as commentator at large. The proceedings of this conference were expanded to become a volume edited by Lynn Hunt and published in 1989 as *The New Cultural History*.[52] In some ways the creation and reception of this volume are strikingly similar to the one edited by LaCapra and Kaplan, and there is some definite continuity between the two. Hunt's volume builds on many of the issues raised in the earlier book, and the presence of Roger Chartier as a key contributor to both created a sense of affinity. Lloyd S. Kramer's essay for the volume focused on "the literary challenge of Hayden White and Dominick LaCapra," so here, too, the earlier volume was present in the latter.[53] But there are also significant differences, especially in terms of tone. Rather than a response to a perceived state of decline and crisis, Hunt's volume is an optimistic affirmation of the new possibilities open to cultural history. In this respect the tone is more like Toews's review, and as with Toews a key component, perhaps the key component, of this "new cultural history" is the interest in language and the "linguistic turn." Furthermore, this emphasis on language leads the "new cultural history" toward interdisciplinarity. Specifically, Lynn Hunt looks to anthropology and literature. In her introduction she points out that "although there are many differences within and between anthropological and literary models, one central tendency in both seems to fascinate historians of culture: the use of language as metaphor. Symbolic actions such as riots or cat massacres are framed as texts to be read or language to be decoded. . . . The use of language as metaphor or model has proved undeniably significant and, I would argue, critical to the formulation of a cultural approach to history."[54] For Hunt, the cultural historian benefits greatly from the strategies of cultural anthropology and literary criticism in regard to their emphasis on language.

For our purposes what is essential are the ways that the linguistic theorists announced in the earlier works on intellectual history are incorporated into the "new cultural history" and the role that deconstruction plays in this amalgamation of linguistic theories. The volume is divided into two parts, "Part One examines, critically and appreciatively, the models that have already been proposed for the history of culture. Part Two presents concrete examples of the new kinds of work that are currently under way."[55] Deconstruction as a method does not figure prominently in either section, and even in Lloyd Kramer's essay on White and LaCapra the term *deconstruction* never appears. Nevertheless, deconstruction haunts this volume, making ephemeral appearances in relation to the other methods and then disappearing from sight.

In the essay by Kramer, included in part 1 (the section on established methods), deconstruction is a constant subtext of the debate between White and LaCapra. Part 2 (on new kinds of work) contains the essay by Roger Chartier, and although Hunt describes Chartier's work in relation to that of Michel Foucault, we should not forget Toews's characterization of Chartier's work as "deconstruction" in his review article for the *AHR*. Indeed, this slippage in and of itself links Foucault to Derrida, a trend that continues to this day. Foucault is probably the most important theoretical figure in the volume, and his work holds the most purchase for the contributors. The first essay in the volume is Patricia O'Brien's "Michel Foucault's History of Culture." O'Brien presents an overview of Foucault's methodology, argues that Foucault studies culture through the "prism of the technologies of power, which he located strategically in discourse," and challenges historians of culture to employ Foucault's "method and tools of analysis" to "rewrite the history of Western civilization" as a "new political history of culture."[56] O'Brien's treatment of Foucault is well measured and judicious, but one can see how the emphasis on "power" in Foucault and the domineering imposition of the "organizing hierarchy" in Derrida could lead one to see these thinkers as two of a kind. This is especially so if one has not actually read Foucault or Derrida but only about them.

In this light, Kramer's assertion that "the call for a more varied approach to history carries the influence of a European tradition that evolves from Friedrich Nietzsche into the recent work of Michel Foucault or Jacques Derrida and that examines critically the founding assumptions of knowledge" suggests that Derrida and Foucault are kith and kin.[57] The edited volume by Kaplan and LaCapra, the review article by Toews, and even the critique by Pocock all push the less-informed reader in this direction, as does *The New Cultural History*. Thus based on a reading culled from the works discussed, one could certainly make the case that Foucault does provide a deconstruction of Western historical paradigms in the sense that he exposes the moment in which power is inscribed and the methods by which it is enforced, but this is no deconstruction in the Derridean sense or as we have previously defined it. Instead, this is a popular perception of deconstruction as the destabilization of authoritative pronouncements.[58] In broad strokes we could distinguish the project of Foucault from that of Derrida insofar as Foucault looked for moments of discontinuity that reveal the underlying epistemic logic at play in any given era, whereas Derrida sought an interminable deconstruction of the structure of thought. Foucault may have been a bigger influence on the "new cultural history," but for the reasons explored above, deconstruction was a far scarier threat to the historical profession, and when criticism is applied to these new trends in historical methods, it is the critique of deconstruction that is most often applied as all the trends morph into one beast.

Hunt's introduction to the volume sets the tone for such a conflation. Her discussion of Chartier and Kramer is one example: "Unlike Roger Chartier, most historians of culture have been reluctant to use literary theory in any direct way. In his essay, Kramer surveys the work of the two historians most closely associated with literary theory. His essay shows clearly how literary approaches have enabled White and LaCapra to expand the boundaries of cultural history, yet it remains sensitive to the reasons for the continued marginalization of such work."[59] Here, Hunt implies that both Chartier and Kramer are sensitive to literary theory but also that the work of White and LaCapra (the figure most closely linked to deconstruction) has expanded the boundaries of cultural history, not intellectual history. She continues: "one of the purposes of this volume is to show how a new generation of historians of culture use literary techniques and approaches to develop new materials and methods of analysis."[60] Deconstruction is not mentioned, but it is no stretch to assume that it is one such "literary technique." How deconstruction relates to the "literary technique" of White, Chartier, or Foucault is unclear, although it is clear that they are related.

One of the most important features of this volume is the way it incorporates the extrahistorical trends that had been making their way into the practice of history. Many of these are the same trends that previously provoked the ire of historians like Pocock. Thus we see the specter of literary criticism and continental philosophy in the articles by O'Brien and Kramer that reference the work of Foucault, Derrida, LaCapra, and White, and the presence of new historicism in the contributions by Thomas Laqueur and Randolph Starn. Furthermore, several other (unwelcome) guests are present in the volume. The inclusion of Alletta Biersack, a cultural anthropologist, is significant both because of her status as a nontraditional historian and because of her substantive discussion of the use of Clifford Geertz, Marshall Sahlins, and cultural anthropology in general, for the history of culture. Likewise, Hunt is keen to announce the importance of women or gender studies for the new cultural history. "In the United States in particular (and perhaps uniquely), women's studies and gender studies have been at the forefront of the new cultural history."[61] The figures invoked are Natalie Davis, whose work *Fiction in the Archives* "puts the 'fictional' aspect of the documents at the center of the analysis"; Carroll Smith-Rosenberg, who "brings to bear both anthropological and literary styles of analysis"; and Joan Wallach Scott, who "has been particularly helpful in linking gender history with the analysis of discourse." Of these three, only Scott is linked to deconstruction, but in all three historians of gender, Hunt tells us, "the rising influence of literary techniques of reading literary theories can be clearly seen."[62] Here women's or gender studies, anthropology, and literary theory are all pushed together. Other figures are introduced in the volume as well, such as the sociologist Pierre Bourdieu and the Marxist literary critic Fredric Jameson. But while the intention of the volume may have been to call on theoretical diversity, it also had the effect of conflating deconstruction with other trends in literary studies, as well as with those in cultural history, cultural anthropology, sociology, and women's/gender studies. All this even though, like a ghostly apparition, deconstruction barely appears in the volume itself.

Jane Caplan's article "Postmodernism, Poststructuralism, Deconstruction: Notes for Historians" (published in *Central European History* in 1989 but originally presented as a discussion paper for the German Women's History Study Group) attempted to disaggregate the disparate strands announced in the title, but in so doing she emphasized a more discrete reduction. "*Deconstruction*, finally, is one variant of the poststructuralist tendencies represented by such different contemporary thinkers as [Roland] Barthes, Foucault, [Jacques] Lacan, [Jean] Baudrillard, or [Julia] Kristeva."[63] Caplan later presents Derrida as the progenitor of the model, but throughout the article all of these theorists are considered representatives of deconstruction. This move takes on greater weight in relation to Caplan's later statement that "while deconstructive method may be borrowed by the historian for the interpretation of single texts, deconstruction as an epistemology is virtually incompatible with the historian's enterprise."[64] This is a statement with which I fundamentally disagree. But the emphasis here is on the way that Caplan's dismissal of deconstruction sticks to all of the figures listed above. If Foucault is a representative of deconstruction and deconstruction is incompatible with history, then Foucault's work is incompatible with history.[65] My point is that if an informed and critical reader such as Caplan is willing to make these conflations, then the "average" conventional historian is likely willing to follow her lead. Thus, to take the other tack, this conflation allows deconstruction to be applied to all sorts of subjects without need for recourse to Derrida's work. Now deconstruction can be affiliated with a large number of theorists and methodologies as it is adapted in the service of cultural history, cultural anthropology, women's and gender studies, subaltern studies, and cultural studies. For both sides the term *deconstruction* took on the weight of a political or ideological position for or against the new trends in American historical practice. Thus the term *deconstruction* became "something closer to 'reverse engineering' or just taking something apart to see how it's made—sometimes with a slight debunking intention."[66]

The End of History

In 1989 Francis Fukuyama's response to the decline of Soviet influence provided another twist to our tale. In an article entitled "The End of History?" published in the *National Interest*, he postulated that the end of the Cold War was in fact the end of "history" in the Hegelian sense of the term. By 1992 the Berlin Wall had come down, the Soviet Union had collapsed, and Fukuyama expanded his essay into the book *The End of History and the Last Man*. At the most superficial level, Fukuyama's work chafed historians by the mere suggestion that the historical endeavor had ended, but the more salient point is that it articulated the end of an ideological conflict that provided poles between which to operate as historians. In the absence of an "enemy," in the Schmittian sense of the term, it became difficult to discern who was "friend" and who was "foe."[67] Throughout the 1990s cultural identity fragmented, and, rather than the stasis predicted by Fukuyama, academics entered into a period of culture wars. It is ironic that Fukuyama's resurrection of the Russo-French theorist Alexandre Kojève led some to the conclusion that Fukuyama himself was a "postmodernist" and in this light was somehow related to other postmodern phenomena such as deconstruction. It is especially problematic given Kojève's reliance on Hegel and Derrida's critique of the metaphysical concept of history.[68]

This period represented a high-water mark for the presence of deconstruction in the practice of history brought about by the work of LaCapra, Hollinger, and Megill, the review article by Toews, the article by Caplan, and especially the work of Joan Scott in *Gender and the Politics of History*,[69] as well as by the expansion of uses that appropriated the name "deconstruction." As one might expect, the increased presence of deconstruction also provoked increased anxiety. John M. Ellis's *Against Deconstruction* of 1989 attempted to exorcise the demon from literary studies, and G. R. Elton's 1990 Cook Lectures at the University of Michigan warned historians of the dangers of "philosophy" for the practice of history.[70] The nature of Fukuyama's claim about the end of history, the ideological free-for-all that resulted from the fall of the Soviet Union, the ascent of multiple academic fields that claimed to do historical analysis (most notably literary studies, gender studies, subaltern studies, and cultural studies), and the willingness of many historians (Hunt, LaCapra, Scott, White) to incorporate the foreign methodologies into the practice of history forced many historians to reevaluate their own work and to ask a larger question: who controls "history" and historical claims?

Joan Scott's "The Evidence of Experience," published in *Critical Inquiry* in 1991, pushed the envelope further. Toews's review article had been adamant that the success of the "linguistic turn" for history must rest on the "irreducibility of experience," and Hunt echoed this concern. By contrast, Scott took issue with the "evidence of experience" and the stability of the subject as the linchpins of historical writing. Scott points out that the innovations in, and expansion of, historical methods, subjects, and types of evidence have led to a "crisis for orthodox history by multiplying not only stories but subjects, and by insisting that histories are written from fundamentally different—indeed irreconcilable—perspectives or standpoints, none of which is complete or completely 'true.'"[71] Thus, the value of "experience" as a historical category has already been undermined by changes in the field that give "voice" to a variety of experiences that had been previously excluded. But this "challenge to normative history has been described, in terms of conventional historical understanding of evidence, as an enlargement of the picture, a correction to oversights resulting from inaccurate or incomplete vision, and it has rested its claim to legitimacy on the authority of experience, the direct experience of others, as well as the historian who learns to see and illuminate the lives of those others in his or her text."[72] Scott is not content to allow the progress that has been made in terms of opening the field of historical discourse to include "fundamentally different perspectives or standpoints" to be recaptured by the "authority of experience," which she characterized as the "conventional understanding of evidence." This is because for Scott, "by remaining within the epistemological framework of orthodox history, these studies lose the possibility of examining those assumptions and practices that excluded considerations of difference in the first place."[73] Scott's argument against "orthodox" or "conventional" history reintroduces the aspects of deconstruction that Hayden White had found so frightening in 1976. Deconstruction reappears as the doppelgänger, the ghost, which troubles history at its core in a way quite different from the conflated understanding of deconstruction examined above.

For Scott, the category of experience and the "project of making experience visible precludes critical examination of the workings of the ideological system itself, its categories of representation (homosexual/ heterosexual, man/woman, black/white, as fixed immutable identities), its premises about what these categories mean and how they operate, and of its notions of subjects, origin, and cause." Given my earlier discussion of deconstruction, it should be clear that it is an appropriate method for providing the sort of critical examination Scott desires. Indeed, Scott echoes Derrida's criticisms of the "metaphysical concept of history" in her diagnosis that "the project of making experience visible precludes analysis of the workings of this system and of its historicity; instead, it reproduces its terms," as well as when she states that "it operates within an ideological construction that not only naturalizes categories such as man, woman, black, white, heterosexual, and homosexual by treating them as given characteristics of individuals."[74] But what is most striking about Scott's attack on conventional history is that her criticisms are not reserved for the "old school" but are applied equally to the "innovators" as well: "Feminist historians critical of 'male-stream' histories and seeking to install women as viable subjects, social historians insisting on the materialist basis of the discipline on the one hand and on the 'agency' of individuals or groups on the other, and cultural historians who have brought symbolic analysis to the study of behavior, have joined political historians whose stories privilege the purposive actions of rational actors and intellectual historians who maintain that thought originates in the minds of individuals. *All seem to have converged on the argument that experience is an 'irreducible' ground for history.*"[75]

The use of Toews's language is difficult to miss, but the key point for our story is the ways that this statement is an indictment not only of the strands of historical investigation that one might expect to be hostile to deconstruction (social historians) but also to those who had appeared to be accepting or at least tolerant of it (feminist history, cultural history, intellectual history). This is an instance of what Derrida termed the re-inscription of the metaphysical concept of history. As we have seen, even the strands that appeared most tolerant maintained a skepticism and distance from deconstruction. Scott exposes the misappropriation of deconstruction and drives a wedge between deconstruction and those historical schools that appropriated it under the umbrella of postmodernism, post-structuralism, or the linguistic turn. In essence, this left deconstruction vulnerable to the attacks of historians who saw it as indicative of "postmodernism" and those who sought to distinguish their brand of "new history" from the stigma of deconstruction.

These attacks converged in the joint effort of Joyce Appleby, Lynn Hunt, and Margaret Jacob entitled *Telling the Truth About History*, published in 1994. Hunt, of course, had been the editor of the volume on the "new cultural history" and was a prominent cultural historian, Appleby a renowned scholar of American history, and Jacob a well-respected historian of science. It is worth noting that two of the three would go on to be presidents of the American Historical Association (Appleby in 1997, Hunt in 2002), that the book was published by a trade press (Norton), and that it is still available in paperback. All this is to say that it was and remains a highly influential book for students of the practice of history. In their chapter "Postmodernism and the Crisis of Modernity," the authors present "postmodernism" writ large as fundamentally incompatible with and irrefutably dangerous for the practice of history. This is a change of position for Hunt, who had earlier championed the possibilities of postmodern strategies, but it is consistent with her skepticism and criticisms of deconstruction in *The New Cultural History*. The authors never disaggregate what is or isn't "postmodern" but instead focus on what they assume to be some common threads. In particular, they propose that "the nature of historical truth, objectivity, and narrative form have all been targeted by postmodernists. The mastery of time becomes the willful imposition on subordinate peoples of a Western, imperialistic historical consciousness; it provides no access to true explanation, knowledge, or understanding"[76]

The larger claim about the questioning of "truth," "objectivity," and "narrative form" is coupled with a specific example that appears to be culled from subaltern studies (though it is uncited), creating the impression that the second is the necessary result of the first. This section is then followed by a discussion of the ways that "postmodernists" are influenced by Nietzsche and Heidegger, both of whom made "notoriously antidemocratic, anti-Western, and antihumanist pronouncements and were associated sometimes fairly, sometimes not, with anti-Semitism." They are then quick to point out that "Hitler cited Nietzsche in support of his racial ideology, and Heidegger himself joined the Nazi Party."[77] Here, we are back at the criticisms leveled at Derrida in 1968, that his philosophy was untenable because it was indebted to the work of the Nazi Martin Heidegger. Rather than engage the issues raised by historians such as LaCapra or Scott, the authors evade them by either presenting straw men (the "willful imposition" of time) or condemning the whole endeavor as secretly National Socialist. What's more, this strategy avoids engaging Derrida and deconstruction on the issue of "time" and temporality, which is a crucial issue for interrogating our relation to the past and the practice of history.

The authors continue to build on earlier trends by presenting Foucault and Derrida as a two-headed beast, but added to this conflation is the filiation to Heidegger and, by association, to National Socialism: "The foremost contemporary apostles of postmodernism are two French philosophers, Michel Foucault and Jacques Derrida. Much of postmodern thought can be traced to their influence and through them back to Nietzsche and Heidegger."[78] Foucault and Derrida are then presented in a joint endeavor: "both Foucault and Derrida sought to challenge the most fundamental assumptions of Western Social Science. Put most schematically, they deny our ability to represent reality in any objectively true fashion and offer to 'deconstruct' (a word made famous by Derrida and his followers) the notion of the individual as an autonomous, self-conscious agent."[79] I am interested in the way that the authors present Derrida and

Foucault as coterminous and equally committed to the project of deconstruction. This is especially important as they enfold other theorists and groups of historians into the term *postmodern* only to return to the influence of Heidegger on this movement. "This debt to Heidegger has further embroiled postmodernism in political controversy, for his unrepentant membership in the Nazi Party has long raised questions about the political meaning of his work."[80] Here, White's ghostly ballet is replaced by another specter, the specter of Nazism.[81]

In the edited volumes by LaCapra and Kaplan we saw how the varying strands of postmodern thought were linked, but we also saw the ways that deconstruction presented problems and unease for many of the historians involved in the endeavor. In Toews's article there is a similar concern about and distrust of deconstruction that is repeated in Hunt's *New Cultural History*, but the underlying effect of these works is that "deconstruction" was uncoupled from Derrida and applied to the phenomenon of postmodernism, poststructuralism, and the linguistic turn as a whole. In *Telling the Truth About History* this trend results in a backlash against postmodernism (provoked by many causes), where deconstruction is again tied to the person of Derrida, and by association to Martin Heidegger and National Socialism, and is then used to indict the whole movement. It is no accident, to my mind, that deconstruction is linked to the representation of pure evil. It is presented as something too monstrous, too horrifying to consider and thus needs to be banished from consideration. This is why Appleby, Hunt, and Jacob conclude that "in the final analysis, then, there can be no postmodern history."[82]

In 1995, *History and Theory* published a forum on *Telling the Truth About History* in which Joan Scott, Raymond Martin, and Cushing Strout all offered their responses, but in many ways this marked the beginning of the demise of deconstruction.[83] In 1999 Lynn Hunt completed her reevaluation of postmodernism in a volume that returned to the issue of methods in cultural history, *Beyond the Cultural Turn*, coedited with Victoria E. Bonnell. Unlike Hunt's earlier volume, this series of essays on the state of cultural history contains no essays by anthropologists or figures associated with literary studies. In their stead we find historians and sociologists (Bonnell is a professor of sociology). It is interesting that the editors chose to identify themselves and the contributors with "social history": "Most of the contributors to this volume, like its two editors, were originally trained in social history and/or historical sociology."[84] This is important because the editors set this volume up as a counter to the crisis of what Hunt and Bonnell refer to as the "cultural turn":

> The cultural turn and a more general postmodernist critique of knowledge have contributed, perhaps decisively, to the enfeebling of paradigms for social scientific research. In the face of these intellectual trends and the collapse of communist systems in Eastern Europe and the former Soviet Union, Marxism as an interpretive and political paradigm has suffered a serious decline. The failure of Marxism has signaled a more general failure of all paradigms. Are the social sciences becoming a branch of a more general interpretive, even literary activity—just another cultural study with claims only for individual authorial virtuosity rather than for a more generally valid, shared knowledge?[85]

Here the aforementioned trends converge (the danger of postmodernism, the fall of Marxism, the rise of cultural studies) and crystallize around Hunt and Bonnell's fear that history is losing its status as a "social science" capable of providing "generally valid, shared knowledge." Thus, there is a valorization of "science" that was decidedly absent from the earlier volume. This defense of history as a "social science" is specifically linked to the dangers inherent in Derrida and Foucault: "During the 1980s and 1990s, cultural theories, especially those with a postmodernist inflection, challenged the very possibility of or desirability of social explanation. Following the lead of Foucault and Derrida, poststructuralists and postmodernists insisted that shared discourses (or cultures) so utterly permeate our perception of reality as to make any supposed scientific explanation of social life simply an exercise in collective fictionalization or mythmaking: we can only elaborate on our presuppositions, in this view: we cannot arrive at any objective, freestanding truth."[86]

This is the ghost story fully formed. It is a tale of the evil specter now named Foucault/Derrida that is the source of the "cultural turn" and that threatens to lead us to a world of total relativism and nihilism. Hunt and Bonnell are not interested in the ways that collective fictionalization or mythmaking might play a role in the scientific explanation of social life but only in disallowing this avenue of investigation because it precludes "objective, freestanding truth." If you are for objective truth and history as ontological realism, then you must join Hunt and Bonnell in purging the poltergeist from the house of history.

To do so, Hunt and Bonnell choose historians and sociologists who have joined them on their crusade. Whereas in the earlier volume, the contribution in intellectual history was quite sympathetic to (if critical of) deconstruction and the postmodern in general, in this volume Hunt and Bonnell enlist Jerrold Seigel, who is far less so. Seigel's contribution, "Problematizing the Self," takes issue with the postmodern critique of the stable self. Seigel provides a substantive engagement with Derrida in an attempt to outline the ways that Derrida's destabilized presentation of the "self" is akin to Nietzsche and Heidegger in that "these thinkers aspired to a higher kind of freedom and power, attainable by way of the dissolution of stable self-hood."[87] Part of Seigel's project is to show this position to be untenable, but the other part is to reanchor knowledge, and thus we presume historical understanding, to the stable self, which is the locus of experience. Seigel terms this experiencing, thinking, and judging self "self-hood," and by the nature of its construction it is at odds with Joan Scott's formulation about the evidence of experience but also with Derrida's critique of the privileging of presence. The larger point is that Seigel represents the field of intellectual history in the volume, and his evaluation of Derrida is resoundingly negative.

Hayden White, who contributed the afterword to the volume, was left as a lone voice in the wilderness. White does not agree with the contributors to the volume in their assessments of "structuralism, poststructuralism, modernism, and postmodernism," all of which he regards as "ideologically progressive movements in their opposition to the pieties of capitalist society and bourgeois culture," nor with their readings of these movements, though he says he will not "correct their misconceptions of what they seem to be."[88] What is ironic, given White's assessment of Derrida in 1976, is that in defense of his position he states that "the significance of the cultural turn in history and the social sciences inheres in its suggestion that in 'culture' we can apprehend a niche within social reality from which any given society can be deconstructed and shown to be less an inevitability than only one possibility among a host of others. I support such a deconstructive enterprise."[89] But White's words seemed to hang in the air as a reminder of the ghost and monster, the danger and evils of a cultural turn that was the raison d'être for the volume.

The tide had turned, and by the year 2000 it appeared that history had indeed exorcized the ghost of deconstruction. In *History and Reading: Tocqueville, Foucault, French Studies*, LaCapra concedes that the high-water mark of theoretical activity has passed even as he again attempts to find common ground between historical and literary studies. His own movement into the area of trauma studies showed a shift in emphasis, where Freud appears to hold a more prominent place in his historical investigation, although these works still show a debt to and deep engagement with Derrida and deconstruction. This is not to say that the issue of postmodernism, or even "postmodern" history, had been put to rest, but figures such as Keith Jenkins and Elizabeth Deeds Ermarth now appeared as outliers rather than innovators.[90] The title of the *History and Theory* theme issue "Agency After Postmodernism" implied that the moment was over, although the volume itself addressed "postmodernist thought and its effects on historiography as a watershed."[91] In his introduction David Gary Shaw states that "while many scholars have recently offered sharp, sometimes even strident or exasperated criticisms of the movement, I think it is as important to stress the contributions of postmodernism and the linguistic turn. It seems to me appropriate to continue to speak of the postmodern moment as our moment."[92] But he also tells us that this "Theme Issue offers examples of how scholars are beginning to do the important work of going through the postmodernist controversy to reconstruct a richer and subtler notion of agency and its self." The subtleties presented by the contributors to this theme issue would be lost on many historians in the early twenty-first century, especially after the terrorist attacks on Washington, DC, and New York on September 11, 2001. The theme issue was not quite a postmortem, but there is a sense that an era had come to a close and that a reevaluation was necessary.[93]

The Ghost Returns

The relation to the aftermath of 9/11 is eerily foreshadowed in Carolyn Steedman's "Something She Called a Fever: Michelet, Derrida, and Dust," published in *American Historical Review* in October of 2001. This essay is something of a novelty because it is a sustained engagement with a text written by Jacques Derrida, rather than one about Derrida. The text in question was *Archive Fever: A Freudian Impression,* and there are two aspects of this article that I would like to explore, both of which relate to a change in the intellectual climate.[94] First, Steedman's article is centered on what she sees as the disconnect between Derrida's understanding of the term *archive* and the historian's understanding and experience of the term. Steedman tells us that "a more serious purpose here is to understand why historians and deconstructionists must continue to talk right past each other, to suggest why this mutual incomprehension may be no bad thing—or at least—nothing to worry about, and along the way to know a little more about what it is that historians do in archives, and in writing about what they have found there."[95] There is some irony in an investigation into Freud that positions itself around the confident assertion that there is "nothing to worry about." The assumption here is that the "deconstructionist," Derrida himself in this case, doesn't understand what historians "do" in the archive. This assumption effectively cuts off the more important, and potentially threatening, aspect of Derrida's meditation on Freud and the archive. This is the question about *why* we ascribe such authority to the archive as the source of legitimation and truth. Steedman homes in on Derrida's discussion of the *arkhe*, a place where things begin, and its relation to the *arkheion*, or superior magistrate's residence, in the Greek city-state as the site where official documents are stored. Derrida's emphasis on civic law and the *arkheion* raised the " puzzling question" for historians "of what on earth an archive was doing there in the first place, at the beginning of a long description of another text which dealt with Sigmund Freud and the topic of psychoanalysis."[96] As discussed in my introduction, the text in question is Yosef Yerushalmi's *Freud's Moses: Judaism Terminable and Interminable*, which seeks to understand Freud's *Moses and Monotheism* in terms of a conflict about the understanding of Judaism as a historical and religious phenomenon.[97] Steedman's obsession with the archive as the source of historical facts leads her to quickly dismiss Freud's book as "famously based on no historical evidence whatsoever" and Derrida's book because it has nothing to do with "real archives."[98] But in so doing she misses a key strand of the argument and the text that makes the relation of the *arkheion* to the work by Yerushalmi or, more specifically, to Freud apparent.

Steedman never makes the connection to Moses and his ark, the Ark of the Covenant, the sacred container that held the stone tablets on which the Ten Commandments were written. Thus, the origins of the Hebrew people and their laws are to be found in an archive of sorts as well. Moses thus serves as the originator of this tradition though the issue becomes cloudy because the Ten Commandments were revealed to Moses by God. Moses is the author of these laws, but his authority is predicated on his relationship to God. This is all tied to history when one considers Moses as the author of the Torah, or Pentateuch, the five books wherein the history of the Jewish people is told. Here, Moses is the first historian, but, again, the validity of his claims rests on the authority of God, and we will return to the relation of religion to history as the theologico-historical in Chapter 4. Thus, Freud's attempt to revise our understanding of Moses based on psychoanalysis may contain no "historical evidence whatsoever," but does the traditional account that he is debunking meet Steedman's criteria for historical evidence? And if not, on what authority does she let one account stand while condemning the other? And what about Yerushalmi's own attempt to conjure the ghost of Freud at the end of his book? Derrida's meditation on the "archive" is an attempt to see it as a site where some traditions, ideologies, practices, and methods are legitimized or granted authority while others are suppressed, suspended, or outlawed.[99] The great irony of Steedman's article is that this is exactly what she does to deconstruction.

The way she does this is by recourse to personal experience. Ultimately, Steedman claims that she can show Derrida's account to be inappropriate for historians based on her personal experience in the archive. "Archive Fever, indeed? *I* can tell you *all about* archive fever."[100] What follows is a well-researched account of the possible origin of an actual medical condition where one gets sick from working in an archive. As it turns out, historians such as Steedman have caught archive fever, whose source is dust coming off the jackets and pages of old manuscripts made from animal skins. This dust contains spores from the "external or cutaceous form of anthrax."[101] So archive fever is not just a catchy title but a real hazard encountered by working historians. Steedman's research and article were written before the events of September 11, 2001, but it was published at a time of increased anxiety and fear about terrorist threats and particularly the threat of letters filled with anthrax powder.[102] Thus, the article played into a heightened sense of fear in the country and among historians but also continued the trend toward regrounding the subject on the bedrock of experience in the face of threats internal and external. But here, too, Steedman evades Derrida's investigation into the authority of the archive and the historian by discussing her own harrowing experience in the archive with little or no reflection about *why* she affords this place such authority or worth. Instead, Steedman tells us:

> The historian's massive authority as a writer derives from two factors: the ways archives are, and the conventional rhetoric of history writing, which always asserts (through footnotes, through the casual reference to PT S2/1/1)

that you *know* because you have been there. The fiction is that the authority comes from the documents themselves, as well as the historian's obeisance to the limits they impose on any account that employs them. But really it comes from having been there (the train to the distant city, the call number, the bundle opened, the dust) so that then, and only then, you can present yourself as moved and dictated to by those sources, telling a story the way it has to be told.[103]

Whether such a claim can still be made given the arrival of the digital archive is an open question. But the point here is that personal experience becomes the basis for the authority of the historian, and while Steedman attempts to head deconstruction off at the pass by asserting that it should come as no surprise that deconstruction made "no difference for this kind of writing [history]" because "there is actually *nothing there*: only absence, what once was: dust," the recourse to this nothingness is based entirely on the living, breathing, presence of the historian who actually goes to the archive, experiences documents, and thus knows what happened. Steedman's article is indicative of the return to a quest for a stable present subject that can provide the grounds for a knowable past even while admitting that the past is somehow unknowable. It is an ontological realist commitment to history as an endeavor concerned with events assigned to a specific location in space and time that are in principle observable and as such are regarded as fixed and immutable. But it is also indicative of the demise of deconstruction as a viable threat to the historical profession. Steedman confronts Derrida on, ostensibly, his own terms to demonstrate his misunderstanding of the historical archive and history in general. In my reading she does this by avoiding or repressing those aspects of deconstruction that are the most troubling and that only appear in the ways that the archive makes her physically sick. In the end, for Steedman there is nothing to fear because deconstruction doesn't actually go into the archives.

But as in any ghost story, the calm would not last. The anxiety and the fear that resulted from the terrorist attacks and the wars that followed led to a general reevaluation of postmodernism and its role in producing a fragmented and hostile war. Coupled with this evaluation was the call to return to more stable grounds; now the issue was not only experience but also judgment. Bruno Latour's "Why Has Critique Run Out of Steam? From Matters of Fact to Matters of Concern," published in *Critical Inquiry* in 2004, suggested that the critical modes of the previous decades (deconstruction included) had run their course, and in this new climate of danger, new methodologies were necessary. It is worth noting that Latour had been something of a poster boy for postmodern critical inquiry into science in the late twentieth century and that *Critical Inquiry* is a journal sympathetic to such methodologies. It is also worth mentioning that Jacques Derrida died on October 8, 2004. Latour wanted to impress on his readers the ways things had changed. "Wars. So many wars. Wars outside and wars inside. Cultural wars, science wars, and wars against terrorism."[104] For Latour these wars are all related, and while his own emphasis is on the history of science, his arguments coincide with larger trends. Thus, the stakes are high as Latour informs us: "entire Ph.D. programs are still running to make sure that good American kids are learning the hard way that facts are made up, that there is no such thing as natural, unmediated, unbiased access to truth, that we are always prisoners of language, that we always speak from a particular standpoint, and so on, while dangerous extremists are using the very same argument of social construction to destroy hard-won evidence that could save our lives."[105] The first example provided by Latour where "critique," which seems to be the stand-in for postmodernism or deconstruction, is indicted is in reference to global warming. Latour indicates that the critique of stable scientific "facts" has allowed conservatives to deny that global warming is a "fact." Clearly, the postmodern moment has gone too far.

It is not only in the realm of science but also in the realm of politics where these postmodern theories have been hijacked to nefarious ends. Latour's anxiety and outrage is palpable when he tells us, "I am now the one who naively believes in some facts because I am educated, while the other guys are too *un*sophisticated to be gullible: 'Where have you been? Don't you know that the Mossad and the CIA did it?'"[106] What has happened here? Latour is telling us that it is the sophisticated intellectual who naively believes in facts while the realm of questions and critique now belong to the *un*sophisticated. And these unsophisticated proponents of critique, these destabilizers of facts, these postmodernists are now akin to revisionist conspiracy theorists who claim that Mossad and the CIA blew up the World Trade Center and the Pentagon. Suddenly, the specter of deconstruction has returned with all its force and fury. "Let me be mean for a second. What is the real difference between conspiracists and a popularized, that is teachable, version of social critique inspired by a too quick reading of, let's say, a sociologist as eminent as Pierre Bourdieu (to be polite I will stick with the French field commanders)?"[107] Latour gives himself some wiggle room by allowing that a careful reading (his own?) of these theorists would lead to a different conclusion. But it is clear that in this day and age one cannot leave these dangerous texts and methodologies unguarded. "Do you see why I am worried? Threats might have changed so much that we might still be directing all our arsenal east or west while the enemy has now moved to a different place."[108] This new climate of wars, "so many wars," clearly differs from the ideological clash of old, and it appears that Latour holds "critique" responsible for this dangerous new world.

Latour has had enough of both the positivist worship of facts and the groundless relativism of critique run amok. But if the former is deemed problematic, the latter is downright dangerous:

> This is why, in my opinion, those of us who tried to portray sciences as matters of concern so often failed to convince; readers have confused the treatment we give of former matters with the terrible fate of objects processed through the hands of sociology, cultural studies, and so on. And I can't blame our readers. What social scientists do to our favorite objects is so horrific that certainly we don't want them to come any nearer. "Please," we exclaim, "don't touch them at all! Don't try to explain them!" Or we might suggest more politely: "Why don't you go further down the corridor to this other department? *They* have bad facts to account for; why don't you explain away those ones instead of ours?"[109]

The quote may be whimsical, but the attack on cultural studies, sociology, and so forth is serious, and we have already discerned how these fields of critical inquiry have been linked to deconstruction. The criticism is all the more serious given the ways that Latour relates these methodologies and fields of study to disastrous results, whether to deny global warming or promote terrorist attacks. The bottom line is that these methodologies lack any basis for sound judgment. For Latour, "Critique has not been critical enough of all its sore-scratching. Reality is not defined by matters of fact. Matters of fact are not all that is given in experience. Matters of fact are only very partial and, I would argue, very polemical, very political renderings of matters of concern and only a subset of what could also be called *states of affairs*. It is this second empiricism, this return to the realist attitude, that I'd like to offer as the next task for the critically minded."[110] In essence, the prior emphasis on the incontrovertibility of "facts" led to the postmodern critique that exposed this as a fallacy. The error occurs when the overthrow of facts leads to the sort of relativistic nihilism that is as much at home providing fodder for revisionist conspiracy theorists as critics of colonialism. In an attempt to disarm the apparatus of critique, Latour calls for social theorists to replace "matters of fact" with "matters of concern." Latour sees the realist attitude, this second empiricism, as our last best hope in a troubled world, and he is heartened because "it is not only the objects of science that resist, but all the others as well, those that were supposed to have been ground to dust by the powerful teeth of automated reflex-action deconstructors."[111] Here deconstruction takes the form of a monster grinding any possibility for truth to dust. But the issue is judgment, and Latour's assumption is that deconstruction, postmodernism, critique, or perhaps those who practice these methodologies, lack this crucial attribute. To his mind, a return to a realist attitude predicated on experience is the only way to achieve this emphasis on "matters of concern."

"Is it not time for some progress? To the fact position, the fairy position, why not add a third position, a *fair* position?"[112] Exasperated by "positivism" (the fact position) and scared to death by "critique" (the fairy position), Latour asks for a position from which one can act fairly, and here, once again, we see the desire for an Archimedean point on which one can rest judgments of fact and fiction, good and bad, right and wrong. This desire for a fixed and stable point characterizes the dominant modes of historical scholarship up to our current moment in the twenty-first century. Furthermore, for Latour "the critic is not the one who debunks, but the one who assembles."[113] The critic should not be engaged in deconstruction but in construction. The critique is eerily similar to the one presented by Hayden White in 1976 when he dismissed Derrida with the question: "When the world is denied all substance and perception is blind, who is to say who are the chosen and who are the damned? On what grounds can we assert that the insane, the criminal, and the barbarian are wrong?"[114] But have we not been here before, and is not LaCapra's response to White equally applicable for Latour? Latour's fear is akin to White's, but in the post-9/11 world the crisis feels more acute because Latour holds deconstruction, at least in part, responsible for the many wars, cultural and military, and this points to the larger issue of the ways that deconstruction and critique have been appropriated and the ways that what Derrida calls the "metaphysical concept of history" and the "logic of identity" are reinscribed in this appropriation.

Up until the 1970s the dominant modes of historical investigation were unmarked in the sense that variations of one general narrative, largely a white male European narrative, laid claim to the field and what was possible to imagine as "proper history." In the 1980s and 1990s postmodernism in general and deconstruction in particular opened up what could be imagined as a past possible and thus possible pasts, allowing for multiple narratives and multiple subject groups. This is what precipitates the crisis for orthodox history "by multiplying not only stories but subjects and by insisting that histories are written from fundamentally different—indeed irreconcilable—perspectives or standpoints, none of which is complete or completely 'true'" as diagnosed by Scott.[115] But the crisis was not isolated to "orthodox historians" as proponents of each of these diverse and differing narratives began to search for firmer ground on which to set their own identity. Here the rejection of deconstruction is the repression of the realization that there is no stable foundation made explicit by a deconstructive approach to the past. As identity politics came into play, a truncated deconstruction appeared that simply sought to invert power dynamics rather than to destabilize them.[116] From this perspective the organizing principle of the historical investigation was no longer put into question but simply redeployed to make the colonizer the colonized. Uncoupled from Derrida's critique of the "metaphysical" concept of history (a "history" that provides an ideological scaffold on which "it" organizes itself but then presents itself as objective and neutral "historical truth"), deconstruction now served to reinforce identity as ideology. This move validates Derrida's reservations about "history" and the possibility of conceptualizing "history" without smuggling in the metaphysical baggage. But to take this a step further, I would argue that it is precisely the fear inspired by the possibility of history or identity that is not predicated on a stable and definitive ground that sends these thinkers (orthodox and iconoclast) "back" to the bedrock of experience, presence, and the stable subject— back to the archive where origins can be found because we "know" they are there, because we experienced them. It sends them back to ontological realism. The *unheimlich* realization that history and identity are moving targets, that the past inhabits an uncanny territory that both is and isn't, is revealed by deconstruction and met by fear and repression.

The problem here is that once all subject groups have recourse to history, there can be no agreement on "truth" if the foundation of evidence is experience or the past is understood via the criteria of ontological realism. In essence this is the source of the culture wars, where each group defends its narrative as more "real" than the others. This is a structural impasse, where the validation of one worldview (or point of view) comes at the expense or suppression of another, where one tradition is inhabited at the expense of another.[117] After the attacks of 9/11 and the "wars on terror," the cultural wars and identity politics took on a much more sinister character. To confront identity politics and to return history to the firm ground of evidence, a ground from which judgment about true and false, right and wrong, good and evil could be formed, history must first exorcise the demons that unleashed this perspectivalism—demons that, we will see, predate deconstruction and that in fact inhabit some formative methodologies of the historical discipline. Faced with a subject position that is jeopardized by other subjects claiming equal or greater authority, the historian retreats into the fortress of the subject and the essentializing metaphysical logic that presents historical "truth" as singular and foundational (and thus restricted and restricting) rather than confronting the possibility that the stable subject, the foundation, like history, is itself a nonessential and problematic construction. But the battle against identity politics was waged against the "relativism" of deconstruction via a return to identity itself through investigations predicated on experience, memory, and truth. Works by Martin Jay, Jerrold Seigel, and Ernst Breisach attest to this trend, as does the recent emphasis on testimony and oral history.[118] All of these works also point toward the return of an emphasis on "presence" as the essential category for the production of history.[119] In this respect the gains of postmodernism have been lost as we return to a logic of essentialism and the reinscription of the "metaphysical concept of history" based on the privileging of presence.

A further twist in the plot is the way that the death of Derrida in 2004 and the subsequent creation of the Derrida archives in Paris and Irvine, California, have allowed historians to revisit his life and work as the subject of historical inquiry. Benoît Peeters published a biography of Derrida in 2010, and Edward Baring's *The Young Derrida and French Philosophy, 1945–1968* came out in 2011.[120] Each of these works attempts to place Derrida's life and work in context. Peeters's work is clearly more interested in the former issue, while Baring provides a sophisticated engagement with the latter. In the case of Baring's book the irony of working in and using materials from the then newly minted Derrida archives is not lost, and Baring addresses the relation of his historical work on Derrida to Derrida's own engagement with history and the archives in the introduction and conclusion. Baring furthers his discussion of what he refers to as the "family resemblance between what [Derrida] suggests and norms already at work within the discipline of history" in his article "Ne me raconte plus d'histoires" from 2014.[121] It is worth mentioning that this article follows the language of "haunting history" I presented in the initial version of this chapter, published as an article in 2007, and in this way my earlier work is entangled with the historiographical narrative presented in this one. But the more salient point for this argument is the ways that Baring wants to read "Derrida historically, outlining what [Baring] consider[s] to be a helpful context for his early work and tracing his thought as it developed."[122] This is, to my mind, both the strength and limitation of Baring's presentation of Derrida and deconstruction in both the book and the article because while Baring's book is a masterful work of intellectual history that enriches our understanding of Derrida in his milieu, his interest lies principally in "reading Derrida historically" rather than reading Derrida and deconstruction for the practice of history.

In her address as president of the American Historical Association, published as "The Task of the Historian" in the February 2009 issue of *American Historical Review*, Gabrielle Spiegel takes a similar tack both in terms of her sense that the deconstructive moment or "linguistic turn" had come to an end and in the ways that she uses Derrida and deconstruction as a cypher to understand and explain a particular historical moment.[123] In this case it is Spiegel's "belief that Derrida alchemized into philosophy a psychology deeply marked by the Holocaust—marked by but not part of its experiential domain—in which the Holocaust figures as the absent origin that Derrida himself did so much to theorize."[124] But to her credit Spiegel does not want to let the remains of deconstruction rest undisturbed and calls on historians to marshal the work of Derrida and deconstruction in the service of their practice. In particular she looks to Walter Benjamin's notes for his "Theses on the Philosophy of History" to assert that "the historian's task [is], therefore, what Hugo von Hofmannsthal defined as 'reading what was never written.' It is in this moment that the past is saved, 'not in being returned to what once existed, but instead, precisely in being transformed into something that never was, in being 'read as what was never written.'"[125] Here, the ontological reality of the past is placed in question, and the entanglement of past, present, and future is exposed. I see this as commensurate to what I refer to as the past that *is*, and I will take this up in Chapters 3, 4, and 5.

But the plea to revisit Derrida and deconstruction is couched in an assessment that the emphasis on language that led historians to him has run its course.[126] This is an assessment shared by other historians sympathetic to deconstruction, such as Michael Roth in his essay "Ebb Tide," from 2007, and Nancy Partner in her piece "Narrative Persistance," for the edited volume *Re-figuring Hayden White*, from 2009. Roth argues that "the linguistic turn that had motivated much advanced work in the humanities is over . . . [and] the massive tide of language . . . has receded; we are now able to look across the sand to see what might be worth salvaging before the next waves of theory and research begin to pound the shore."[127] Citing and building on this, Partner points to the "tentative alternate candidates vying for attention," such as ethics, intensity, postcolonialism, empire, the sacred, cosmopolitanism, trauma, memory, agency, experience, the sublime, and presence. She argues that all of these proposed "topics or focal points share a common desire to escape language, to restore a pure and immediate connection with the past or at least some central aspect of experience, and generally deny the power of language to contaminate 'history' with its own uncontrollable meanings."[128] The sense of despair at the inadequacy of "language" emboldened historians and theorists to seek solace in seemingly nonlinguistic methodologies and theories such as that of "presence," which we will explore in the following chapter.

But as Spiegel suggests, the specter of deconstruction has not been laid to rest, and the sureties of experience and presence for the project of history are more tenuous than they may appear. Much like the specter, the past is a *revenant* brought back to the present by the historian. It visits us but does not belong to our time or place. This is to say that it has no ontological properties of its own but is conjured by the medium of the historian. By revealing the play of *différance*, deconstruction unhinges the past from the "as it really happened," problematizing the belief in a fixed and stable past (which is the myth of a fixed and stable present), and returns it to the realm of possibilities. To be sure, the historian arrests certain of these possibilities in his or her telling of the story, but this does not negate these possibilities of the past that can return. Furthermore, deconstruction reveals the moment of decision when the story is structured according to a hierarchical ordering that privileges certain possibilities and discounts others (presence/absence, stable/relative, postmodern/traditional). In this way deconstruction reveals the legitimizing strategies of the author/historian while upsetting the authority of this particular telling. This destabilization creates, in turn, the possibility of a revised history or interpretation based on a reevaluation of the possible ordering strategies. Deconstruction is perhaps most visible as the spirit of historical revision where it lays open the possibility of new tellings, new readings, and new facts and where it forces the historian to confront her- or himself in the creation of the history revised. But it is most forceful as a critique of our conventional assumptions about space and time as the coordinates of identity. This is the double, the unheimlich, the ghost that terrifies us because in it we see our "darker purpose" and the limits of the project of history: the aporia of the chaotic, heterogeneous and polysemic past. "'Unheimlich' is the name for everything that ought to have remained . . . secret and hidden but has come to light."[129] For history to be uncomplicated "truth," this secret must remain hidden, but each time a historical event is revised, the very act of revision reveals the instability of historical truth, identity, and the possibility of recounting what "actually happened." It reveals the possibility of alternative pasts that had been previously unimagined. This is a moment of possibility and communication when the understanding and presentation of historical events is put into play so that it is not "owned" by anyone. But this is also a source of great anxiety for a discipline with "scientific" aspirations to know the "truth." The spectral nature of the past is revealed in revision so as to expose this moment of possibility, but, ironically, this specter has been continually exorcised under the name of deconstruction. But "in this case too, then, the *unheimlich* is what was once *heimisch*, familiar; the prefix '*un*' is the token of repression."[130] Thus, as we have seen, in revision the deconstruction itself is repressed and the mantle of "truth" is awarded to the revised version.

The reaction against deconstruction by conventional historians and historical theorists alike has been consistent and strong. Thus, to present a deconstructive approach to the past and the practice of history I will first turn to one of the most prominent schools of historical theory and then to an investigation of ontological realism in disciplinary history as it is currently practiced. This will be the subject of the next two chapters, after which the specter of deconstruction will rise, as if from the dead, to haunt history once more.

§ 2   Presence in *Absentia*

> If we were not perfectly convinced that Hamlet's Father died before the play
> began, there would be nothing more remarkable in his taking a stroll at night,
> in an easterly wind, upon his own ramparts, than there would be in any other
> middle-aged gentleman rashly turning out after dark in a breezy spot—say
> Saint Paul's Churchyard for instance—literally to astonish his son's weak
> mind.
> —Charles Dickens, *A Christmas Carol*

"Marley was dead: to begin with."[1] So opens Dickens's classic tale of
Christmas redemption, and it is with the ghost of Jacob Marley that I
want to begin this exploration of the concept of "presence" as a historical
theory in relation to deconstruction. Dickens's point is that if time were
not out of joint, if Marley was not dead and we were not absolutely sure
of his ghostly, spectral, and immaterial nature, then "nothing wonderful" could come of the story. To be sure, Marley is not the only ghost in
Dickens's story, but the other three have a strikingly different nature. For
Dickens, Marley is the only ghost whose death concerns us because he is
the only ghost who is out of time. This is to say that unlike the ghost of
Marley, the Ghosts of Christmas Past, Present, and Future appear to be
well jointed in terms of our classic understanding of temporality. The past
precedes the present that is followed by the future, and each is announced
by the ordered sounding of the clock. But while these three ghosts are
bound by this temporal structure, they, too, are each unique. Not unlike
the past itself, the Ghost of Christmas Past is a figure that "fluctuated in
its distinctness: being now a thing with one arm, now with one leg, now
with twenty legs, now a pair of legs without a head, now a head without a body: of which dissolving parts, no outline would be visible in the
dense gloom wherein they melted away. And in the very wonder of this, it
would be itself again; distinct and clear as ever." In the gloom the Ghost
of Christmas Past emits a "bright clear jet of light" from the crown of its
head though it also possesses a "great extinguisher of a cap."[2] This ghost
will visit us again in Chapter 4. The Ghost of Christmas Yet to Come is

a figure shrouded in a "deep black garment which concealed its head, its face, its form" and whose "mysterious presence filled him [Scrooge] with a solemn dread."[3] By contrast, the Ghost of Christmas Present is a gregarious fellow, a "jolly Giant, glorious to see," before a "mighty blaze that roared up the chimney" and seated upon a "kind of throne" made up of "turkeys, geese, game, poultry, brawn, great joints of meat, sucking-pigs, long wreaths of sausages, mince pies, plum puddings, barrels of oysters, red-hot chestnuts, cherry cheeked apples, juicy oranges, immense twelfth-cakes, and seething bowls of punch, that made the chamber dim with their delicious steam."[4] And here we should think about the way Hans Ulrich Gumbrecht differentiates "presence effects" from "meaning effects" in that "presence effects appeal exclusively to the senses."[5] A more sensuous or welcoming figure could not be imagined: "'Come in!' exclaimed the Ghost. 'Come in! and know me better, man!'"

Thus, even beyond the material comfort one receives in his presence, there seems more to be gained from the Ghost of Christmas Present than from the others. The past is gone, and the future is yet to come. It is only in the present that one can actually do things, that one can change in ways that of course cannot rectify the past but can serve the future. This is precisely what happens to Scrooge, and in this light one can certainly see the attraction of a focus on presence and the present: on a philosophy of history that eschews the endless turning over of the past or fruitless speculation on the future in favor of an emphasis on actual things that are present here and now. "'Presence,' in my view, is 'being in touch'— either literally or figuratively—with people, things, events, and feelings that made you into the person you are."[6] Thus "before" and "after" meet in the very real place of the present, safe from the brackish ontological waters of the past and the uncertainty and anxiety of the future.[7] One might say that the present "is what it is," and in this respect the present distinguishes itself from the past and the future because it positions itself as a category of space and not time.[8] As such, the interpretive paradigm of "presence" takes priority over the other temporal modes because it investigates the place where a "whisper of life" is "breathed into what has become routine and clichéd—it is fully realizing things instead of just taking them for granted."[9] It is a place of change and a place of redemption, or so it appears.[10] This certainly seems to be the case for Scrooge, who "fully realized things" that he had previously "taken for granted" that fine Christmas morning. For Scrooge, as for thinkers such as Frank Ankersmit, Hans Ulrich Gumbrecht, and Eelco Runia, the present is where they want to be, and the present of "presence" is a place of experience and unmediated contact with material things freed from the ambivalence and multiplicity of recollection, interpretation, and narration embodied in the shape-shifting Ghost of Christmas Past and protected from the deathly specter (or specter of inevitable death) of the future embodied in the Ghost of Christmas Yet to Come. It is the realm of experience, empirical evidence, and self-certainty. Thus, one can understand Scrooge's compulsion to retreat to the inviting chamber of the present and away from the specters of absence and death that haunt both his past and future. But on what is our current compulsion for "presence" predicated? I ask this not only in relation to the work of Ankersmit, Gumbrecht, and Runia but also in relation to the current prevalence of the use of empirical studies, neuroscience, material culture, archaeology (in the traditional—i.e., not Foucauldian—sense), oral testimony, affect, and memory studies, as well as the ontological realist fetish to provide the absent past with the same ontological properties they attribute to the present.

The Return of the Real

For Eelco Runia the publication of Hayden White's *Metahistory* was a watershed moment that led to a "process in which the philosophy of history was emptied of reflection on what had actually happened in the past . . . and inaugurated the heyday of 'metahistoriography.'"[11] Runia laments the ways that the historical profession became obsessed with the construction of narratives about the past at the expense of losing touch with the past itself. Gumbrecht and Ankersmit expand this critique by enlarging the field to include other figures and movements of the "linguistic turn" that we explored in the previous chapter. Gumbrecht tells us that he has "grown weary of this intellectual one way traffic as it has been based on and upheld by a certain narrow and yet totalizing understanding of hermeneutics. I also have long experienced the absolutism of all post–linguistic turn varieties of philosophy as intellectually limiting, and I have not found much consolation in what I want to characterize as the 'linguistic existentialism' of deconstruction, that is the sustained complaint and melancholia (in its endless variations) about the alleged incapacity of language to refer to the things of the world."[12]

Thus, Gumbrecht believes that the current emphasis on the production of meaning via language that dominates higher academia, the "culture of interpretation" as he calls it, has led to "intellectual relativism" and our estrangement from the past.[13] "In the last three or four decades— philosophers of history have tried to purge their discipline of attempts to establish meaning."[14] Runia, Gumbrecht, and Ankersmit all seek to move beyond this climate of constructivism and to return to what is real. Ankersmit describes a shift "away from language toward experience" and attempts to reclaim "meaning" from the clutches of language and representationalism.[15] To Ankersmit's mind, "philosophy of history, in the last half century, has predominantly been an attempt to translate the success of philosophy of language to historical writing," but "'theory' and meaning no longer travel in the same direction; meaning has now found a new and more promising traveling companion in experience."[16] All three call for a turn away from the seemingly endless interpretations manufactured by "theory" and a return to a relationship with the past predicated on our unmediated access to actual things that we can feel and touch and that bring us into contact with the past. This is a position that shares affinities with ontological realism insofar as it attributes material properties to the past but differs and goes further because the thinkers of presence wish to explore the ways that the past actually visits us in the present. "Rather than having to think, always and endlessly, what else there could be, we sometimes seem to connect with a layer in our existence that simply wants the things of the world close to our skin."[17] In the same vein, Ewa Domanska states, "I am trying to rethink the material aspects of traces of the past in a context other than semiotics, discourse theory, or representation theory, and to focus the analysis of those traces on an aspect that is marginalized or neglected by traditional notions of the source. That is, I mean to focus on the materiality or thingness of the trace rather than on its textuality and content."[18] In this sense the paradigm of presence is an explicit rejection of deconstruction, discursive theory in general, and can be seen as part of a larger backlash against postmodernism and the perceived dominance of language. It is an attempt to reconnect "meaning" with something "real," and here we should recall our discussion of Nancy Partner in the previous chapter and the way these thinkers fit into the "desire to escape language, to restore a pure and immediate connection with the past or at least some central aspect of experience, and generally deny the power of language to contaminate 'history' with its own uncontrollable meanings."[19]

The most obvious target is Derrida but also thinkers like Richard Rorty, Hayden White, and those historical theorists who have advocated a constructive or deconstructive approach to the study of history via the investigation into language.[20] But this trend is also indicative of a larger social unease about secularism, proceduralism, and a social contract that is no longer guaranteed by either God or a fixed "human nature." If all there is is "language all the way down," then there is nothing to assure the validity of the contract. I have argued elsewhere that as "we grow less and less confident in humankind's ability to provide a moral or ethical scaffold to guide us, we are left searching for a new authority to validate that which humankind has surveyed and measured."[21] This desire for stability became all the more acute in the wake of September 11, 2001. The rise of "presence" as a category of historical reflection in its more or less sublime incarnations is a direct response to a growing unease that seeks to grab the past and hold it in the present to help us divine guidance for the future. This is what Runia describes as his "focus not on the past but on the present, not on history *as what is irremediably gone*, but on *history as an ongoing process*" and the basis for his claim that "the concept of presence is a convenient way to put an edge on the issue of how exactly the past can be said to exist."[22]

"Presence" is a movement away from an absent past and toward a past that actually exists. But it would be a mistake to assume that it is a return to the positivism or realism that characterized the philosophy of history before the "linguistic turn" and that still characterizes much conventional history. Ankersmit puts it this way: "It is certainly distressing that the liberation of philosophy from the narrow straights of transcendentalism that we may find in their [Derrida, Gadamer, Rorty] writings did change so desperately little that it left the world of history, of representation, of our experience of art, music, and of the more existential aspects of the *condition humaine* as unexplained and devoid of philosophical interest as had been the case in the heyday of logical positivism."[23] Indeed, in some ways it is the failures of these earlier movements that allowed for the ascendancy of the later ones. But this is because "in the philosophy of history we have long been led astray by the phenomenon of 'meaning'—first by pursuing it, then by forswearing it."[24] So while on one level "presence" is presented as a counter to meaning, it is also presented as a response to the attack on meaning (whether Derrida's deconstruction, White's representationalism, Gadamer's hermeneutics, or Rorty's contructivism) that conserves the category as essential for understanding and communication but demotes its status in terms of our relation to the past. Runia states:

> I take the position that, on consideration, it is not meaning we want, but something else, something that is just as fundamental, something that outside the philosophy of history, in society at large, is pursued with a vehemence quite like the vehemence with which we—within the discipline—believe only meaning can be pursued. For it is, I think, not a need for meaning that manifests itself in the enthusiasm for remembrance, in the desire for monuments, in the fascination for memory. My thesis is that what is pursued in the Vietnam Veterans Memorial, in having a diamond made "from the carbon of your loved one as a memorial to their [*sic*] unique life," in the reading of names on that anniversary of the attack on the World Trade Center, in the craze for reunions, and in a host of comparable phenomena, is *not* "meaning" but "presence."[25]

For Runia, "presence—being in touch with reality—is just as basic as meaning," but our quest for "meaning" has been misguided because it is actually a response to our desire for "presence."[26] So presence offers a return to the real that can in turn help us rehabilitate our belief in meaning, and it does so by literally bringing the past into the present. But what is the transhistorical mechanism by which one can do this? What brings the past into the present?

The Storehouse of Presence

Runia suggests that it can be gleaned in the way that presence allows the past to be both present and absent at once.[27] To my mind, this is a claim that a deconstructive approach to history holds as well. In what follows, I want to disaggregate the two positions and demonstrate the way that the position held by the theorists of presence privileges presence over absence and disallows the possibility that the past be both "present and absent at once." For Runia, investigations into "meaning," of both the epistemological and ontological order, focus on either presence or absence and thus miss out on the connection between the two. This is a position I believe we can conserve. Runia presents this connection in terms of the "problem of continuity and discontinuity," which is in turn a "symptom of the determination to account for the fact that our past—though irremediably gone—may feel more real than the world we inhabit." So the trick for Runia is to establish a discourse of presence that does not "explain discontinuity away in some kind of 'meaning,' but gives it its due," and for Runia, *metonymy* is a "surprisingly suitable tool to do so. . . . My thesis is, to put it somewhat paradoxically, that metonymy is a metaphor for discontinuity. Or rather, that metonymy is a metaphor for the entwinement of continuity and discontinuity."[28] Runia asserts that the trope of metonymy allows one to take account of the ways that the past is contiguous with the present, that is, the way the past touches the present to affect both continuity and discontinuity. But "coming to grips with discontinuity requires an adjustment many philosophers of history will hesitate to make." As previously noted the adjustment is "to focus not on the past but on the present, not on history *as what is irremediably gone,* but on *history as an ongoing process.*" Furthermore, Runia tells us that this adjustment is

> not unlike the momentous modification Freud came to make in his approach to the past of his patients. Somewhere around 1900 Freud stopped heading for that past *straight away.* Instead of delivering himself to the alluring stories his patients volunteered to tell him, he opted, not for a Rankean "turning to the sources," but for a radical (and counterintuitive) "presentism." By sticking to the present as steadfastly as he could, by exploring the symptoms and the transferences that made themselves felt in the here and now of the analytic encounter, Freud was able to come forward with much more "original," much more "convincing," much more "effective," versions of the past of his patients than they had entertained themselves.[29]

This quote gives us some purchase on the transhistorical workings of presence, and we will need to return to Freud, but for Runia what is important is that Freud recognized the ways that focusing exclusively on the past "never takes you anywhere but to places in sight of your departure, whereas exploring the present may have you somewhere, someplace, tumbling into depths you didn't suspect were there." Thus, the historian of presence "walks the plane of time," as Runia calls it, scanning the surface of both "present day reality" and the "discipline of history" ("the assemblage of texts, codes, habits, topics, trends, and fashions") with an "evenly suspended attention" as in the therapeutic session advocated by Freud.[30] In doing so, we come to see that both surfaces are "*at one and the same time*, a tightly knit, 'organic,' functioning whole as well as a jumble of things that are genetically, ontologically, and existentially separate." In other words, the Freudian attention to the surface of the present reveals a wonder of continuity and discontinuity—"'continuity' and 'discontinuity,' that is, not in a historical, temporal, 'vertical' sense, but in the spatial 'horizontal' sense of 'being thoroughly interwoven' and 'radically contiguous.' Trying to envision continuity and discontinuity in its temporal sense is so hard as to be virtually impossible. To understand continuity and discontinuity requires being able 'to walk around' the events in question—but as soon as we start to look backwards, the second dimension needed for approaching events from different angles somehow gets lost."[31]

Here, Runia asks us to cede temporal investigation in favor of a spatial one that will expose the ways that the past is contiguous with the present. Rather than focusing on an impossible object irretrievably lost in the past, we should concentrate on things and places in the here and now, even if these things are metonymical markers for other things or events that are temporally absent. "Consequently, a metonymy is a 'presence in absence' not just in the sense that it presents something that isn't there, but also in the sense that in the absence (or at least the radical inconspicuousness) that *is* there, the thing that isn't there is still present." It is this contiguous relation that the present has with the past that allows the past to affect the present in real ways through the experience of the individual. "Metonymical 'presence in absence,' in other words, works both ways: up *to* the present, and downward *from* the present." For Runia, these two ways correspond to two aspects of Giambattista Vico's "topics": invention and storage. "As *inventio*, metonymy transposes something to the present, or more correctly: as *inventio*, metonymy has *made* the surface as we know it; the present consists of metonymies that were once *Fremdkörper* but are now taken for granted. As 'storage,' metonymy contains what was left behind. But what it stands for can still be found in—or, as Vico would say, 'invented' out of—what he may find on the plane of time."[32] Of course it is storage, what was left behind, that provides the material for invention that may be innovative and shocking at first but soon comes to be accepted as convention or forgotten and again filed away in storage. But invention never runs dry because there is always plenty of the past (all of it, in fact) left in storage waiting to be unpacked. In both cases, however, this takes place in the here and now of the present through actual engagement with material things and places.

As the name suggests, the "plane of time" is a spatial category where the temporal past is accessed in the places of the present. These are common places "in the sense that anybody can visit them, that they lie open for examination. . . . But they are not 'commonplaces'—they are not empty but full, they are not shallow but deep, not dead but alive. They are repositories of time—or, perhaps even better, the places where history can get a hold of you. Places are, in short, storehouses of 'presence.'"[33] This has an enormous impact on the writing of history because, as Ankersmit notes, it broaches the question of whether "the past can actually be carried into the present by historical representation, in much the same way that one may carry a souvenir from a foreign country into one's own." Ankersmit responds that "under such conditions, the past would be made 'present' in the present in the most literal sense of the word."[34] It is not surprising that to support this claim he turns to an earlier article by Runia, and it is with this article that we will return to Freud in an attempt to understand the transhistorical workings of this storehouse and its relation to space and time.

Parallel Processes: Presence *in Absentia*

Ankersmit turns to Runia's article "'Forget About It': 'Parallel Processing' in the Srebrenica Report," published in *History and Theory* in October 2004.[35] The article itself is illuminating because it precedes Runia's fully formed articulation of "presence" and focuses instead on the phenomenon of "parallel processes."[36] In this piece Runia sought to articulate one way that the past is literally present in the here and now by exploring the ways that historical accounts of past events parallel those very happenings. Specifically, Runia sought to show the ways that the NIOD Report, the Dutch report on the massacre in Srebrenica, parallels the event it describes. Runia presents the "way the NIOD researchers unwittingly replicated several key aspects of the events they studied, and discusses some instances in which paralleling highlights precisely those features of the events under consideration that are hard to come to terms with."[37] The starting point for Runia's analysis is Dominick LaCapra's assertion that "when you study something, at some level you always have a tendency to repeat the problems you are studying," and there is something ironic in this connection as LaCapra's work is regularly associated with the language-based construction/deconstruction of meaning that becomes a target of the presence movement in its return to the real.[38] Building on this assertion, Runia tells us "parallel processes are an important manifestation of this tendency." The concept of "parallel processes," in Runia's usage, originates in psychoanalytic supervision and refers to instances when "supervisees manifest toward their supervisors many psychic patterns which parallel processes that are prominent in their interactions with their patients."[39] In essence, the behavior of the patient is transferred to the analyst, who then exhibits this same behavior toward the supervisor. But the key to this move in relation to the formation of "presence" does not lie in the issue of transference or countertransference but in the relation of two aspects of the parallel process:

> When a parallel process is operative there is always a dual set of transferences and countertransferences involved—the one, the patient/therapist set, as it were *in absentia*, the other in the here and now of the supervision. Yet parallel processes are not reducible to transferences or countertransferences. Key to parallel processes is a 180 degree turn of the "middle man"—the therapist. Paralleling occurs when therapists, in the supervision setting, unconsciously identify with their patients, enact this identification, and elicit responses from the supervisors that replicate the difficulties they themselves have encountered—as *therapists*—in the therapy.[40]

In the Srebrenica article the emphasis is on the ways that historians, like therapists, unconsciously identify with their objects of study and thus unwittingly replicate the difficulties present in the object of study. Thus, aspects of the past that are not actively sought for smuggle themselves into the present through the historian. This then justifies the turn to Freudian surface analysis articulated in the "Presence" article but already announced in this earlier piece. "Instead of delving deep, one had better stay at the surface. The important thing, as Freud said, is to conceive of the illness 'not as something of the past but as a force that influences the present.'"[41] It is precisely these unconscious reenactments of the past that allow us access to what was actually there but only if we pay attention to the ways they surprise us in the present. This is one aspect of Runia's "plane of time."

There is another aspect of this statement in the Srebrenica article that is undeveloped but becomes the most important, and problematic, factor in the later articulations of "presence." In his move toward the, at the time, more important point of showing how therapists and historians unconsciously mirror their object of investigation, Runia quite casually tells us that the parallel process operates as a dual set of transferences and countertransferences, "the one, the patient/therapist set, as it were *in absentia,* the other in the here and now of the supervision." This move, uncoupled from explicit reference to the transferences and countertrans-ferences of the individual, is the basis for his presentation of the plane of time as "present day reality" and the "discipline of history." In effect, the *in absentia* of the patient/therapist set is the absence of the past event, and the here and now of supervision is the presence of present day reality. This becomes the embodiment of the entwining of continuity and discontinu-ity that is exposed by metonymy as "presence."

But the entire move is predicated on, tied to, the unconscious reenact-ment of the past event. Thus, the transhistorical mechanism that allows the past to literally be present is a psychohistorical one, as in Freud's *To-tem and Taboo* and *Moses and Monotheism.* In this psychohistorical model it is an early trauma that is conserved and repeated not by the individuals but by their descendants. Here Freud asserts that there is a permanent psychic mechanism that is at play, and given the correct conditions, the archaic memory of the event can be triggered. Thus, in Freud's telling, the murder of the Egyptian Moses turns out to be the repetition of the killing of the primal father as enunciated in *Totem and Taboo.*[42] Richard J. Ber-nstein tells us this acting out is the result of a psychic memory but trig-gered by specific historical events. "The great deed and misdeed of prime-val times, the murder of the father, was brought home to the Jews, for fate decreed that they should repeat it on the person of Moses, an eminent father substitute."[43] Freud goes on to show that as with the first patricide, this crime is also repressed, and the memory lies latent until such histori-cal conditions occur as to bring it forth again with the arrival of a second Moses and the transformation of the Yahweh religion. Freud's analysis of Moses is not based on any hard evidence of what happened in the past but is predicated on the discoveries of psychoanalysis in the present. As in Runia's presence paradigm, the analysis of the historic event (Moses's role in founding Judaism) *in absentia* is predicated on a psychoanalytic investigation of the here and now (the current condition of Judaism in Freud's present). Freud is a perfect touchstone for Runia and the other thinkers of presence because he advocates a scientific, secular, and mate-rial methodology for investigating the past based on the immanent condi-tion of the present. This is to say that he advocates a means by which one can literally access the past but that denies the possibility of transcendent meaning. This transhistorical mechanism is modified by Runia and appropriated to greater and lesser degrees by Ankersmit and Gumbrecht. But, as I have argued elsewhere, the belief in the transhistorical nature of these models (Freudian, evolutionary, environmental, neuroscientific, biological, or presence-based) requires the same sort of "leap of faith" that is necessary in religious belief but now applied to the infallibility of scientific or material (modern secular) thought. Thus the seemingly neutral term *transhistorical* assumes that the model itself is able to transcend time and place to be universally applicable.[44] Even though Gumbrecht is surprised by "the suspicion (or was it rather meant to sound like praise?) that [he] had turned into a religious 'thinker'" and counters that his "desire to reconnect with the things of the world" is as strictly immanentist as "one could possibly imagine," I would argue that "presence" as conceived by these thinkers is really a postsecular articulation of transcendence that conceals its temporal leap of faith by keeping the emphasis on the material and spatial focus on what is present in the here and now.[45] This is to say that one must simply believe that the past can visit us in the present as it once was, as present rather than absent. In this way it is always presence that defines absence and never the converse.[46] What's more, the transhistorical/transcendent mechanism allows one to freeze a moment in time and transport it to the present, thus reinscribing assumptions of a static past always available to us in the present.

The *Wunderblock*

Here I would like to turn to a different piece by Freud, his "Note Upon the 'Mystic Writing Pad,'" in an effort to discern what is going on in "presence" both in relation to the "meaning-based" construction/deconstruction of history and to the issue of immanence and transcendence in relation to presence and absence.[47] The note on the mystic writing pad, the *Wunderblock*, is a meditation on the nature and limits of perception in relation to memory. The *Wunderblock* itself is a device composed of a "dark slab of brown resin or wax; over the slab is laid a thin transparent sheet, the top end of which is firmly secured to the slab while its bottom end rests on it without being fixed. This transparent sheet . . . consists of two layers, which can be detached from each other except at their two ends. The upper layer is a transparent piece of celluloid; the lower layer is made of thin translucent wax paper."[48] The trick is that one can write on the *Wunderblock* as much as one likes and then lift the two sheets to make the writing disappear. "The close contact between the waxed paper and the wax slab at the places which have been scratched (upon which the visibility depended) is thus brought to an end and it does not recur when the two surfaces come together once more."[49] Freud finds that the *Wunderblock's* "construction shows a remarkable agreement with my hypothetical structure of our perceptual apparatus" in that it can provide "both an ever ready receptive surface and permanent traces of the notes that have been made upon it," just as our mental apparatus has an "unlimited receptive capacity for new perceptions and nevertheless lays down permanent—even though not unalterable—memory traces of them."[50] On first glance the *Wunderblock* seems to affirm the mechanism presented by the thinkers of presence in that it demonstrates the way that the past is always available to the present via the imperceptible but undeniably present etchings on the wax slab below the two sheets. Indeed, "it is easy to discover that the permanent trace of what was written is retained upon the wax slab itself and is legible in suitable lights."[51] On this reading the wax slab represents the past, and the two sheets represent present-day reality. We can extend the analogy and say that what the theorists of presence consider problematic in meaning-based models is that they either focus on the means of writing on the top of the pad or ceaselessly lift the two sheets together to erase the writing and expose the limits of meaning.

But here, too, the mechanism warrants a closer look. At the end of his note Freud asserts that the parallel between the *Wunderblock* and the perceptual apparatus of our mind reveals more than the way that the system perception-consciousness is infiltrated by the unconscious.

> It is as though the unconscious stretches out feelers, through the medium of the system *Pcpt.-Cs.* [Perception-Consciousness], towards the external world and hastily withdraws them as soon as they have sampled the excitations coming from it. Thus the interruptions, which in the case of the Mystic Pad have an external origin, were attributed by my hypothesis to the discontinuity in the current of innervation; and the actual breaking of contact which occurs in the Mystic Pad was replaced in my theory by the periodic non-excitability of the perceptual system. *I further had a suspicion that this discontinuous method of functioning of the system* Pcpt.-Cs. *lies at the bottom of the origin of the concept of time.*[52]

Freud had previously articulated this claim in *Beyond the Pleasure Principle*:

> We have learnt that unconscious mental processes are in themselves "time-less." This means in the first place they are not ordered temporarily, that time does not change them in any way and that the idea of time cannot be applied to them. These are negative characteristics which can only be understood if a comparison is made with *conscious* mental processes. On the other hand, our abstract idea of time seems to be wholly derived from the method of working of the system *Pcpt.-Cs.* and to correspond to a perception on its own part of the working method.[53]

So while the unconscious is permanently timeless and thus not suscep-tible to any temporal ordering, our abstract idea of time is based on the functioning of the system Pcpt.-Cs. that necessarily orders our percep-tions so that consciousness can make sense of them. But we can only think the timelessness of the unconscious based on the abstract or vulgar idea of time.[54] Thus, the key to what we call "historical understanding" is linked to the question of temporality, as in Martin Hägglund's discussion of the "negative infinity of time," which we will explore in Chapter 4.[55]

By contrast, Runia and the thinkers of presence claim that the past is made present not in a spatiotemporal sense but in the purely spatial-horizontal sense of being thoroughly interwoven and radically contigu-ous; thus, they manage to avoid what is most uncanny and unsettling about the wax block, the unconscious, and the past: that is its radical alterity in relation to the vulgar concept of time.[56] In this light we see that "presence" only appears to bring the traces on the wax block to the surface of the two sheets of our present; at best, it lifts the protective sheet to reveal what was written below.[57] It never gets to the confused, conflicting, and polysemic wax block below. This is all the more so when one moves beyond the psychoanalytic investigation of the individual mind and to the psychohistorical investigation of the past because of its character *in absentia* that eschews the spatial component that "presence" demands. This is to say that the past has no "there" in the spatial sense. Runia is certainly aware of this when he states, "Trying to envision continuity and discontinuity in its temporal sense is so hard as to be virtually im-possible. To understand continuity and discontinuity requires being able 'to walk around' the events in question—but as soon as we start to look backwards, the second dimension needed for approaching events from

different angles somehow gets lost."[58] Clearly, Runia wants to make sense
of the past in some fashion but this assertion leads us to another possible
reading of the parallel process that is especially illuminating in light of a
deconstructive reading of space and time. What if the parallel process is
not about accessing the past but about recognizing the forces in the past
that press on us but that are not accessible? What if what is at stake is not
the ability to walk around the events in question, to make them understandable, but to recognize our relation to continuity and discontinuity
in a "temporal sense" that "is so hard as to be virtually impossible"? It is
in this sense that one can speak of the parallel process as "uncanny."[59] On
this reading it is precisely "when the therapist does *not understand* the
meaning of a patient's enacted communication, [that] he may convey the
meaning to his supervisor by parallel enactment."[60] Despite the appeal to
space, the thinkers of presence never get to the timeless place of the past,
the negative infinity, because they remain in the most comforting moment in time: the here and now of the present.

Conclusion

So perhaps we can think more on the comfort "presence" affords in all
its material splendor by critically examining the comfort Scrooge finds
in the Ghost of Christmas Present. After all, neither presence nor the
Ghost of Christmas Present is exactly what it appears to be. To begin, the
ghost's encounter with Scrooge escapes the present by pressing into the
future, the near future, to be sure, but a near future far more definite than
anything revealed by the Ghost of Christmas Yet to Come. And this near
future is made all the more meaningful to us because of its relation to
Scrooge's recent past. We see Christmas at the Cratchit household, then
Christmas for miners on a bleak and distant moor, and finally Christmas
at Scrooge's nephew's house. The emphasis on space, on material things,
and on experience conceals the way the ghost moves in time much in
the way that Ankersmit does when he tells us that "the past *itself* can
be said to have survived the centuries and to be still present in objects
that are given to us here and now. . . . Hence, the notion of historical
experience does not necessarily require a sudden disappearance of time
or some mystical union with the past, for the past can properly be said
to be present in the artifacts that it has left us. They are protuberances,
so to say, of the past in the present."[61] Similarly, Runia pushes the past

through the present up into the future as in the ways that "in the cells and corridors of Abu Ghraib, Saddam Hussein's torture practices were so overwhelmingly present, and the sheer possibility of using them—though horrifying—loomed so large, that sooner or later the Americans *had* to repeat them."[62] The emphasis on space downplays the role of time. There is another troubling aspect of the Ghost of Christmas Present that initially went unnoticed. At the end of the evening we are told, "It was a long night if it were only a night; but Scrooge had his doubts of this, because the Christmas Holiday appeared to be condensed into the space of time they passed together. It was strange, too, that while Scrooge remained unaltered in outward form, the Ghost grew older, clearly older. . . . 'Are spirits' lives so short?' asked Scrooge. 'My life on this globe, is very brief,' replied the Ghost. 'It ends to-night.'" [63] Thus the spatial presence of the present is constricted and bound by a conventional or vulgar concept of time in ways that are not apparent when one focuses primarily on space.

But perhaps the strangest secret concealed by the Ghost of Christmas Present is the "two children: wretched, abject, frightful, hideous, miserable" hidden under his robes. "'They are Man's,' said the Spirit, looking down upon them. 'And they cling to me, appealing from their fathers. This boy is Ignorance. This girl is Want.'" Ignorance and want, both concealed by the present. The Ghost continues: "'Beware them both, and all of their degree, but most of all beware this boy, for on his brow I see that written which is Doom, unless the writing be erased. Deny it!'"[64] And it is in relation to the ignorance that the present conceals that I would like to return to Dickens's musings on Hamlet's father. There is a strange way in which "presence" ignores what is most troubling about ghosts and about the past, and perhaps the future, by shifting the emphasis to place, thus privileging "presence" over "absence." Presence is comforting because it affords a place to posit oneself as self in time and in relation to real phenomena, but in so doing it empties the category of its force and potency as it asserts the dominance and mastery of presence over absence. Deconstruction takes the opposite tack, making this discomfort explicit. This is to say that what is uncanny about the ghost is effaced as metonymy makes absence present and in so doing "insinuates that there is an urgent *need* for meaning."[65] In this light the turn to presence is a return to meaning, the traveling partner of experience, and as such it is a retreat from the meaninglessness revealed in the parallel process and attributed to deconstruction. What is troubling and powerful about the ghost of Hamlet's father is not that it is present (which it is) but the ways that its presence disturbs all the spatiotemporal categories by which we have come to make sense of the world around us. The ghost troubles both time and space; thus, one cannot "walk around" it in the way that Runia suggests. We cannot actually say what the ghost means. Indeed, if one could, if Hamlet's father was actually there, "there would be nothing more remarkable in his taking a stroll at night, in an easterly wind, upon his own ramparts, than there would be in any other middle-aged gentleman rashly turning out after dark in a breezy spot."[66] In other words, if time were not out of joint, there would be nothing dramatic, remarkable, or eventful (to use Gumbrecht's phrase) at all.[67]

Unlike the ghosts of Christmas who are all circumscribed by the temporal marker of Christmas Day and who imbue their moment with an otherworldly authority, the ghost of Jacob Marley represents an existence without end and in this way evokes Emmanuel Levinas's category of the *il y a*, the "there is," of impersonal existence. For Levinas the *il y a* is the recognition of being in all of its strangeness and alterity, as that which is beyond representation or localization and thus is completely beyond our control. It is this lack of control that makes the *il y a* so frightening because in it "the *private* existence of each term, mastered by a subject that is, loses this private character and returns to an undifferentiated background."[68] For Levinas this anonymous and infinite being is in fact the opening to ethics because of the way it displaces the primacy of the subject as the original and proprietary owner of a position in place and time and, instead, asks one to consider the way that one's own presence compromises the existence of an other. For our purposes, what is important is the way that Levinas characterizes the present as a "situation in being where there is not only being in general, but there is a being, a subject."[69] Here, as in Freud's meditation on time, the timeless space of anonymous being is interrupted by the hypostasis of an individual subject that posits itself in time. All access to time and meaning now flows through the spatial position of this subject. In presence this positing is presented as a transhistorical/transcendent portal through which meaning flows from the past to the present. What is not considered in this emphasis on space, secretly coupled to time, is the "spot trampled in a subject's taking position" and the way this spot/space serves "not only as a resistance, but also as a base, as a condition for the effort."[70] This can also be seen in the way that some possible pasts are trampled underneath dominant historical accounts rendering them invisible or illegible.

There is a way in which the movement of "presence" actually forecloses the possibility of change and justifies the *status quo* through its claims to produce unmediated access to the past via a return to the real. Runia's discussion of the ways that Abu Ghraib's past conditioned the actions of individuals in the present absolves those actors of agency and, in fact, cedes agency and responsibility to a past that we are doomed to repeat. Hans Gumbrecht's emphasis on Heideggerian *Gelassenheit,* the patiently waiting or letting things be, also describes a condition where one passively waits for something to appear and takes no action in the meantime.[71] For Ankersmit, too, the past is literally present and thus conditions the present, but in his presentation this relationship takes on a radically individualistic and seemingly incommunicable character through "sublime historical experience."[72] Thus, despite the rhetorical move away from the endless game of interpretation and a return to things that really matter, there appears to be nothing to do but wait for sublime historical experience or presence to come to us. Here we must wait patiently for the hidden or repressed past to come to us. The desire for control, for a position, for real presence comes at the expense of others, and it is in this sense that "nothing wonderful" can come from it. This is important, for it is not the "presence" of the Ghost of Christmas Present and his heartening display of material goods or real material objects to engage every sense nor the other two ghosts of Christmas, important as they all may be, that is the catalyst for Scrooge's journey of redemption. No, it is the untimely return of the uncanny ghost of Jacob Marley that provokes the change in Scrooge, and Marley was dead: to begin with.

§3   Chladenius, Droysen, Dilthey:
Back to Where We've Never Been

There is a story by Franz Kafka about the Great Wall of China that he wrote in 1917, though it was not published until 1931. Most interpreters have argued correctly, I think, that this story is not at all about China but about the Habsburg or Austrian Empire, though there is certainly more at stake: there are the parallels Kafka draws between the building of the Great Wall and of the Tower of Babel, the fascination with the "endless space" of the empire, and the reflection on power and tradition in the fable of the "imperial message" embedded in the heart of the story, where the message is received only after the emperor is dead and a new emperor, presumably with a new message, has been installed. But I want to focus on one aspect of this story in a way, perhaps forced, that will gather together many of its themes in relation to the figures of Johann Martin Chladenius (1710–59), Johann Gustav Droysen (1808–84), and Wilhelm Dilthey (1833–1911) to explore the German historicist tradition and its relation to one of the most resilient underlying assumptions in the current practice of history that I refer to as "ontological realism." But I also want to suggest that a closer look at these thinkers sheds light on the utility of deconstruction for the project of history, as well as the possibility of a hauntological historical approach to the past that is guided by, though not beholden to, Derrida.

In *Beim Bau der chinesischen Mauer* Kafka's narrator begins by telling the reader of the curious manner in which the wall was constructed:

It was carried out in the following manner: groups of about twenty workers were formed, each of which had to take on a section of the wall, about five hundred meters long. A neighboring group then built a wall of similar length to meet them. But then afterwards, when the sections were fully joined, construction was not continued on any further at the end of this thousand-meter section. Instead the groups of workers were shipped off again to build the wall in completely different regions. Naturally, with this method many large gaps arose, which were filled in only gradually and slowly, many of them not until after it had already been reported that the building of the wall was complete. In fact, there are said to be gaps which have never been built in at all, although that's merely an assertion which probably belongs among the many legends which have arisen about the structure and which, for individual people at least, are impossible to prove with their own eyes and according to their own standards, because the structure is so immense."[1]

What interests me is a possibility intimated by Kafka but left unexplored. What if, in fact, some sections of the wall were never built at all? And what if later, over time, it came to be believed that these gaps were missing portions of the wall that had been destroyed, decayed, or lost? And what if a later generation seeking to understand the origins of the wall, its original intentions and meanings, decided to pursue the reconstruction (physical or theoretical) of these sections, thus discerning and recounting the properties of an "original" that never actually existed? On this reading Kafka's Great Wall is a story about our relationship with the past and the gaps in that immense structure, gaps between points that are fixed and available in the present but that may be impossible for individual people to prove with "their own eyes and according to their own standards."

In these murky epistemo-ontological waters Chladenius, Droysen, and Dilthey each sought to account for the relation of part and whole to determine a "historical science" that could reconstruct the wall as it was in the past. For Chladenius this was done using a hermeneutic strategy for interpreting the past as one would a text, all the while keeping the historian's viewpoint (*Sehe-Punkt*) or perspective. For Droysen, and contrary to Ranke, the historian's perspective and understanding was paramount. The perspectival approach of the historian in his or her moment was an opportunity to realize an optimum methodology for the study of the past. For Dilthey it was precisely our lived experience as historical beings that fostered our abilities as observers of history, though it would be through the imaginative act of transposition that one could gain access to past understandings and events.

It is true that although these thinkers were also practicing historians, the texts under consideration here serve primarily as methodological and philosophical reflections on how *to do* history rather than simply *doing* it. Thus, I accept that there is a risk of falling into what Dominick LaCapra has referred to as "theoreticism," which he defines as "thought that operates primarily on a speculative, purely conceptual, often self-referential, level that feeds on itself (at times to the point of tying itself in quasi-transcendental knots) and construes history as a source of illustrations or signs, a repository of incommensurable particularities or singularities, or a transhistorical abstraction."[2] LaCapra cites Giorgio Agamben and Slavoj Žižek as indicative of this trend, and although it seems unlikely that Chladenius, Droysen, or Dilthey would be placed alongside any of these thinkers, Derrida has been cast in this light.

But neither should we unreflectively privilege the historical emplotment of a chain of transmission, a German historicist tradition that leads to our own historical practices today. Such reference to context or historical situation and connection should not serve as a cipher that historically decodes the thought of these three figures to simplify it. Instead, the difficulty of what these thinkers have to say about our relation to and use of the past, as well as the way that their statements simultaneously coincide with and diverge from conventional contemporary historical practices, should serve to complicate our understanding of how to engage historically with these theorists in the most productive ways.[3]

Chladenius

The eighteenth-century thinker Chladenius has found renewed interest because of the recent popularity of the work of Reinhart Koselleck. For Koselleck, Chladenius was the "harbinger of modernity" because of his theory of perspective or standpoint.[4] Chladenius held that "histories are accounts of things that have happened. If one intends—as is presumed—to speak the truth about an event, one cannot recount it in a way that differs from one's perception of it."[5] Thus while any past event is itself singular, conceptions of it are many because "different people perceive that which happens in the world differently, so that if many people describe an event, each would attend to something in particular—if all were to perceive the situation properly."[6] Koselleck acknowledges that "to state that every historical statement is bound to a particular standpoint would *today* meet with hardly any objection. Who would wish to deny that history is viewed from different perspectives, and that change in history is accompanied by alterations in historical statements about our history?"[7] But, according to Koselleck, such an understanding of history and the historian was not always the norm and is thus a modern phenomenon that began with Chladenius. What's more, this position conceals within it two mutually exclusive demands on the historian: "to make true statements, while at the same time to admit and take account for the relativity of these statements."[8] This problem is worth exploring both on Chladenius's terms and our own.

At first glance, Chladenius's writings on history seem to support the position I refer to as ontological realism, where in the end, getting the past "right" is a question of historical method. In his *Einleitung zur richtigen Auslegung vernünfftiger Reden und Schriften* Chladenius designates "the term view-point (*Sehe-Punkt*) to refer to those conditions governed by our mind (*Seele*), body (*Leibes*), and entire person (*ganzen Person*), which make or cause us to conceive of something in one way or another. . . . A King, for example, has no accounts of events which take place in distant provinces other than those reported to him by the governors whom he has relegated to the different areas."[9] This distance can be spatial, as noted above, or temporal, as in the case of a historical event, but in either case there is only one reality, though it may be seen from differing perspectives. "Clearly, the [historical] event itself cannot contain contradictions; it alone may be presented to the observers so differently that the accounts of it contain something contradictory in themselves."[10] For Chladenius historical reality itself is never in question, but the representation of history is always a matter of interpretation. "It is not the historical event itself but the concept of the historical event which is unclear to another person and is in need of an interpretation. . . . The historical event is one and the same but the concept of it different and manifold."[11] Here we have to account for the epistemological method that can lead us to an exact representation of the past reality as well as the ontological grounds on which Chladenius can argue for the singular historical reality of the past event.

One place to start is by examining the ways that Chladenius narrows the definition of what he means by "historical" knowledge in his work of 1752, *Allgemeine Geschichtswissenschaft*. Here, Chladenius differentiates between the German term *Geschichte* and the term *Historie*. For Chladenius, *Geschichte* denotes our concern with a series of events (*Begebenheit*) and the connections between them that ultimately allow us to determine change over time.[12] At their most basic and irreducible level, these are bare-bones singular events, such as a man riding a horse or an apple falling from a tree. In practice we usually present a series of events in sequence, but in principle the reduction is possible and allows us to come to terms with these basic building blocks. *Historie* denotes our concern with this as well but also must account for the narratives and descriptions by which we relate and describe these events and changes as "what happened."[13] Thus, *Historie* is the more ambiguous concept because while *Geschichte* restricts its purview to historical events as the basic building blocks of change over time, *Historie* must account for the problem of representation, which determines the articulation of the historical event as narrated or described. In the *Allgemeine Geschichtswissenschaft*, Chladenius focuses on the narrower and more restricted concept of history as the basis for his "science of history."[14] We should also note that Chladenius is working with this more narrow definition in his discussion of the *Sehe-Punkt* or viewpoint in chapter 5 and 6 of the *Allgemeine Geschichtswissenschaft*. It is entirely likely that the recent use of Chladenius assumes an expanded definition of "history" and thus pushes the work of Chladenius onto ground he would consider beyond the parameters of his historical science. But it is also the case that, in practice, Chladenius was caught between these two definitions of history (*Geschichte* and *Historie*) and was unable to resolve the underlying tensions between the historically conditioned and thus contingent nature of narration and description and the fixed immutable building blocks of historical events that constitute "reality" by means of an increasingly narrow definition of *history*.

This is apparent in his discussion of the *Sehe-Punkt* (viewpoint or perspective) in the *Allgemeine Geschichtswissenschaft* as opposed to that of the *Einleitung zur richtigen Auslegung vernünfftiger Reden und Schriften*. On the one hand, and as noted above, Chladenius argues in the *Einleitung* that despite the possibility of multiple (and potentially conflicting) perspectives, the historical event itself is one and thus in theory is perfectly accessible.[15] But on the other hand, in chapter 6 of the *Allgemeine Geschichtswissenschaft*, "Transformation of History Through Narration" (*Verwandelung der Geschichte im erzehlen*), Chladenius asserts that we do not see historical events as if we were looking into a mirror that simply reflects back what was once there. Instead, we see historical events in accordance with the concept or image (*Bilde*) that we construct of them.[16] This means that historical events are never fully there for us but are recreated based on the images and concepts we, or others, have constructed and deployed via narrative. Beiser puts it this way: "Chladenius explains that the transformation of history takes place especially in narrative, which alters the material given to us in sensation according to images or concepts. Not content with vague generalizations, he carefully spells out the many specific ways narrative transforms the material of history: by omitting detail and leaving out many circumstances (§3; 117–18); by saying in distinct times what happened at the same time (§5; 119); by confusing terms that describe our reaction to phenomena with phenomena themselves (§5; 119); by making things seem smaller or larger than they really are (§6; 120–21); and by formulating a whole series of events into a single generalization or phrase (§10; 125–26)."[17] History is itself transformed in the process of narration that alters the historical material given to us. What's more, the past event is twice altered, first by the witnesses, each of whom approaches the event from his or her own perspective or viewpoint, which is subject to all of the possible alterations listed above, and then again by the historian, who must weave the myriad accounts into a single story (again from his or her *own* perspective or viewpoint). Chladenius is thus on an edge of sorts because despite his claims to one single reality, the relativism of the *Sehe-Punkt* makes it impossible to imagine a neutral standpoint from which to access the historical event as it happened. What's more, it appears that whatever "reality" might be, it is invariably a construction generated from the subjective perspective of the viewpoint and, as such, multiple rather than singular and fixed. Here, Chladenius's assertion that there is "one historical reality" seems to rest entirely on the restricted definition of history as articulated in *Geschichte* rather than the more full and ambiguous one announced in *Historie* despite the fact that there seems to be no way to access the discrete building blocks of *Geschichte except* through the narrative strategies contained within *Historie*.

Thus, for Chladenius we have to distinguish between events and knowledge of those events. Somehow, the ontological properties of the past are fixed and definite whereas our epistemological understanding of such events is subject to error, so for Chladenius attention to method is paramount. Here it becomes clear that Chladenius's hermeneutic approach to the interpretation of texts is the key to his science of history. Our ability to get back to where we've never been is predicated on our ability to interpret past events as one interprets a text. Indeed, Chladenius is absolutely confident that so long as later generations do not alter the wording of original accounts or documents, the history of past events can be faithfully and accurately passed down from generation to generation. This is to say that there *is* a consistent historical truth of the past event even if it is understood from different perspectives and at different moments in time. The truth adheres in the event, not in the account. The example that Chladenius provides in chapter 11 of the *Allgemeine Geschichtswissenschaft* is the way that reading ancient documents makes it as if we were transported back in time so that the original author was speaking to us.

The key to retrieving the past is by adopting a correct and appropriate methodology of interpretation. This interpretation is conditioned by one's *Sehe-Punkt* (perspective) and one's historical situation (*Standortgebundenheit*), but Chladenius does not allow for either subjectivism or relativism because to his mind "understanding a speech or writing completely and understanding the person who is speaking or writing completely ought to be one and the same thing."[18] Therefore, assuming that later generations are able to accurately report what is written in the original document, the historical record can be handed down and understood with no change in meaning.[19] If one faithfully understands the historical texts or documents, then one can access the past event, and this is the historical truth. Thus, our ability to get back to the past is predicated on our ability to correctly read and understand texts in the present, but as noted, Chladenius is also aware that "because people cannot survey the whole, their words, speech, and writings can mean things they themselves did not intend to say or write. It follows that in trying to understand their writings one can with good reason think of things which did not occur to the authors."[20] This would certainly be the case for readers approaching a text from a later or otherwise different historical perspective. Thus, rules of interpretation are necessary to completely and fully understand a text or passage, "to think of all the things which the words can awaken in us in accord with reason and the rules of our mind [*Seele*]"; and for Chladenius "there can be no doubt, then, that a science springs up when we interpret according to certain rules. For this we have the Greek name 'hermeneutic' and in our language we properly call it the art of interpretation."[21] It is as if Chladenius is telling us that we can come to know all of the properties of the Great Wall so long as we correctly interpret the documents that chronicle it because the wall itself, as it was in the past, still conditions the meaning of these documents or words in the present.

Again, this appears as a fairly direct problem where any errors that occur are due to our epistemological uncertainty in regard to a fixed ontological reality. But given our previous discussion of the *Sehe-Punkt* and the historically conditioned position of the historian, we need to again ask what holds the ontological certainty regarding the past event given the possibility of epistemological uncertainty in recounting that event. How is Chladenius so confident about the properties of the Great Wall given the entanglement of past and future retellings in our conception of what this artifact is? If, in fact, some sections of the wall were never built, and over time it came to be believed that these gaps were missing portions of the wall that had been destroyed, decayed, or lost, our investigation would *begin* by seeking to discern and recount the properties of an "original" that never actually existed. Here it is essential for us to understand Chladenius's own historical standpoint (*Standortgebundenheit*) and perspective (*Sehe-Punkt*) and the way his "historical science" is predicated on his religious beliefs. "For Chladenius, who gave the first independent lecture on *Historik* in Erlangen in the winter semester of 1749–50, an explicit belief in divine providence is basic."[22] Chladenius makes this evident in the preface to the *Allgemeine Geschichtswissenschaft*, where he declares that his purpose is "to defend and extoll these high truths" and the work is punctuated by this claim throughout.[23] What's more, writing in the first half of the eighteenth century, Chladenius must be considered as a precritical thinker in the Kantian sense of the term because despite his innovations determining the role and place of the observer in relation to the thing observed, this relative relation is uncritical, in the Kantian sense, because questions about the conditions under which cognition is possible are never raised.[24] Chladenius does not question the knowability of things in themselves because to do so would have contradicted his orthodox Lutheran belief that the sole rule of faith is Scripture. For Chladenius, the historical record of Scripture could never be in doubt, for if it were, faith itself would rest on an unstable foundation.[25] Thus Chladenius's project of establishing a historical science that could establish the hermeneutic certainty of historical truth via the immediate sense of an author was predicated on his desire to secure the theological foundations of his faith. It is essential that the truth of the "book" be accessible and faithful regardless of one's historical distance from it. This is what I will refer to as the theologico-historical underpinning that holds his precritical understanding of the "past" and our ability to access it.

Our current appropriation of Chladenius (as in Koselleck, Rüsen, and others) avoids his theological motivations and requirements by focusing solely on the rules of interpretation, and we will explore this further in our discussion of Droysen and Dilthey. But for this to hold in the absence of God, Chladenius's certainty about the fixed status of past events must be based instead on rules of textual investigation, and this requires a further narrowing of terms. It also requires that we retain a belief in language where words "have something in themselves through which one could reach a certain or probable understanding."[26] Peter Szondi's work on Chladenius is useful in demonstrating the ways that Chladenius's approach is distinct from "latter-day hermeneutics," which "neither demands that 'words' have something 'in themselves through which one could reach a certain or probable understanding,' nor does it demand of itself that interpretation be codified in rules which need only be applied."[27] But what intrigues me is the theological remains that continue to haunt our "latter-day" use of Chladenius (and ontological realism) via the privileging of the text as the site by which we access the past. It is precisely by investigating Chladenius's rules for proper interpretation that we see the privileged role of the text and what Chladenius calls the "complete sense" of the text as the mechanism by which he can claim access to the past "as it happened." It is also here that the work of Derrida exposes the strategy of textual interpretation that allows Chladenius to make this claim.

In *Voice and Phenomenon* Derrida is keen to trace the ways that Edmund Husserl attempts to define the concept of sign (*Zeigen*). Husserl begins his investigation into the sign, so Derrida tells us, by distinguishing between two entangled though distinct types of sign but in "proposing from the start a radical dissociation between two heterogeneous types of sign, indication and expression, he does not ask himself what in general the sign is." Derrida goes on to say that "for many reasons our ambition is not to answer this question. We only want to suggest the sense in which Husserl may seem to evade it."[28] By focusing on the distinctions about what makes up the sign, Husserl evades and defers the question of what the sign *is*. For Chladenius, too, investigation into the "complete sense" of a passage begins by distinguishing the different distinct-though-entangled concepts that make up this "complete sense" (*vollkommener Verstand*):

The complete sense is composed of numerous concepts that can be awakened by the passage in question. These concepts fall into three categories. . . . First of all, we discover in a passage a particular concept which arises from the passage simply as a result of our attentiveness when we approach the text with the requisite knowledge and background. Teachers of the art of interpretation call this type of concept, brought forth by mere attentiveness to the words of the passage, the *unmediated sense* [*unmittelbarer Verstand*]. This immediate sense then gives rise to all kinds of other concepts that are brought forth by the various faculties of the mind [*Seele*], with the exception of the imagination. These concepts are called the *application of a passage* [*Anwendung einer Stelle*], or the *mediated sense of a passage* [*mittlebarer Verstand einer Stelle*], as well as the *conclusions* [*Folgerungen*], because this type of concept usually consists of deductions and logical conclusions. Third, the unmediated sense gives rise to concepts that are brought forth by the imagination, and these are called *digressions* [excesses] [*Ausschweiffungen*].[29]

Like Husserl with the concept of sign, Chladenius does not attempt to provide an answer about what the "complete sense" of a passage *is* in general but to distinguish and define the "numerous concepts" of which it is composed. These are (1) the unmediated sense of a passage; (2) the mediated sense of a passage in the form of application or conclusions; and (3) digressions (excesses). Thus to understand the "complete sense," one must understand these three concepts and the relations between them.

It is clear that for Chladenius, the most important of the three is the "unmediated sense" because "the unmediated sense is present in all texts, regardless of what they are called or what characteristics they have."[30] Thus, one could imagine the unmediated sense itself as the "true meaning" of a passage or text even though the "complete sense" comprises all three concepts. In §677 Chladenius tells us:

The unmediated sense is the one about which the author of the passage and all the readers who comprehend the passage must be in agreement. That is to say, the complete sense of a passage consists of many concepts, and the unmediated sense constitutes one component thereof. Thus it is that a reader can understand a passage even though he does not think certain thoughts that the author had in mind. It follows that the author will not concur with all of those readers who can be said to have understood the passage. Nevertheless, with regard to the unmediated sense the author must be in agreement with all of his readers, provided that they have understood him.[31]

Thus, despite the possibility of applications, conclusions, or digressions that might deviate from the author's intention, the "certain thoughts that the author had in mind," those thoughts are still available to the reader in a pure and unadulterated form via the unmediated or immediate sense of the passage. This is because this "level of meaning is the result of mere attention to the words of the passage and demands the least amount of attention from the reader; the unmediated sense can remain concealed from no one so long as he has properly prepared himself beforehand."[32] Here, Chladenius asserts that regardless of what a reader brings to the reading of a passage or text and regardless of temporal or geographic distance, the original meaning is always available in the form of the unmediated sense of a passage, and this is the case for all texts. By contrast, the "mediated sense" (*mittlebarer Verstand*) of a passage, while derived from the unmediated sense, moves beyond those thoughts that the author had in mind when composing it. Chladenius introduces the term *application* (*Anwendung*) to describe the way this "mediated sense" consists of "those things which the mind [*Seele*] continues to think of and feel after it has called to mind the things contained in the unmediated sense, and this occurs through the application of all kinds of capacities of the mind [*Seele*]."[33] The key issue for Chladenius is that while the application of the meaning of the passage exceeds the original meaning, as gleaned in the unmediated sense, it is nevertheless dependent on that unmediated sense. But here we must consider the way that Chladenius relates the mediated sense of a passage to the mind or soul and how this is indicative of his attempt to revise and rehabilitate hermeneutics. Szondi states that Chladenius's "distinction between the straightforward and mediated senses represents a generalized and secularized reformulation between the old distinction between the *sensus literalis* and the *sensus spiritualis*, undertaken in the interest of establishing a *general* theory of interpretation."[34] Whereas in traditional hermeneutics the "literal sense" was placed in distinction from the "spiritual sense," in Chladenius's model the "literal sense" is but a "particular type of unmediated sense," and the spiritual sense appears in the realm of the mediated sense of the passage, here mediated by the soul.[35] For Chladenius, it only makes sense to speak of a "literal sense" in relation to a "spiritual sense," but one can always speak of the unmediated sense of a passage. Szondi takes this as indicative of how Chladenius expands the scope of his interpretative methodology beyond pure theology: "The terminology 'straightforward sense' and 'mediated sense,' and within the latter, 'application' and 'digression,' is conceived in keeping with the goal of a general art of interpretation so as to be valid for all types of speech and writing."[36] Nevertheless, we should not lose track of the theological implications of Chladenius's hermeneutics.

The final term, *Ausschweiffungen*, which can be translated as "digression" or "excess," diverges from the mediated sense of the passage as application because although it is still related to the unmediated sense, it is not necessarily dependent on the passage.

> That which we call digression [excess] (*Ausschweiffungen*) is [like application] also brought forth by a particular capacity of the soul upon the occasion of reading a passage. It is therefore not easy to distinguish the applications from the digressions/excesses. Nonetheless, the differences should become clear in the following way. As long as in our thoughts we must still have the passage in mind by which the thoughts were stimulated, we are still dealing with the application of the passage. When, however, we no longer need to think of the passage, then the concepts involved are to be called a *digression* even if they were stimulated by the passage.[37]

To put this in relation to historical thought, the application of a passage is when the text or meaning of the text is applied to a specific case or instance to make sense of a contemporary or past historical situation. Here the content of the passage can be applied to judgment or belief or a current situation that does not belong to the intention of the author. Digression, however, is when the passage in question inspires the reader to issues or thoughts that are no longer dependent on the text itself and thus exceed the passage in question. This could be seen as a movement away from the text to issues stimulated by, but unrelated to, the passage in question, but it could also be an interpretation of the passage based on the author's biography, context, or external events that may have conditioned the author's situation but remained unavailable to the author at the time and is, in any case, extrinsic to the contents of the text itself.

Thus the criterion of application seems to apply to digression/excess except that the former still adheres to the text or passage while the latter is only inspired by it. Both of these interpretive positions seem to be conditioned by the interpreter's own historical standpoint (*Standortgebundenheit*) or perspective (*Sehe-Punkt*), and here, the hard realism of the unmediated sense presented in the *Einleitung* seems to contradict the theory of the viewpoint as articulated in the *Allgemeine Geschichtswissen-*

schaft and as taken up by later readers of Chladenius. Chladenius explicitly acknowledges the problem of digression as a destabilizing force that could potentially lead to a sort of subjective relativism:

> But since the imagination and the memory function differently in every person, presenting things to one person on this or that occasion which cannot occur to other people even though they are knowledgeable, it follows (1) that every reader is inclined to his own particular digressions whenever such are in order; (2) that the author of a text, because he is not all-knowing, cannot anticipate the digressions, especially when they concern things that had not yet occurred in his time, or did not yet exist, or had not yet been invented; (3) that therefore the author of a book cannot be in agreement with his readers in regard to digressions, and therefore (4) they also do not belong to the meaning of the book and the passage, since he has not expressed himself on the subject.[38]

Chladenius acknowledges that the historical position of the reader has an impact on the reader's ability to understand the text, but rather than accept the possibility that the reader determines the meaning of the passage based on the circumstances of her or his historical situation, he asserts that digressions/excesses "do not belong to the meaning of the book and the passage." But earlier, in §690, and again later, in §736, he argues that "the understanding of a book contains the unmediated sense, the applications, and the digressions."[39] Thus, it is unclear whether the ultimate arbiter of meaning is the text/event itself or the understanding of the text/event in the mind of the reader. Szondi seizes on this seeming contradiction and the parts that comprise it to ask if "the motive for division—namely, the recognition that understanding depends on the position of the interpreter—admits the possibility of a core of 'straightforward sense' beyond all relativity? Should we not pose and solve the problem of the validity of understanding and interpretation *within* the theory of their historical situatedness [*Standortgebundenheit*] rather than try to rescue the traditional criteria of the objectivity of understanding by postulating a 'straightforward sense'?"[40]

The question is fair but shifts the focus to the receiver without fully interrogating the logic of inclusion and exclusion by which the past event is made available in the present. The movement between inclusion and exclusion can be clarified when we place Chladenius in proximity to a comment Derrida makes about J. L. Austin in "Signature Event Context." There, Derrida tells us that Austin's procedure "consists in recogniz-ing that the possibility of the negative (in this case, of infelicities) is in fact a structural possibility, that failure is an essential risk of the operations under consideration; then in a move which is almost *immediately simul-taneous*, in the name of a kind of ideal regulation, it excludes that risk as accidental, exterior, one which teaches us nothing about the linguistic phenomenon being considered."[41]

Chladenius likewise accounts for the structural possibility of the fail-ure to understand the unmediated sense of the passage (in this case, di-gressions/excesses) by including digressions as part of the makeup of the "complete understanding" of a passage but then excludes that risk as con-tributing nothing to the unmediated meaning of the passage. Thus the ideal of the unmediated understanding affords a stable connection be-tween the author's intention and the reader's understanding that remains uncontaminated.[42]

But the unmediated meaning that is ultimately to be conferred to the reader in the present (or the future) is predicated on an ideal meaning in the past that is always already in danger of being contaminated by the mediated understanding as application or digression. The absent ideal meaning of the unmediated sense, therefore, is deferred until such a time as the stable connection between the author's intention and the reader's reception can be established. In this sense "this structure presupposes that the sign [ideal meaning for Chladenius], which defers presence, is con-ceivable only on the *basis* of the presence that it defers and *moving toward* the deferred presence that it aims to reappropriate."[43]

Conventional history, in its attempt to recuperate the past, makes this sleight of hand apparent because there is nothing to actually reappro-priate. The past event cannot be made present; any reappearance is the untimely visitation of a ghost. Thus, "the substitution of the sign for the thing itself is both *secondary* and *provisional*: secondary due to an original and lost presence from which the sign thus derives [this is the past event, the 'as it really happened']; provisional as concerns this final and missing presence toward which the sign in this sense is a movement of mediation [the ideal unmediated sense]."[44]

The contamination of the past event or author with the present inter-preter is manifest in Chladenius's attempt to solidify the original intention of the author in the past as the basis for true understanding in the pres-ent. This maneuver should be familiar to most present-day historians who continue to operate under the assumption that their interpretative actions in the present are entirely guided by adherence to the event or historical actor in the past. Toward the end of the *Einleitung* Chladenius tells us, "In the historical interpretation of an author, the interpreter should note the point of view according to which he imagined and make this known to his student."[45] One way to read this is as the interpreter accounting for his or her own position and inevitable infelicities in his or her ability to understand the "true meaning" of the text. But another reading is possible in light of a quote from an earlier passage where Chladenius states that the interpreter must "imagine the history he wants to interpret from both points of view, partly as it appears to whoever finds it unbelievable and partly as the writer imagined it."[46] Here, we see that the ability to bring the past artifact into the present is predicated on the imagination of the interpreter. It is in the recuperation of the author's imagination, "the point of view from which he [the author] imagined the history," that the direct line between past and present is achieved. In essence, we are asked to replace the reader's point of view with that of the author in order to achieve the unmediated understanding, but this is itself an act of imagination, thus either an application or digression, which then becomes the interpretive ground for discerning the straightforward meaning from which application and digression (mediated understandings) should be excluded. But for Chladenius any interpretation that differs from the immediate sense is a perversion of meaning in the religious sense and a deviation from the theologically given true sense.

Chladenius opens the possibility of the ontological problem of the subject's historical position (*Standortgebundenheit*) via perspectivalism in the concept of the *Sehe-Punkt* but also closes it via the noncritical theological hold. The correct meaning is available and accessible but deferred until such time as the methodological and interpretive strategies of the reader can acquire the true meaning conveyed by the author. Thus, the issue is primarily an epistemological one about method but only so long as the ontological reality of the past is backed up by a theological guarantee. This epistemological claim makes Chladenius a good touchstone for ontological realists reading him back through the lens of Koselleck or Gadamer, where the burden of meaning is placed on the reader rather than the author so that the problem of the ontological properties of the past opened by the contamination of interpreter and artifact is simultaneously closed. The question remains one of method and epistemology rather than that of the theologico-historical hold that allows for the past event to be transported to the present. What is key is that for Chladenius, the epistemological instability of the human interpreter of history is mitigated by the divine authority who holds the past and renders it both meaningful and accessible. This is what allows us to go back to where we've never been. In modern incarnations the theological side of the theologico-historical hold is effaced, creating the illusion that the past event or object simply holds itself. But absent the divine, the bond is broken, and one must wonder what, if anything, allows the historian to account for the properties of an absent past given the contamination by the historian's subject position in the present?

Droysen

As with the work of Chladenius, the work of Droysen as a theorist of history has undergone a revival since the 1970s, especially as a result of the work of Jörn Rüsen and the publication of Peter Leyh's edition of Droysen's *Historik* in 1977. But we should not underestimate the sustained influence of Droysen for teaching historical method either through courses in the German tradition of *Historik* or in the American historical tradition. In terms of the latter, one can look to Kerwin Lee Klein's account of Droysen's influence on Herbert Baxter Adams and Frederick Jackson Turner.[47] Here we must also keep in mind Peter Novick's discussion of the influence of a particular understanding of Leopold von Ranke for American historians such as Turner. For the Americans, "Ranke's reputation as an unphilosophical empiricist underwrote an already existing American predisposition to disparage philosophical speculation about history; and this, in turn, served to perpetuate the reputation."[48] Thus, despite the deep disagreements and divides between the approaches of Droysen and Ranke, in the American context the two could sit comfortably together insofar as Droysen's "infinitely practical accounts" of the practice of historical research meshed with "Ranke's epistemology 'naturalized' into an English empiricist idiom." Here, both thinkers become examples of history as *Wissenschaft*, understood as Anglo-American "science." Hayden White has argued that while not many historians systematically set forth and defend claims to the autonomy of history as *Wissenschaft*, they do "simply assume that autonomy and criticize anyone who import[s] interpretative methods into history from other fields and uses them to guide the formation of either their narratives or their explanations of what really had happened in the past. This is an effective tactic, since it permits the practice of historians to substitute for the theory which their enterprise lacks."[49] But such a move effectively effaces the theoretical aspects of Droysen's investigation in favor of solely the methodological aspects. What's more, the understanding of *Wissenschaft* in terms of Anglo-American "science" demotes or disregards the role and place of the theologico-historical in the work of Droysen and its residual effect on ontological realism.

Droysen was keenly aware of the issue of indeterminacy inherent in the perspectivalism of the "point of view" (*Sehe-Punkt*), "position" (*Standort*), or "standpoint" (*Standpunkt*) but believed that emphasis on the historian's place and role in recounting the past was an essential component of the process of history. This stood as a stark counter to the Rankean position that Droysen characterized as a "eunuch-like objectivity" and also reveals the strong influence of Hegel on Droysen.[50] If for Ranke the historian should aspire to a position of neutral objectivity in order to let the facts speak for themselves, for Droysen the historian should, and in fact must necessarily, play an active role: "Objective impartiality is inhuman, [because] to be human is rather to be biased";[51] the historian makes the facts speak and does so on the basis of her or his historically conditioned circumstances.[52] The temporally and culturally specific goals of the historian will ultimately dictate what the facts tell us. Thus, the noble dream of objectivity is merely that—a dream never to be achieved, and on this reading Rankean *Anschaulich*, or vivid history, reveals more about the imagination of the historian than it does about the subject of inquiry.

This is a key move reflected in the structure of Droysen's work, where he "turns the ambiguity of the word 'history' into a principle for organizing his analysis of all the problems connected with historical representation. Accordingly, he divides his work into two principal parts: I. *Methodik*, having to do with the forms and contents of a distinctively historical mode of thinking ('heuristic,' 'criticism,' 'interpretation,' and 'representation'), and II. *Systematik*, having to do with the forms and contents of a distinctively historical mode of existence (the 'Ethical Powers' that inform historical being and the concepts of 'Man and Humanity' that comprise history's basis and goal respectively)."[53]

We will turn to the contents of these sections presently, but I want to emphasize that for Droysen the position of the historian in the present holds a greater weight and burden than it did for Chladenius. Unlike Chladenius, Droysen did not see any way for our relationship to the past itself to be direct or unmediated because "all empirical investigation governs itself according to the data to which it is directed, and it can only direct itself to such data as are immediately present to it and susceptible of being cognized through the senses. The data for historical investigation are not past things, for these have disappeared, but things which are still present here and now, whether recollections of what was done, or remnants of things that have existed and of events that have occurred."[54] Thus, if there is an *unmittelbarer* or unmediated sense for Droysen, it refers only to those portions of the past that remain available for us to take up in the present and not the "ontological reality" of the past event itself. It is the extant remaining sections of the Great Wall that can tell us about the missing portions. What's more, our understanding of these artifacts is conditioned by our historically determined circumstances. Whereas for Chladenius the problem of getting back to where we've never been, the ontological reality of the past, is an epistemological one that can be managed through proper method, for Droysen there is a split between the epistemological problems one encounters in the section on *Methodik* and the ontological issue of our existence as historical beings, which determines our epistemological understanding as discussed in the section on *Systematik*. Thus, for Droysen history refers to both the past we seek to understand through sound investigation and our ontological condition as historical beings. "Historical investigation presupposes the reflection that even the content of our 'I' is a mediated content, one that has developed and is thus an historical result."[55] The God-held meaning of the past in itself gives way to the subjective position of the historian in the present. Because the "I" is not a self-sufficient mental substance, it is formed by the social, political, and cultural conditions that surround it. These make up the norms or shared practices of collective groups of people. Following Hegel, Droysen refers to these shared practices or norms as the ethical world (*die sittliche Welt*), and this is the basic unit of history encompassing our historical mode of thinking and our ontological condition as historical beings.[56]

Here, Chladenius's perspectivalism is conserved to counter Rankean objectivity (source criticism), but Droysen parts ways with Chladenius when he concedes that the past is itself ontologically inaccessible. Access to the past only exists by and through our own historical-ontological condition in the present. For Droysen the project of history is not about "knowledge" which is the realm of philosophy, or "explanation," which is the realm of math and science, but "understanding." Droysen employs the verbs *to know/ erkennen, to explain/ erklären,* and *to understand/ verstehen.*[57] "The essence of the historical method is understanding by means of investigation."[58] In this way Droysen moves from a position where the ontological reality of the past is held by God, even if we are epistemologically uncertain about that past, to one where the past itself is not held at all. "What becomes clear is not past events as past. These exist no longer. It is so much of those past things as still abide in the now and the here. These quickened traces of past things stand to us in the stead of their originals, mentally constituting the 'present' of those originals."[59] What we do have is our ontological condition as historical beings and the remnants of the past we seek to understand. Thus, Droysen should be distanced from the ontological realist position, or, at least, there are indications that Droysen was not ready to commit to such a position. It is in this light Droysen can state that while he is "thankful for this kind of [Rankean] eunuch-like objectivity . . . I do not want to appear to have more or less than the relative truth of my standpoint, insofar as my fatherland, my political and religious conviction, and my earnest study have helped me to reach it. That is by far not meant to be the work for eternity, and in every respect it is one-sided and limited. But one must have the courage to confess this limitation and to console oneself that the limited and particular is richer than the universal."[60]

Here we see that the criteria for doing history, no matter how earnest one's study, are inextricably bound to the situation of the historian. Thus, for Droysen any "realistic" representation of the past should require sound method but is always actually based "on a criterion not of truth, but of plausibility, which has reference to the social practices of the historian's own time, place, and circumstances."[61]

The weight of historical study rests firmly in the present, but, to be sure, the object of study is the past, and it is through the historian's concern with what remains of the past that we can come to understand it. "Historical material is partly what is still immediately present, hailing from times which we are seeking to understand (*Überreste/*Remains), partly whatever ideas human beings have obtained and transmitted to be remembered (*Quellen/*Sources), partly things wherein both these forms of materials are combined (*Denkmäler/*Monuments)."[62] These materials make up the empirical data of historical analysis and what allows for Droysen to consider history an empirical science. Because "the three kinds of materials will differ in relative value according to the purpose for which the researcher is to use them," there is no "right" answer in terms of truth but only understanding predicated on one's current historical condition. "Even the very best of these sources give the researcher, so to speak, only polarized light."[63] Nevertheless, the soundness and accuracy of historical work can be vouchsafed through the appropriate use of source critique as outlined in the section on Method. For Droysen source critique should serve to determine whether the historical materials we have are reliable to answer the questions we pose of them.[64] Thus, the historian must "inquire whether the material actually is what it is taken to be or pretends to be . . . whether the material has maintained its original and pretended character unchanged, or, if not, what changes are to be recognized as having occurred in it and as therefore to be left out of the account . . . and whether the material, under the circumstances of its origin, did or could involve all that for which it is, or offers itself to be, taken as a voucher."[65]

For Droysen the critical method is misused when the critical examination of sources is taken to be tantamount to the recovery of the past itself. As Beiser notes, a large part of the "critical historians' naive confidence is that they seemed to think that, if they only sifted and sorted enough, they would finally be able to distinguish truth from falsehood, and so see 'how things actually were.'"[66] But as I have noted, for Droysen such a view is based on the faulty premise that the past is an object available for discovery. The "facts" that can be verified by way of source criticism never constitute a past whole but instead are fragmentary remains of a past that no longer exists. Criticism allows us to account the best we can for the veracity of the materials in order to do away "with all sorts of imperfections and impurities which the material initially had." What's more, it allows us to "organize them so that they may lie well ordered before us."[67] Here again we see that our understanding of the past is created by the historian in the present because the material remains are both myriad and partial; thus, even once verified as "authentic" the coherency of these many partial pieces has to be constructed. "Each of these facts arises as a rule from interaction with many other facts and some were formed in such a way that they opposed and acted against one another."[68] Thus, for Droysen the goal of historical inquiry is not merely the accumulation of "facts" but the understanding of the volition or will of the actors at that time:

"Criticism does not seek 'the exact historical fact'; for every so-called historical fact, apart from the means leading thereto, and the connections, conditions and purposes which were active at the time, is a complex act of will, often many, helping and hindering, and acts of will which, as such, passed away with the time to which they belonged, and lie before us now only either in remnants of contemporary and related transformations and occurrences, or as made known in the views and recollections of men."[69]

But, Droysen asks, "how should we react to facts, that is evidence or remains of facts, in which (as with the remains of the Old Roman Wall, or the *leges barborum*, or the founding of Knights' Orders in Jerusalem) there are no longer any traces of a personal will and what is left to speak to us is merely something general, like the genius of a people, the insight of an age, the same uniform attitudes of countless believers?"[70] This is to ask how do we account for the gaps in the Great Wall that is the past given the absence of data or evidence? Here, we encounter the crucial functional role of imagination for the historian that was both opened and closed in the work of Chladenius. Droysen is explicit in articulating the appropriate methodology for handling and verifying sources, but he is equally explicit to note that even under the best conditions our understanding will still be incomplete. We cannot actually get back to where we've never been. What we can do, however, is imagine how things were. "It is precisely the imagination which is immediately active in producing a picture of the events past—be they recorded or not—and the saga illustrates to us just how historic necessity is forced to proceed in such a manner."[71] The combination of criticism and imagination allows the historian to sift and order the particular facts into a coherent whole so that the facts now have meaning for us as a sequence of causally linked events.

Because of the prominent role of imagination in the project of history, Droysen cautions us: "the greatest danger is that we involuntarily bring in the views and presuppositions of our own time and the present interferes with our understanding of the past."[72] Here, as with Chladenius, the crucial role played by imagination in presenting the past reveals the necessary contamination of the past with the standpoint of the historian in the present. But as soon as it is announced, it is effaced and deferred. Hayden White describes this move as "historical representation permitting the reader of it to give free reign to the 'imaginary,' while not remaining bound to the constraints of a 'symbolic system,' but in such a way as to engender in the reader a sense of a 'reality' that is 'more comprehensible' than one's present social existence."[73] When this overly comprehensive representative system is taken for the "reality of the past," it becomes the basis for the contemporary ontological realist position that effaces the imaginary by emphasizing the coherency derived from the "facts." In this way the work of Droysen can be marshaled as a defense of the ontological realist position. "Historical representation is especially well [suited for this] since it purports to deal with the 'real' rather than the merely 'imaginary' (as literature is supposed to do), but distances this 'reality' by construing it under the modality of a 'pastness' which is both distinct from and continuous with the present."[74] But for Droysen it is clear that the retrieval of the past itself is an ideal, not a reality: "Every point in the present is one which has come to be. That which it was and the manner by which it came to be—these have passed away. Still, ideally, its past character is yet present in it. Only ideally, however, as faded traces and deferred gleams. Apart from knowledge these are as if they existed not."[75] Droysen's language is closer to Derrida's than to that of most conventional historians, and we will follow this path presently.[76]

But it is worth asking, given the empirical uncertainty surrounding our access to the past and the contamination of the historian's standpoint or perspective with the object of study, what is to keep history from being a purely presentist endeavor? For Droysen this is not a problem of the same magnitude as it is for those modern historians seeking to follow his work. This is because Droysen's theory of history had a decidedly Hegelian inflection wherein what holds "history" is the "moral world" of our historical moment and this is the guarantor of our certainty:

> The moral world [*die sittliche Welt*] moved by many ends, and finally, so we instinctively surmise and believe, by the supreme end, is in a state of restless development and of internal elevation and growth, "on and on as man eternalizes himself" [Dante]. Considered in the successive character of these, its movements, the moral world presents itself to us as History. With every advancing step in this development and growth, the historical understanding becomes wider and deeper. History, that is, is better understood and itself understands better. The knowledge of History is History itself. Restlessly working on, it cannot but deepen its investigations and broaden its circle of vision.[77]

Two things are at play here. One is that individuals and communities are in a state of constant development that is both conditioned by and conditions its historical circumstances in a sort of reciprocal feedback loop. We create the world as much as we are created by it. What's more, this condition of creative struggle between the individual and the world in which we live is one where our opposition to our current or past condition brings us forward to a higher level, which leads to further struggle but also further advancement.[78] As we advance historically, our understanding of history becomes more full and more substantial. "History is humanity becoming and being conscious concerning itself."[79] What's more, it is from the privileged and enlightened vantage of the present that we come to understand and make sense of facts and events in the past that appear contradictory either to each other or to a logic of progress:

> All development and growth is movement toward an end which is to be fulfilled by the movement thus coming to realization. In the moral world end links itself to end in an infinite chain. Every one of these ends has primarily its own way to go and its own development to further, but at the same time each is a condition for the others and is conditioned by them. Often enough they repress, interrupt, and contradict one another. Often appear here and there temporary and partial steps backwards; but always only that presently, with so much stronger advance and with exalted elasticity may be pushed forward at some new spot or in some new form, each form impelling the rest and impelled by them.[80]

Thus for Droysen, *Historik*, as an approach to history that accounts for our place in the moral world as both historical actors and as selves who act upon history, is an advance that places scientific reason in relation to our moral condition. History's service in our understanding and development of the moral world is itself the guarantee of its success.

Here it is quite clearly the progressive nature of history that serves to guarantee our surety about historical discourse, but this leads to the second point: what guarantees Droysen's notion of progress? For Droysen it is God, the highest end, "which conditions without being conditioned, moving them all, embracing them all, explaining them all, that is, the supreme end," which, however, "is not to be discovered by empirical research."[81] Thus, God is as present for Droysen as for Chladenius. But whereas in Chladenius's model the presence of God is felt in God's hold over the past (itself a guarantee of the past's properties), for Droysen God's presence is in the present, the now, through the actions of the historian discerning the moral world of his or her time, thus reconciling the problematic contradictions or seeming regressions that litter the past. Though God's hold on the past is itself beyond the methodology of empirical research, "without the consciousness of ends and of the highest end, without the Theodicy of History, [History's] continuity would be a mere motion in a circle, repeating itself."[82]

But for more recent historians working in the secular scientific tradition, the theologico-historical underpinnings are swept aside in favor of the emphasis on the subject position of the historian and the proper method of investigation. Felix Gilbert summarizes Droysen's understanding of history as a "continuing development in which only the valuable survived. The road into the past therefore began in the present, and Droysen's demand that historical research must focus on understanding was not meant to lead to relativism but to widen our knowledge of the possibilities of the present by attaining awareness of all that has gone into its making."[83] The statement is certainly apt in many ways but neglects the theological mechanism by which Droysen is able to avoid falling into relativism, one surmises because the reliance on God is no longer relevant or crucial to Gilbert and modern historians. One key aspect of this move, however, is that the transcendental authority to dictate what is "real," which once belonged directly to God, is now ascribed to "History" detached from its divine author. "What better substitute for this absolute ground than 'reality' itself, but now identified with 'History' rather than with 'God' or 'Nature'?"[84] Thus, we arrive at a tautology of sorts because it is not the presence of God that provides the absolute ground but the ontological reality of the past that now becomes the guarantor of the historical endeavor that itself defines what the ontological reality of the past should be. On these grounds Gilbert can assert that "Droysen is closer to the modern historical approach than many historians of the generation which followed him" and that Blanke, Fleischer, and Rüsen can claim that "for Droysen it is not possible to endanger [the empirical character of history] for he still explains the historical research epistemologically and finds the beginnings of his philosophy of history in the epistemological foundations of historical studies."[85] One could argue, however, that it is not the epistemological foundation of historical studies per se that grounds the empirical character of history but the supreme end, which "is not to be discovered by empirical research" except insofar as we experience the condition of our moral world, which is directed toward the "highest end which conditions without being conditioned."[86]

Rational or scientific discourse is substituted for theology as the guarantor of the empirical nature of historical studies. But "essential to this
sleight of hand is the necessity of hiding the fact that all 'history' is the
study, not of past events which are gone forever from perception, but
rather the 'traces' of those events distilled into documents and monuments, on the one side, and the praxis of present social formations, on
the other. These 'traces' are the 'raw materials' of the historian's discourse,
rather than the 'events' themselves."[87]

The point here is not to advocate for the return to, or privileging of,
a religious understanding of history but to make explicit the move by
which ontological realist historians conserve Droyen's empirical methodology absent its extrahistorical theological aspects without accounting for
the extrahistorical mechanism that guarantees its success. By exposing this
false floor, I want to remove the safety net under both the theologico-
historical and ontological-realist positions in order to explore the instabilities of the past exposed by Droysen. In doing so we will also discover
Droysen's affinities with Derrida.

Let us revisit Droysen's claim that "what becomes clear is not past
events as past. These exist no longer. It is so much of those past things
as still abide in the now and the here. These quickened traces of past
things stand to us in the stead of their originals, mentally constituting
the 'present' of those originals."[88] Here we see that the place to begin is
not by assuming an origin, a hold, or the materiality of the past itself but
by following the "trace"—by going back to where we've *never* been. But,
Derrida asserts, "one can only expose that which at a certain moment can
become *present*, manifest, that which can be shown, presented as something present, a being-present in its truth, in the truth of a present or the
presence of the present."[89] Thus, the past is exposed only as that which is
present for us, and this is the basis for the empirical nature of historical
research in Droysen's account. But following Droysen, we are told that
the basis of this "being-present" is not the past itself, for this has passed
away, but "faded traces" and "suppressed gleams" that shine forth from remains (*Überreste*), sources (*Quellen*), and monuments (*Denkmäler*). Here,
I want to link history and the historical endeavor to Derrida's *différance* in
a way that modifies and borrows from this term.

For Derrida the term *différance* "derives from no category of being,
whether present or absent" and thus is "literally neither a word [n]or a
concept" that can be exposed but serves to expose that "which is main-

tained in a certain necessary relationship with the structural limits of mastery."[90] Locked within the sonically imperceptible presence of the *a* in *différance* is both the difference and deferral of meaning. This is to say that it avoids positing an origin, beginning, or foundation, replacing these with a logic of deferral, difference, and displacement that refuses to present a definitive statement of mastery. This is certainly a dangerous proposition for the historian in fear of losing his or her grip on the past, but it is also a liberating movement in accounting for revision, unaccounted voices, repressed histories, and the Droysenian proposition that our constantly moving position or standpoint within a historical moment conditions and informs our understanding of the past and, thus, history. *Différance* also serves to replace the two coordinates used to hold Droysen's historical model, unhinging it from either the theologico-historical, as in Droysen's *sittliche Welt*, or via recourse to ontological realism as the foundation of empirical historical research, as in Gilbert, Assis, or the American appropriation. Derrida tells us "in the delineation of *différance* everything is strategic and adventurous." This is certainly also the case in the deployment of *différance* for history because of the reasons discussed in Chapter 1. As it pertains to Droysen, it is "strategic because no transcendent truth present outside the field of writing can govern theologically the totality of the field. [And it is] adventurous because this strategy is not a simple strategy in the sense that strategy orients tactics according to a final goal, a *telos* or theme of domination, a mastery and ultimate reappropriation of the development of the field."[91] In the case of the former, historical investigation denies the dominance of a transcendent truth or theological master narrative that is the measure of historical accuracy and efficacy, be it in the form of a theological hold, as in Chladenius, or the teleological progression toward a "higher end," as in Droysen's Hegelian formulation. I believe most modern historians would welcome this strategic intervention as compatible with most current historical practices. The application of *différance* articulated in the latter assertion is more adventurous and troubling. This is because such a move would require historians to embrace a strategy that denies ultimate truth claims or definitive analysis, asking them instead to "read what was never written."[92] On this model the historian would no longer have a "final goal" of mastery and reappropriation through either the scientific presentation of the past "as it was" (that noble dream) or the teleological sense that our understanding of the past improves as we ourselves advance historically (Rüsen, Assis).

While such a move denies the empirical hold articulated by Droysen and appropriated by contemporary historians and some theorists of history, it does not reject Droysen's methodological emphasis on empirical research, where such an investigation proceeding "from the present and from certain elements given in the present used as historical material . . . is two things at once: it is the enrichment and deepening of the present by clearing up past events pertaining to it, and it is a clearing up of these past events by unlocking and unfolding certain remnants of them, remnants of facts which were relatively obscure and perhaps exceedingly so, even when present."[93]

Instead, it rejects a logic of origins and originals that dictate the "truth" of the historical investigation because "no matter how productive the investigation may have been, the ideas arrived at in the endeavor are far from reaching the fullness of content, movement, manifoldness of forms, and of real energy which the original things had when they constituted 'the present.'"[94] For Droysen it is ultimately "illusory to search for the origin of something with the belief that it is possible to find the true essence of that from which this development proceeded," whereas for Derrida "what is put into question is precisely the quest for a rightful beginning, an absolute point of departure, a principal responsibility."[95] Thus, historians should not assume a definite object or point or event to which they seek to return and which serves as the guarantor of the "reality" of the past because "to arrive at a point which is the origin, in its complete and eminent sense, it must be sought exclusively outside the realm of historical research."[96] Instead, it is in the "nature of the narrative to portray historical events as a process and to allow these to present themselves genetically to the ear of the hearer, thus allowing them to virtually unfold before him. However, it is equally clear that we, in so narrating, are only seeking to imitate the sequence as it appears to us to be 'becoming' and that we reconstruct this sequence by inquiry."[97] The problem here is that the "origins" historians seek are constructed in the present and then posited as the ground upon which the veracity of the investigation should be held. "This is important to note because in explaining the origin of that which has become, the genetic mode of narration consistently leads one to the misconception that it is possible to verify historically why things had to come into being and why they had to become what they became."[98] The incompatibility of the fixity of origins with the play of *différance* is no small matter for the historian when considering the way that the idealized origin or event comes to hold the past event as a permanently present sign for an event that is decidedly absent. That is, because the origin is only ideal and because it is past, it can never really be present; its presence as the actual guarantor of the historical reappropriation must always be deferred. For if the past is what makes possible the presentation of the being-present of history, it is never presented as such. The past itself is never offered to the present.[99] We will take this up more fully in my final chapter.

For now, we can think about this conundrum in relation to Derrida's discussion of the "practice of language or of a code supposing a play of forms without a determined and invariable substance, and also suppos- ing in the practice of this play a retention and protention of differences, a spacing and a temporization, a play of traces—all this must be a kind of writing before the letter, an archi-writing without a present origin, without archi-. Whence the regular erasure of the archi-, and the trans- formation of general semiology into grammatology, this latter executing a critical labor on everything within semiology, including the central con- cept of the sign, that maintained metaphysical presuppositions incompat- ible with the motif of *différance*."[100] Historians engage in precisely this practice of language or a code when doing/writing history because they suppose the play of forms, the past events, actors, ideas, that lack any de- termined or invariable substance. And as presented in both Chladenius's and Droysen's concept of the standpoint, the historian supposes a play of retention and protention of differences, of casting back and reaching forward, which is enacted in the spacing and temporization of the traces of the past.[101] This requires the sort of archi-writing Derrida describes, a positing of something that precedes the writing itself, that lacks a present origin, that lacks an archi-. The key issue is the way that the instability of the past, which is both an openness and closedness, is replaced by a sense of fixity that only sees the closedness or takes the closedness to be an opening. This understanding is based on the reappropriation and rep- resentation of the past event, not on the originary event itself "as it hap- pened," but then erases or effaces the priority of the reappropriation/rep- resentation in favor of the holding power of the "originary event" itself. The proof of the historical account becomes its adherence to an originary past event, though one that has yet to be accessed, and the role of the historian contaminated by his or her own historical moment is rendered moot. Here the historian simultaneously "grants to the 'living present' the power of synthesizing traces, and of incessantly reassembling them" while claiming the veracity of the reassembly on the basis of an "orginary presence" located in the past.[102] Representation here "regularly *supplants* presence. However, articulating all the moments of experience insofar as it is involved in signification . . . , this operation of supplementation is not exhibited as a break in presence but rather as a continuous and homogeneous reparation and modification of presence in the representation."[103] The absent past is made present but in a manner noncoincident with the past present it represents.

But, following Droysen, "it is not the [past] object but our understanding of the object" where "our knowledge is at first something received, a something which has passed over to us, ours, yet not ours."[104] Here, Droysen tells us that we are moving in a circle, where our historical investigation seeks to understand the context of events in the past but is conditioned by our current context in the present, which itself is conditioned by the past.[105] Thus, we are starting "from the place and the time in which 'we' are, even though in the last analysis [my] opening is not justifiable, since it is only on the basis of *différance* and its 'history' that we can allegedly know who and where 'we' are, and what the limits of an 'era' might be."[106] I want to pair the standpoint or perspective (the historically conditioned moment from which we begin our investigation into history) with *différance*, which places this entry point into the hermeneutic circle into question. Indeed, the very notion of context is placed in question by the complex relation between the historian operating within the context of his or her historical moment and the sources (*Quellen*), remains (*Überreste*), or monuments (*Denkmäler*) through which the past haunts the present and the historian attempts to understand the context of the past. For historians a context is never absolutely determinable because it is always gathered/ascertained within another context.

Historical works, such as Ranke's *History of the Romanic and Germanic Peoples* or Droysen's *History of Hellenistic Civilization*, are each histories of past events written on the basis of historical sources, and from this perspective they provide the context of the subject under investigation written from the particular standpoint of each author; but they can also become historical sources themselves, to be used in a future history about historians in the nineteenth century, for instance. In this way the remnants of the past carry "a force that breaks with [their] context, that is, with the collectivity of presences organizing the moment of [their] inscription."[107] The source thus drifts (*dérive*) from context to context. For the conventional historian "this allegedly real context includes a certain 'present' of the inscription, the presence of the writer to what he has written, the entire environment and the horizon of his experience, and above all the intention, the wanting-to-say-what-he-means [*vouloir-dire*], which animates his inscription at a given moment."[108] "But," Derrida continues, "the sign possesses the characteristic of being readable even if the moment of its production is irrevocably lost and even if I do not know what its alleged author-scriptor consciously intended to say at the moment he wrote it, i.e. abandoned it to its essential drift."[109] The former statement relates to the ideal of historical inquiry and the latter to its actuality because in most cases we do not know what the author-scriptor intended, and our understanding of the source material is entangled with our own particular moment. Thus, when Droysen tells us that "as a rule the earliest historical composition respecting an event governs all subsequent tradition," it does so not as a definitive representation of that event but as the first in a chain of citational grafts.[110] And here "one can perhaps come to recognize other possibilities in it by inscribing it or *grafting* it onto other chains. No context can entirely close it."[111] Thus, we can account for the transformation of historical understanding over time articulated by Droysen without relying on the scaffold of either a Hegelian theological or rational teleology of progress, introducing instead the play of *différance*.

Here, what Derrida refers to as "finally, a strategy without finality, what might be called blind tactics of empirical wanderings,"[112] aligns with Droysen's assertions that empirical "facts" do not tell us anything in and of themselves but need to be understood in the context of our times. This interminable contextual drift allows for the possibility that new understandings of what is, or was, possible be revealed. This fits with Droysen's sense of transformation, where the past is understood through the condition of the present: as we change, our historical understanding changes, and as our historical understanding changes, we change. Because of the possibility of disengagement and citational graft, which belongs to the structure of every trace [in the Droysenian sense], "every sign can be *cited*, put between quotation marks; in so doing it can break with every given context, engendering an infinity of new contexts in a manner which is absolutely illimitable."[113] Thus the source material can be put to work to reimagine possible historical conditions in the past that were unimaginable in previous historical accounts. "This does not imply that the mark is valid outside of a context but on the contrary that there are only contexts without any center or absolute anchor."[114] Indeed, the inclusion of vast amounts of sources, voices, language, and concepts from "others" is actually what history has done best over the last fifty years. The problem is that conventional history has remained beholden to ontological realism committed often to chronology, if not narrative, but also to the "art" of the archive and the quotation. The historian should not be searching for the origin or the anchor but working through the trace. "Since the trace is not a presence but the simulacrum of a presence that dislocates itself, displaces itself, refers itself, it properly has no site—erasure belongs to its structure."[115] This is the condition of the past. The past is always out of context.

Dilthey

In a forum for the *American Historical Review* in 1989, David Harlan argued that the influence of literary criticism and the work of theorists such as Saussure, Barthes, Foucault, and Derrida had facilitated a sufficiently strong critique of the nineteenth-century positivist view of history "established on the solid foundation of objective method and rational argument" so that "now, after a hundred year absence, literature has returned to history, unfurling her circus silks of metaphor and allegory, misprision and aporia, trace and sign, demanding that historians accept her own mocking presence right at the heart of what they had once insisted was their own autonomous and truly scientific discipline."[116] In response, David Hollinger presented a defense of *Wissenschaftliche* historical practice based, to a large extent, on the claim that historians are neither as positivistic nor epistemologically naive as Harlan indicated. Hollinger countered that "historians of the contextualist persuasion have generally been content to labor within Wilhelm Dilthey's 'hermeneutic circle': interpretations are circular in that they cannot be expected to touch an Archimedean point. The 'progress' made is thus not of the positivist sort."[117] Here, Hollinger relies on the authority of Dilthey to concede the fallibility of the historian but not the definite nature of the object of inquiry and remains highly skeptical of any theory that would do so. The issue is not the existence of the Great Wall in its original state but our access to it. What interests me is the way that Harlan's own reply to Hollinger's response, while conserving Harlan's interest in the possibilities offered by literary theory, ends up in accord with Hollinger on this point. "Hollinger is right: the return to literature does raise critical problems about interpretation, about meaning and about evaluation—in other words, about relativism. It is not difficult to understand why the deconstructionist's seemingly joyous affirmation of a world without origin or truth reawakens, for many people, a dark undercurrent of dread. . . . But to assert that there are no *universal* truths is not to assert that there are no *particular* truths."[118] Hollinger's invocation of Dilthey is intended to serve as indication of a more nuanced understanding of the project of history that can account for the role and place of literature and imagination while remaining a scientific project interested in the "truth" of the past though "the 'progress'" made toward that end should not be considered of the "positivist" sort. Here Dilthey, like Droysen, represents history as *Wissenschaft*, understood as Anglo-American "science."

Harlan's affirmative response to the invocation is indicative of the way historians routinely use Dilthey as a kind of guardrail or anchor where the hermeneutic nature of his project is deemed sufficient to account for the problematic nature of the past while the scientific aspects of his project assure its rigor. This is to say that for both Hollinger and Harlan, Dilthey authorizes the conclusion that we should consider the past as an object with ontological properties that are discernible and obtainable when approached with correct method. This is a past with definitive properties that exists independent of the historian and that is accessible when approached correctly and directly. On this understanding, the historian may not "be expected to touch an Archimedean point"; nevertheless, this point does exist, and here we see an example of the way a "hard" ontological realist position can be at work in a "soft" one.[119] But as Martin Heidegger suggested as early as 1927, such an image of Dilthey, while "superficially correct," nevertheless "covers up more than it reveals."[120] This coincides with Michael Ermarth's conclusion that Dilthey's assessment of Goethe should be ascribed to Dilthey himself: "For him everything was a problem; every solution contained a new problem—nothing left him in rest."[121] Historians would be wise to maintain a similar state of unrest and vigilance before appropriating Dilthey in the service of ontological realism lest their untroubled application of his troubled and conflicting critique of historical reason serve to cover up more than it reveals.

Like Chladenius and Droysen, Dilthey was taken with the problem of the indeterminacy inherent in the historian's position or standpoint in the present in relation to the past event that is the historian's object of study. Chladenius, Droysen, and Dilthey held a shared commitment to hermeneutics and the ideal of making true statements about the past while also accounting for the perspectival nature of these statements. But unlike either Chladenius or Droysen, Dilthey did not look for a theological solution to the vexing problem of getting back to where we've never been. Dilthey's approach is certainly closer to that of Droysen, emphasizing the position of the historian in her or his present moment rather than Chladenius's God-held meaning of the past. This creates a tension in Dilthey akin to the one we saw in Droysen, where it is our ontological condition as historical creatures that dictates the epistemological methodologies by which we do history and come to ascribe meaning to the past. "We are historical beings before being observers of history, and only because we are the former do we become the latter."[122] But Dilthey's secular understanding of history as science did not allow for the teleological progression toward a "higher end," as in Droysen's Hegelian formulation; thus, our progress forward in time alone was no guarantee that we could come to understand the events of the past.

Instead, Dilthey presents a formulation wherein the science of history must be based solely on our own faculty of reason, not in the strictly Kantian sense but reason understood as historically determined. Dilthey attempts to distinguish his understanding of "reason" from that of Kant in his *Drafts for a Critique of Historical Reason*, where he begins with the issue of temporality: "Temporality is contained in life as its first categorical determination and the one that is fundamental for all others. . . . Time is there for us by means of the gathering unity of our consciousness. Life, and the external objects encompassed by it, share the relationships of simultaneity, succession, time interval, duration, and change. It is from them that the mathematical natural sciences derived the abstract relations on which Kant based his doctrine of the phenomenal nature of time."[123] Thus Kant's "mathematical" framework of temporal relationships is not the primary way in which we experience temporality but a derivative and abstracted understanding of time. This is because for Dilthey, Kant's framework does not sufficiently engage what Dilthey calls the "lived experience of time through which the concept receives its ultimate fulfillment."[124] According to Dilthey, our lived experience of time is as the "restless advance of the present, in which what is present constantly becomes past and the future present."[125] Here, our experience of the present as full of our reality creates a sense of continuity, permanence, and cohesion that inoculates us from the ways that the content of our lived experience is constantly changing. Because the representations by which we possess the past and the future are always only available for us in the present, it is solely through the lens of this present that we come to view future or past. Here we should remember our visit with the Ghost of Christmas Present in the previous chapter and the ways that the "presence" paradigm allows one to freeze a moment in time and transport it to the present, thus reinscribing assumptions of a static past that is always available to us in the present. But strictly speaking for Dilthey, the present never *is*: "what we experience as present always contains the memory of what has just been present. . . . The ship of our life is carried forward on a constantly moving stream, as it were, and the present is always where we enter these waves with whatever we suffer, remember, and hope, that is, whenever we live in the fullness of our reality. We constantly sail into this stream, and the moment the future becomes the present, it also begins to sink into the past."[126] Thus for Dilthey, there can be no Archimedean point on which our knowledge of the past can rest, but neither is there any sort of external perspective from which we can do history as there is for Ranke or Hollinger and Harlan.

The idea of such an external position is a Kantian one for Dilthey, and this is why he asserts that "no real blood flows in the veins of the knowing subject constructed by Locke, Hume, and Kant, but rather the diluted extract of reason as a mere process of thought."[127] As with our experience of the present, this construction of abstract reason as an a priori category is derivative of our lived experience but also isolates the category of reason, thus denying a rigorous investigation into the historical conditions that led to its construction. In this abstracted form reason appears as a constant, stable, and always available basis on which to assess truth claims. But in doing so, it proposes a stability that is no more available in the present than it is in the past. For Dilthey "the questions which we ask of philosophy cannot be answered by rigid *a priori* conditions of knowledge but only by a history which starts from the totality of our nature and sketches its developments."[128]

But if Dilthey was critical of the philosophical application of abstract reason because it did not sufficiently account for history, he was equally critical of the Historical School because its proposed methods for history lacked sufficient philosophical foundations. Thus, while Dilthey

lauded the "Historical School—taking that term in its broadest sense—
[for bringing] about the emancipation of historical consciousness and
historical scholarship," he also derided the school because "its study and
evaluation of historical phenomena remain unconnected with the analysis
of facts of consciousness; . . . it has, in short, no philosophical foundation."[129] In particular, Dilthey considered the Rankean ideal of extin-
guishing oneself (*Selbstauslöschung*) in order to see the past as it "really
was" to be philosophically naive.[130] For Dilthey, there was no separation
between our ontological position as historical beings and the epistemological coordinates by which we make sense of the past.

The Thus, Dilthey follows Kant and the neo-Kantians in looking to the
category of "reason" to provide the philosophical foundation lacking in
the Historical School, but he does so by historicizing reason, and in this
regard he follows the Historical School. "Hereby, I incorporate the theory
of the conditions of consciousness as instituted by Kant, but critically
transformed, into the theory of self-actualizing knowledge and of the history of science . . . Kant's a priori is fixed and dead; but the real conditions of consciousness and its presuppositions, as I grasp them, constitute
a living historical process, a development; they have a history, and the
course of this history involves their adaptation to the ever more exact,
inductively known manifold of sense-contents."[131] Dilthey transforms
the Kantian epistemological subject into one whose ontological makeup
is primarily historical. As Gadamer describes it, "Dilthey does not limit
himself to reflect only on historical knowledge as it is present in the science of history, rather he reflects on the being of human being which is
conditioned by a knowledge of its own history."[132] For Dilthey, our ability
to do and understand history is, itself, historically contingent.

The collective historical condition in which we find ourselves and
which makes up the epistemological framework for the possibility of
knowledge in the human sciences, and thus for our understanding/defi-
nition of reason, is what Dilthey, following Hegel, calls the "objective
mind." By this he means "the manifold forms in which what individuals
hold in common have objectified themselves in the world of senses. In
this objective mind the past is a permanently enduring present for us."[133]
The "objective mind" represents the intersubjective or communal nature
of a specific community at a specific point in time and space, but each of
these communities takes its own epistemological framework to be eternal,
a priori, and unconditional. Within this framework the past is seen as a

"permanently enduring present," and here we should revisit the ways that this notion aligns with Derrida's diagnosis of the metaphysics of presence insofar as "it means first the certainty which is ideal and absolute, that the universal form of all experience (*Erlebnis*) and therefore of all life, has always been and always will be in the present."[134] What's more, Dilthey's objective mind can be productively engaged through the lens of Derrida's concept of archi-writing that we discussed in relation to Droysen. Here we would think about the given coordinates that make up our shared world as "a kind of writing before the letter, an archi-writing without a present origin, without archi-. Whence the regular erasure of the archi-," which leads to the illusion of an ever enduring present or unconditional epistemological a priori.

In 1924 Heidegger prepared an extended article titled "The Concept of Time," prompted by the publication of the correspondence of Dilthey and Count Yorck von Wartenburg. Following Dilthey, Heidegger diagnosed how disciplinary history lacks sufficient awareness of the way it operates within, and is biased by, its own historical horizon. "People think that indifference to what is settled in advance for every interpretation within the inevitable hermeneutic situation amounts to the exclusion of subjective viewpoints. Such obliviousness to the explicit appropriation of the hermeneutic situation and its constant *revision* in the ongoing interpretation reveals the kind of historicalness from which such investigation of the past emerges. This is the kind of presencing we have described as inauthentic temporalness."[135] To place this quote in conversation with our current climate of ontological realism, the error of ontological realism is that it fails to recognize the limitations of our own historical horizons, the extent to which our personal perspective is determined and directed by our past. The current epistemological understanding of the past is taken to be the ontological reality of the past. It is this indifference to the epistemological understanding that allows one to take our historically contingent mode of understanding as indicative of a method that is universally valid for all time. And it is here that we can see the ways that the current attempted rapprochement between our historical methods and our historical condition is predicated on a mistaken understanding of our current practices as contained within a permanently enduring present that fosters a similarly misconceived representation of a permanently enduring past. This is the erasure of archi- from archi-writing. Dilthey's own work is characterized by an irreconcilable tension between his epistemological desire to ascertain a universally valid scientific methodology for historical research and his understanding of the ontology of humans as finite beings conditioned by their historical circumstances in a particular time and place. This tension accounts for the split between those philosophers who focus on the ontological aspect of Dilthey's project such as Heidegger, Gadamer, and the thinkers of presence and historians such as Harlan and Hollinger but also those we encountered in Chapter 1 who have focused on the epistemological aspect.

The issue forced Dilthey to confront the problem of relativism and led him to believe that only a sufficiently rigorous hermeneutic investigation into *Verstehen* (understanding) could reconcile the problem of relativism unleashed by perspectivalism. For Dilthey, Verstehen is "both an ordinary or 'natural' (i.e., unreflected) form of human awareness and a method of inquiry in the human sciences."[136] In "The Rise of Hermeneutics" (1900) Dilthey asserts that "because hermeneutics determines the possibility of universally valid interpretation on the basis of an analysis of understanding [*Verstehen*], it ultimately arrives at a solution to the quite general problem with which the essay began," that is, the reconciliation of the singular and historically contingent human experience with that of a universally valid scientific analysis.[137] But as Dilthey recounts his own history of the "rise" of hermeneutics from ancient Greece to the works of Schleiermacher, the reader comes to realize that this "universally valid interpretation" has yet to be achieved. Dilthey was unable to achieve it and instead presents a story of intellectual assent that, to his mind, will ultimately lead to such a method but that as yet has failed to do so. In this sense his solution to the problem of the standpoint, our ontological condition as beings who are made up by our historical conditions, is in line with those proposed by Chladenius and Droysen: a rigorous methodology that will ultimately allow us to go back to where we've never been . . . but not yet.

Historians who use Dilthey, such as Harlan and Hollinger, have focused on the epistemological issue of a universally valid rigorous method to stabilize this investigation into the past. But in doing so they take Dilthey's future task as already accomplished. Here, it is not an ideal origin that is deferred but an ideal methodology that promises to "preserve the universal validity of historical interpretation against the inroads of romantic caprice and skeptical subjectivity, and to give a theoretical justification for such validity, upon which all the certainty of historical knowledge is founded."[138] Dilthey was never to achieve this ideal, nor is it likely that such an ideal could be achieved given his emphasis on the historicity of the subject. In the end, for Dilthey, no objective universal methodology could sufficiently explain our ontological condition as historical beings.[139] As Gadamer describes it: "He pondered a great deal on the question of how to assure objectivity in the midst of all these relativities, how to conceive of the relationship of the finite to the absolute. . . . Nevertheless, we ask Dilthey in vain for an effective answer to this problem of relativism."[140] Dilthey's attempts to reconcile the historicist (perspectivalist) position with the scientific empiricist position remained purely aspirational, and contemporary historians who employ Dilthey in defense of ontological realism mistake this aspiration for achievement.[141]

But the result of such an approach is that the historical work serves to fill in the gaps that have occurred over time without addressing the challenges Dilthey was unable to overcome. Dilthey does assert that "in many cases, the understanding of human creations is directed merely at the nexus in which the successively apprehended parts of a work form a whole."[142] The gaps in the Great Wall are filled in so as to present a whole derived from the extant parts. In this way "the tale of the novelist or the narrative of the historian that follows the historical course of events produces an act of re-experiencing in us. The triumph of re-experiencing is that it completes the fragments of a course of events in such a way that we believe them to possess a continuity."[143] The key issue here is that as a result of this approach, the instability of the past is replaced by a sense of fixity that is based on the representation and re-experiencing of the past event. It is one's belief in the continuity of events as if they really happened as such that is proffered, not the reality of those events. But the priority of the representation in securing this belief is effaced in favor of the holding power of the originary event itself. Once the proof of the historical account is considered to be its adherence to the ontological reality of the past event, the role of the historian in assembling the fragments into a whole is demoted to one of epistemological method rather than ontological construction. That is, the role of the historian in constructing what is to be considered the ontological reality of the past event is effaced. The repercussion is that the historically contingent nature of the particular historical representation is considered to be valid for all time. In this way, "the presence of the past replaces immediate experience for us. When we want to observe time, the act of observation destroys it because it fixes things by means of attentiveness; it halts the flow and rigidifies what is in the process of becoming."[144] The attentiveness of the historian makes a definite, fixed and present object of the past event, but in doing so isolates the ostensibly present past from its relation to the historian in his or her moment. In this way "representation regularly *supplants* presence. However, articulating all the moments of experience insofar as it is involved in signification . . . , this operation of supplementation is not exhibited as a break in presence but rather as a continuous and homogeneous reparation and modification of presence in the representation."[145] The absent nature of the past is presented as eternally available but, once again, this absent past is made present in a manner noncoincident with the past present it supplants. Representing, reexperiencing, recalling come "into being at the same time as imagination and memory, the moment it is necessitated by the absence of the object from present perception."[146]

Here I want to emphasize the important role of imagination in establishing the continuity between any series of past events thus filling in the gaps in the wall. On this count Dilthey is clearly more concerned with those presences he can gather than with the absences he cannot. But as Derrida states, the absence of the object necessitates imagination to bring it back or perhaps better put, to bring us back to it: back to where we've never been. As was the case with Chladenius, the ability to bring the present interpreter to the past event is predicated on the imagination of the interpreter. Dilthey tells us "re-experiencing attains its fulfillment when an event has been processed by the consciousness of a poet, artist, or historian and lies before us in a fixed and permanent work."[147] Thus the fixed and permanent work of the historian that appears after the fact to be the result of scientific inquiry is actually predicated on imagination. But, as with Droysen, for Dilthey it is the combination of criticism and imagination that allows the historian to sift and order the particular facts into a coherent whole.

"Put generally: Human beings bound and limited by the reality of life are liberated not only by art—as has often been claimed—but also by the understanding of the historical." According to Dilthey, it is this imaginative capacity, not our scientific method, that gives history its special status and allows us to move beyond the limits of our temporally bound historical conditions:

Understanding [*Verstehen*] opens up a wide realm of possibilities that are not available within the limitations of a person's real life. The possibility of experiencing religious states in my own life is narrowly delimited for me, as for most of my contemporaries. But when I survey the letters and writings of Luther, the reports of his contemporaries, the records of religious disputes and councils, and those of his dealings with officials, I experience a religious process of an eruptive power and intensity commensurate with issues of life and death, which is beyond the possibility of direct experience for a present-day human being. But I can re-experience it. I transpose myself into circumstances in which everything supports such an extraordinary development of religious emotional life.[148]

Despite the demotion of the imagination that coincided with the fashioning of history as a social science, for Dilthey it is the power of imagination that enables us to bridge the temporal and geographic distance between our own culture and that of the past.[149] It is by means of what Dilthey calls transposition that he believes it possible to move beyond the limits of our own time and place to imaginatively enter into the world of Martin Luther and reexperience the religious culture of early modern Europe. Here we see the way that historical representation is predicated on the imaginary, engendering in the reader a sense that the ontological reality of the past is fixed and immutable.[150] Dilthey is clear to state that the historian must follow a combined inductive and deductive hermeneutic method wherein one formulates the understanding of the whole based on the careful study of the parts, which leads to the reinterpretation of the parts based on knowledge of the whole, but the key to this investigation is an ideal methodology that has yet to be perfected. Perhaps more important, this approach is unable to resolve the inevitable contamination of the standpoint of the historian in the present with the object of transposition that is the past.

If we retrace the steps in this chapter, we can see that whereas for Chladenius and even Ranke the past object or event was considered to provide access to the past, with Droysen and Dilthey the position is flipped, and it is now our position in the present (as *Verstehen*, lived experience, and objective consciousness) that is the access point. For Chladenius and Ranke the focus was on the historical event, object, or artifact. For Droysen and Dilthey the focus is on our position in the present as historical beings. For all, the goal is to take us back to where we've never been. But where Droysen still adhered to a theological scaffold to safeguard our ability to access the truth of the past event, Dilthey does away with this theological scaffold, replacing it with science.[151] In a speech given in honor of his seventieth birthday, Dilthey stated that the historical worldview articulated in his work "has liberated the human spirit from the last chains that natural science and philosophy have not yet broken."[152] I take these chains to be the religious understanding that was strained but not yet broken in the work of Chladenius, Ranke, or Droysen: the theologico-historical. Dilthey breaks with this understanding by presenting a purely historical methodology wherein the only guardian of our access to the past is the universally valid method of historical science. But as we have seen, for Dilthey "an apparently irreconcilable antithesis arises when historical consciousness is followed to its last consequences. Every historical phenomenon is finite—be it a religion or an ideal or a philosophical system—therefore the relativity of every kind of human conception about the connectivity of things is the last word of the historical worldview (*Weltanschauung*). Everything flows in process, nothing remains."[153] Relativism is inscribed in the very work that Harlan and Hollinger invoke to ward off the dread brought on by deconstruction. The position of ontological realism cannot guarantee its "hold" on the past, and those historians who claim it can only do so by secretly adhering to the theologico-historical position they profess to have supplanted like a Marrano, the crypto-Jew whose identity is bound up with the ignorance of that identity.

Conclusion

Chladenius, Droysen, and Dilthey all placed a heavy emphasis on the methodology of the historian in response to the instability unleashed by the realization and articulation of the historian's own role as a historical being for whom history is an issue. But in so doing, their chief concern was with those aspects of the past that remain. To return to Kafka's story of the Great Wall, all three of these thinkers focused on the extant portions that remain "in the present" with an eye toward filling the gaps in the Great Wall. But let us ask again what it would mean for these approaches if some sections of the wall were never built at all? What if the absent portions were not indicative of a missing piece, to be discerned by our reading of the parts in relation to a presumed whole, but instead were never there? In such a case the methodological verification of the ontological reality of the past Great Wall would only indicate our view of the Great Wall from our own historical horizon, objective conscious, or tradition. To be sure, our investigation into the past is predicated on the traces that remain, but as we have seen, these are often entangled with prior tellings and inextricably linked to the project of archi-writing. The relation of part to whole should never be simply or certainly understood as a means to fill in the gaps by rendering them the missing original key-stones to provide us with a definite understanding of the past event lest we discern and recount the properties of an ideal "original" that never actually existed. But neither should we assume our relationship to the past to be purely presentist, solely privileging our ontological condition in an ideal stable present as historical beings inhabiting a tradition. This is to say that we should not consider the historical approach to the past from the position of either the ontological realist or the constructivist.

Indeed, for both the ontological approach of those philosophers of history whose focus is our historical mode of being in the present (Chapter 2) and the epistemological approach of those historians who focus on the importance of method for ascertaining the reality of the past (Chapter 1), the emphasis is always on what is present. The former do so by arguing for the presence of the past in the present. The latter argue for the enduring presence of the past as past. But following Yorck, I would like to suggest that "up till now, the question has been formulated in a way that is false, even impossible; but this is not the only way of formulating it."[154]

In contrast to the search for origins or the material past made present, Derrida embraces the perturbations that the past returned convokes. In *Archive Fever* Derrida discusses our relation with a tradition or legacy—one could even call it Dilthey's objective world—as a "performative repetition" in which "the interpretation of the archive can only illuminate, read, interpret, establish its object, namely a given inheritance, by inscribing itself into it, that is to say by opening it and by enriching it enough to have a rightful place in it."[155] Thus, Derrida sees the relation with the past as a process of self-inscription wherein one reads and interprets the archive of the past in order to create a space for oneself in it in the present. But at the same time the traces of the past carry with them "a force that breaks with [their] context, that is, with the collectivity or presences organizing the moment of [their] inscription."[156] This opening onto the relation of presence and absence through a hauntological approach to history predicated on a logic of différance accounts for the entangled relation of presence and absence without privileging one over the other.

Like the Great Wall, the past is and is not, or better yet it is. The past comes and goes, and the pieces we do have are shot through with the nonsynchronicity of prior historical tellings. The past is here, and it is also constructed, and we do get entangled with it when we do history. "In fact, there are said to be gaps which have never been built in at all, although that's merely an assertion which probably belongs among the many legends which have arisen about the structure and which, for in-dividual people at least, are impossible to prove with their own eyes and according to their own standards, because the structure is so immense." What is certain is that when we seek to engage with the past, we do so by going back to where we've never been. But given the indefinite status of the past, its hauntological presence of absence, the question remains about why the ontological realist position persists as the dominant one among most historians. That is the focus of the next chapter.

§ 4   The Analog Ceiling

I want to revisit the story by Kafka about the Great Wall of China from the previous chapter to focus on another, related, aspect of Kafka's tale: the fable of the "imperial message" embedded into the heart of the story where the message is received, if it ever could be received at all, only after the emperor is dead and a new emperor, presumably with a new message, has been installed. The narrator tells us:

> Just so, as hopelessly and as hopefully, do our people regard the Emperor. They do not know what Emperor is reigning, and there exists doubts regarding the name of the dynasty. In school a great deal is taught about the dynasties with the dates of succession, but the universal uncertainty in this matter is so great that even our best scholars are drawn into it. Long-dead emperors are set on the throne in our villages, and the one that only lives on in song recently had a proclamation of his read out by the priest before the altar. Battles that are old history are new to us, and one's neighbor rushes in with a jubilant face to tell the news.[1]

I can't speak for certain about the situation in other regions of the world, but it strikes me that this passage is a perfect description of the current state of historical methodology in most American history departments.[2] Long-dead methods of, and assumptions about, historical inquiry are set on the thrones in our history departments and libraries, and one that only lives on in song recently had its virtues extolled by the president of the American Historical Association. Battles that are old history are new to them, and one's colleague rushes into the department meeting with a jubilant face to tell the news of the death of "historical theory."

The emperor has a name, "ontological realism," although there is "universal uncertainty" about whether this is the dynasty of empiricism, neo-positivism, ontological materialism, or historical realism. As previously discussed, what I mean by "ontological realism" is a commitment to history as an endeavor concerned with events assigned to a specific location in space and time that are in principle observable and as such are regarded as fixed and immutable. Central to this position is a commitment to empirical data that serves as something of a false floor to hold it up. Hayden White argued in 1976 that this "empiricist prejudice is attended by a conviction that 'reality' is not only perceivable but is also coherent in its structure,"[3] and in a recent review on an anthology of essays by White, Paul Roth explains that "whether discrete or extended, events within a realist conception of history constitute the stuff of true chronicles, so they form an analog to an empiricist's foundational data on which to build historical knowledge/representation. But as goes the notion of singular statements or simple descriptions that have their own determinative truth conditions, so goes the conception of events as an untheorized given that supports realist representation."[4]

Ontological realism is ultimately beholden to a Rankean-like belief that history can (at least partially) represent the past "as it really happened," but as Alun Munslow has pointed out, proponents of this view often hold it while simultaneously making concessions to philosophers of history or theorists of the historical in regard to the properties of the past or issues of writing and representation.[5] Of course, we've read Hayden White or Dominick LaCapra, or Keith Jenkins, or Joan Scott. We are not naive empiricists. We understand that historical work always involves an interpretative shaping of material and that what is 'given' is itself dependent upon various factors of personal or collective interest, the character of the historical evidence, current debates in historiography, and so forth. Nevertheless: whatever the interpretative shaping of the past, that past itself preexists our interpretative shaping. This is to say that in the practice of actually doing history—research, writing, teaching—conventional historians both acknowledge and ignore, if they do not dismiss outright, the criticism, concerns, and constructions articulated in theory of history during what I will limit to the last fifty years, and here I want to return to Kafka's parable, imagining that his subject is not dynasties but history: "The teachers of . . . history in the schools of higher learning claim to be exactly informed on these matters, and to be capable of passing on their knowledge to their students. The further one descends among the lower schools, the more, naturally enough, does one find teachers' and pupils' doubts of their own knowledge vanishing, and superficial culture mounting sky-high around a few precepts that have been drilled into people's minds for centuries, precepts which, though they have lost nothing of their eternal truth, remain eternally invisible in this fog of confusion."[6]

This willful ignorance, in the more sophisticated variant articulated by Alun Munslow as opposed to the superficial culture described by Kafka, is what I propose to call the "analog ceiling" because of the ways that current practices in academic publishing, reinforced by disciplinary historical training, serve to justify the use of ontological realism as the primary and only viable mode of thinking (or not thinking) about the past.

The analog ceiling functions because it allows one to argue that even though the past may not really correlate to the narrative reconstructions of ontological realism, this form is nevertheless the best analogy to make the past intelligible, understandable, and comprehensible. What's more, so this argument goes, the constraints of publishing, advanced degrees, and tenure all make this the best and most viable format for writing about the past and for "doing" history. One could of course write a historical account that takes another form, say that of a modernist novel or a series of aphorisms, but the argument and causal connections of such an endeavor would be hard to follow and thus difficult to judge. Indeed, there is much to be said for the ways that the narrative form of ontological realism is incredibly well tailored to the technological constraints of analog publishing (the codex, the modern monograph, and the article) in terms of crafting a causal argument but especially in regard to the pleasure principle of reading these historical accounts. This coincides with Hayden White's argument in *Metahistory* about the ways that historical writing took the form of nineteenth century realist fiction. But it is also for this reason that I believe *Metahistory* came too soon, arriving before the platforms and media that would allow us to explore the alternative narrative possibilities that were at our ready disposal.

Thus, the argument for ontological realism as the most useful analogy to represent the past is reinforced by the analog limits of traditional publishing that shepherd historians toward the form of realist fiction. Even as publishers and departments champion and encourage the move toward digital publishing and scholarship, we are restricted from innovation because of the ways that the assumptions of ontological realism and the limitations of analog publishing practices serve to substantiate each other as necessary. If anything, recent advances in the digital humanities have led us toward a resurgent neopositivism, chasing empiricist dreams toward the grail of history as a hard science. The cliometric origins of digital history and the recent infatuation with neuroscience are the bookends of this development. And it is on to this naturalized and thus unquestionable field of explanation that digital history has provided us with an incredible array of tools for acquiring and processing data, but because there is no critical theoretical or imaginative historical scaffold, we have entered a zone of neoempiricism. By and large, what we are doing is discovering new means of acquiring evidence and then putting them in the same buckets. We are not innovating the historical discipline with the data, codes, or maps we now can acquire, nor are we doing the epistemological work of inquiring about what is happening to key historical apparatuses such as the archive and how this affects our discipline.[7]

The tools and the possibilities have changed, but we are in danger of using them to simply replace the old ones. Thus, the article online looks exactly like the one published in the journal. The e-book is indistinguishable from the codex. We are hitting our heads against the analog ceiling rather than crashing through to see how these innovations can change the way we research, write, and teach about the past—the way we do history. Indeed, it seems that historians, publishers, and administrators are more focused on the technology than on what the technology can do. In a piece for *Perspectives on History*, Paula Findlen addressed the need for history departments and administrators to open their minds to the changes underfoot "lest we fall back on a conservative ethos that fails to capture the sense, indeed the possibilities, of where and how intellectual conversations occur," lest we lead colleagues to miss "the chance to do . . . exciting things because some administrator told them they could not be promoted" by doing so.[8] While Findlen engages the issue of "what should count," and thus addresses the shifting terrain, she doesn't engage the deeper question about what these changes mean for the project and writing of history. These changes in scholarship, writing, and teaching need to be addressed theoretically because it is not the tools and technologies employed for history that set the digital apart from the analog but the novelty of the ideas and assertions. As Jonathan Sterne observes, "By this measure, the digital humanities have produced a lot of infrastructure and resources, a host of experiments and new textual forms. But they have not fully delivered at the level of ideas."[9]

Here, I want to point out that I am not averse to analog technology itself, be it writing with pen and paper or strolling the library stacks. Nor do I begrudge ontological realism as a particular choice of narrative representation to tell certain kinds of stories. What I do condemn is what I call the "analogic" that fuses analog constraints to ontological realism so that the only analogy for the past is the ontological realist one. Here the function is "not only to orient, balance, and organize the structure—one cannot in fact conceive of an unorganized structure—but above all to make sure that the organizing principle of the structure would limit what we might call the *play* of the structure."[10] The analog restraints create the impression that the structure is fixed and necessary, leaving no room for play. But, as Louis O. Mink observed in "On the Writing and Rewriting of History" (1972), such a belief "in the actuality and immutability of the past is based on a cluster of unconscious and invalid analogies."[11] For Mink these included such analogies as those between temporal distance and spatial difference, between memory and perception, and between a past present and a present past. To these I would add the faulty analogy between the formal narrative presentation of a past "as it happened" and the "ontological reality" of that past. According to Mink, the ability to hold these analogies is indicative of the incompatible views we hold about the reality of the past: about the relation of historical knowledge to its object, whatever that may be, and about the relevance of historical knowledge to the possibilities of action that lie before us.

Mink sums up this paradox by articulating the way historians hold the simultaneous views that "everything which belonged to the action when it was taking place in its own present belongs to it now that it is past," alongside the conflicting realization "that the past isn't there at all."[12] Mink sees this paradox as the motivating force behind all serious philosophy of history. I see it as proximate to what I refer to as the latent ontology of the past that *is*, where the past appears as present and absent, available and yet restricted, here and gone. One of the most salient values of a deconstructive approach to history is that it draws attention to these properties of the past rather than denouncing them in the pursuit of ideal origins or properties that are always to be deferred. In the case of ontological realism in our current moment, the deconstructive approach exposes the ways that historians maintain the teleological power of a principle whose possibility they simultaneously refuse. But it is worth asking about the motivation that allows one to hold such incompatible views.

In "History and Fiction as Modes of Comprehension" Mink reflects on why some stories bear repeating, and I think his response to this question will help us gain purchase on the previous one. Mink tells us that some stories bear repeating "because they aim at producing and strengthening the act of understanding in which actions and events, although represented as occurring in the order of time, can be surveyed as it were in a single glance as bound together in an order of significance, a representation of the *totum simul* (that Boethius regarded as God's knowledge of the world) which we can never more than partially achieve."[13] Latency is removed from the equation as is the surprise of the unexpected possible. One can of course imagine or read a history as if one did not know the outcome, or one might not know the outcome, and thus one follows the story from beginning to end. But in the "configurational comprehension of a story which one *has followed*, the end is connected with the promise of the beginning as well as the beginning with the promise of the end, and the necessity of the backwards reference cancels out, so to speak, the contingency of the forward references." The indeterminacy of the future is canceled out by the givenness of the past that is grasped in the present. Thus, "to comprehend temporal succession means to think of it in both directions at once, and then time is no longer the river which bears us along but the river in an aerial view, upstream and downstream in a single survey."[14] This aerial view can be considered as a God's-eye view or that of La Place's omniscient scientist in his *Philosophical Essay on Probabilities*. Each of these points to the issue of temporality and the desire for a static snapshot that arrests the temporal flow. These are the problems that vexed Chladenius, Droysen, and Dilthey as they attempted to reconcile the possibility of a universal historical method that could account for the temporal instabilities of lived experience. In Chladenius's model the properties of the past are held in perpetuity by the hand of God. Droysen's approach takes the progress of the historian's methodology in the present as indicative of, and thus vouchsafed by, the presence of God. Dilthey attempted to develop a universal historical method predicated on historicized reason that would supplant such a theological hold but account for the malleable and temporally determined category of reason itself. But in our current understanding, these complex problems of temporality are flattened out in favor of the static snapshot. On such a reading, and by and large this is the conventional historian's reading, time is never out of joint, and assuming one has the right methodological tools, one can master the past and recount it in the form of a realist narrative.

The shift from the theological hold on the past to that of scientific method and the relation of God, the omniscient scientist, and history as *totum simul* is particularly telling when considered in light of Constantin Fasolt's assertion that "history, far from being opposed to religion, is one of the forms religion has taken in the modern age."[15] Fasolt is careful to state that by "religion" he does not mean any of the particular institutional or confessional varieties such as Catholicism, Protestantism, Judaism, or Islam; instead, he takes religion to be "a human practice designed not to solve, but to contain the problems arising from the asymmetry between first-person and third-person statements."[16] Another way to put this is the asymmetry between the self and the other. By contrast, Fasolt sees philosophy as an endeavor that seeks to abolish this problem by clarifying the confusion from which it arises. But religion, in the form of the particular institutional or confessional varieties, can no longer fulfill the purposes of religion, contain the problem of asymmetry, as it once did. "This is largely because modern science has made it increasingly difficult to reconcile our knowledge of the world with the statements ritually repeated by the institutional or confessional religions."[17] Thus, it has become harder to believe in the explanatory function of these institutions, and the result is that they are a source of increased tension rather than comfort. For Fasolt, it is now history that contains the problem because in "the act of reading history readers reconcile their liberty with their existence in the world in the same way in which Adam reconciled his liberty with the will of God by listening to God's commands."[18] This is to say that it is history that now holds the place of religion insofar as it provides the explanatory scaffolding for meaning and order.

Extending our discussion from Chapter 3, it is "history" that came to hold the position previously held by God in terms of reconciling the God's-eye omniscient view of the meaning of the whole with the chaotic plurality of events that make up the parts. This coincides with the argument offered by Koselleck in "Modernity and the Planes of Historicity," where he states that "it was the philosophy of historical process which first detached early modernity from its past [the fundamentally Christian plane of expectations] and, with a new future, inaugurated our modernity."[19] The key point is the way that Koselleck presents modernity as the result of the introduction/invention/discovery of "historical times" and how this coincides with the rise of philosophy of history and the development of the historical discipline. The historian of Jewish thought

David Myers makes a similar case in his description of the historicization of the Jewish religion in his book *Resisting History*, where he describes Moses Mendelsohn's (1729–86) turn to history as "an ontological category increasingly relevant as a source of authority to confirm events of great religious import."[20] This can be seen as part of the rationalist project that came to prominence during the scientific revolution, dominance during the Enlightenment, and crystallization into the disciplinary forms of historical inquiry most associated with Ranke.

To take things a step further, and reconnect to ontological realism and the analog ceiling, in *Gramophone, Film, Typewriter*, Friedrich Kittler presents the turn to history as facilitated by first the printing press and then the typewriter. To his mind, "what will soon end in the monopoly of bits and fiber optics began with the monopoly of writing. History was the homogenized field that, as an academic subject, only took account of literate cultures."[21] The explanatory transition articulated in different ways by Fasolt, Koselleck, and Myers roughly coincides with the rise of the technological apparatus that became the primary mode for the transmission of history. The rise of ontological realism was the result of a belief that a value-neutral description of facts, prior to interpretation or analysis, was possible.[22] The narrative strategies for explaining these facts turned out to be particularly well suited to the structures and forms of traditional publishing and to a public interested in reading them. As a result, conventional historians have held on to these forms even as our understanding of the past has drifted further and further away from the tenets of ontological realism.

This disconnect between the position of ontological realism and the shifts facing the practice of disciplinary history is pronounced in Gordon S. Wood's *The Purpose of the Past* (2008) when he tells us: "Yet when all is said and done, when all the concessions to subjectivity, imaginative reenactment, and the use of 'regulative fictions' have been made, historians must still remain necessarily tied to . . . the 'epistemology of nineteenth century positivism,' the view that the past 'out there' really existed and that they can through the collection and ordering of evidence bring us closer to knowing the truth about that past 'as it really was,' even if the full and complete truth about the past will always remain beyond their grasp."[23] The use of scare quotes indicates Wood's acknowledgment that the methodological gesture does not adequately map onto the object of investigation and goes so far as to admit that only by an act of faith can the historian maintain such a position. What's more, he tells us that "this faith may be philosophically naive, may even be philosophically absurd in this skeptical and relativist-minded age; nevertheless, it is what makes history writing possible." Wood does not tell us why it would be impossible to imagine history writing under other conditions, but he does warn us that "historians who cut loose from this faith do so at the peril of their discipline."[24] Thus, the argument for the status quo of ontological realism relies on an act of faith built on the fears that abandoning such a stance would cause the discipline of history to tumble into relativism, absurdity, or unintelligibility. As one historian told me in response to a paper I presented, historians must be ontological realists unless they want to think of the past itself as blinking in and out of existence like a Christmas light.

There are several issues to be addressed, but first I want to point out that in many ways Wood's use of quote marks to bracket off the "out there" from the past as it really existed embodies the conflict articulated by Louis Mink between the assertion that past events are fixed immutable objects and the realization that past events are not objects at all. I should also say that it does not adequately recognize the connection between the analog form of historical narrative that enables ontological realism to appear virtuous as a faithful representation of the past. This is all to say there is no "past" to be recovered in the form of the realist narrative because that is not the structure of the past. This is neither the ontology nor the reality of the past; thus, I think there is light to be gleaned in thinking of the past itself as "blinking in and out of existence like a Christmas light." It certainly gives me occasion to revisit the Ghost of Christmas Past from Dickens's *A Christmas Carol.*

Dickens describes the Ghost of Christmas Past as "a strange figure—like a child: yet not so like a child as an old man, viewed through some supernatural medium, which gave him the appearance of having receded from view, and being diminished to a child's proportions. Its hair . . . was white with age; and yet the face had not a wrinkle in it, and the tenderest bloom was on the skin." Here one can imagine this spirit as the object of history: an aged object from the past transported to the present by the historical author, who imbues it with youth and the "tenderest bloom" on the skin even while signaling its age, the whiteness of its hair. In this way the historian presents the "old man" of the past event as a "child," as though through some supernatural medium. "But the strangest thing

about [the ghost] was, that from the crown of its head there sprung a
bright clear jet of light," though it also possessed a

> great extinguisher for a cap. Even this though . . . was *not* its strangest quality.
> For as its belt sparkled and glittered now in one part and now in another, and
> what was light one instant, at another time was dark, so the figure itself fluc-
> tuated in its distinctness: being now a thing with one arm, now with one leg,
> now with twenty legs, now a pair of legs without a head, now a head without
> a body: of which dissolving parts, no outline would be visible in the dense
> gloom wherein they melted away. And in the very wonder of this, it would be
> itself again; distinct and clear as ever.[25]

The past here is no fixed and immutable object but a fluctuating bundle
of physical and temporal contradictions. Young and old, near and far,
light and dark, a figure that is at one moment indecipherable and the
next "distinct and clear as ever," blinking in and out of existence like a
Christmas light. Most important, the past is a ghost. Its strangest quality
is never strange enough, and here one must wonder what, if anything, is
gleaned by the tautological assertion that "it would be itself again," which
prefaces the statement "distinct and clear as ever," the ontological realist's
dream.

But I want to go back to the quality of the ghost that is and is not the
strangest thing about it: the bright clear jet of light that sprang from its
head, though I also note the "great extinguisher for a cap, which it now
held under its arm." The strangeness of this light evokes images of Freud's
category of the "uncanny" or "unheimlich" as "the name of everything
that ought to have remained hidden and secret . . . and has become visible."[26] On encountering the ghost, Scrooge had a special desire "to see
the Spirit in his cap; and begged him to be covered," to keep hidden and
secret that which ought to remain so, but the ghost would not comply.
Nevertheless, after a long evening of strange encounters Scrooge could no
longer bear to be haunted by the past and began to wrestle with it: "In the
struggle, if that can be called a struggle in which the Ghost with no visible
resistance on its own part was undisturbed by any effort of its adversary,
Scrooge observed that its light was burning high and bright; and dimly
connected that with its influence over him, he seized the extinguisher cap
and by a sudden action pressed it down upon its head."[27]

On my reading, ontological realism bears an uncanny resemblance to
the extinguisher cap and the historian who wields it to Scrooge. For like

Scrooge, the historian who wrestles with the past does so with an adversary that offers no visible resistance on its own part and is undisturbed by any effort on the part of the historian. The disturbed remains haunt us and not vice versa. But more important is Scrooge's "sudden action" in response to his observation that the light of the past exerted influence over him. The conjuring trick of ontological realism is that it allows the historian to exert his or her own influence over the past, by restricting its light and all that its light reveals, in the same way that Scrooge pressed the extinguisher cap down on the Ghost of Christmas Past. "But though Scrooge pressed it down with all his force, he could not hide the light: which streamed from under it, in an unbroken flood upon the ground."[28] You cannot kill a ghost.

Following the argument in Chapter 3 about the role of the theological hold on the secular assumptions of ontological realism, my earlier analysis of how "history" has taken the place of religion as our modern explanatory scaffold, and the ways that ontological realism, as framed by the analog ceiling, maintains itself as the dominant disciplinary mode of history, I contend that conventional history has done so by means of the properties normally ascribed to "negative theology." Negative theology presents God as the condition for everything that can be while emphasizing that God is not a being, as such. The God of negative theology is presented as without being, insofar as "being" is understood as a category of finitude. Following this logic, "to predicate God is deemed inadequate since God transcends the determinations of time and space that all predication entails."[29] The aerial view of history, the *totum simul* or static snapshot that arrests the temporal flow, likewise takes itself to be outside the determinations of time and space, and here we should keep in mind Dilthey's critique of such external positions that purport to reside outside the temporal flux of lived experience.[30] But the "history" of ontological realism is most akin to negative theology insofar as it determines what is "real" and what is "ontological" without determining what "history" is beyond its properties as that which determines (or creates) what is "ontologically real."

Now one can only assert such a position, a position outside of time and space, if one does so with the extinguisher cap pulled firmly down because the problem of temporality cannot be so easily bracketed or brushed aside. For try as we might to contain it, the past, like the ghost, disturbs the categories by which we conventionally make sense of the world around us, troubling both time and space. And this is why I want to offer a counter to these conventions that embraces the investigative and narrative possibilities offered by advances in digital publishing and scholarship in the service of a hauntological approach to the past based on the logic of différance, "where the assemblage to be proposed has the complex structure of a weaving, an interlacing which permits the different threads and different lines of meaning–or of force—to go off again in different directions, just as it is always ready to tie itself up with others."[31] Derrida was keenly interested in subverting traditional forms of publishing in works such as "Tympan," *Glas, Of Grammatology,* and "La double séance" but also frustrated by the limitations of the form.[32] Thus, there is a certain irony to the self-imposed limitations of the analog ceiling given the proliferation of innovative alternatives that now lie before us.[33]

But here I think it important to differentiate Derrida's category of *différance* from that of negative theology, and Martin Hägglund's book *Radical Atheism* is particularly instructive for this purpose. Derrida describes *différance* as the condition for everything that can be, while emphasizing that it "is" nothing in particular. It isn't present or absent, sense or nonsense, active or passive, and in this way one can see it as formally similar to the account of God in negative theology. But whereas God, on this reading, transcends time and space as a *positive* infinity that is absolute in itself, *différance* articulates what Hägglund calls the *negative* infinity of time, which he describes as "an infinite finitude since it entails that finitude [that] cannot ever be eliminated or overcome."[34] So like the God of negative theology or the "history" of ontological realism, *différance* is without being but not because it is something ineffable outside of time and space as the arbiter of ontological content. Instead, it serves to designate the "spacing of time that makes it impossible for anything to be in itself."[35] Such an understanding pairs well with Droysen's historical methodology, which rejects a logic of origins and originals that dictates truth and embraces the active investigation of a play of forms, the past events, that lack any determined or invariable substance. But it also should be seen as akin to Dilthey's presentation of "the restless advance of the present, in which what is present constantly becomes past and the future present."[36]

Let me clarify what I mean by returning to Louis Mink and the paradox he described between our belief that everything that belonged to the action when it was taking place in its own present belongs to it now that it is past and the belief that the past isn't *there* at all. To quote Mink: "Events don't withdraw from the present to the past as an actor withdraws from the stage to the wings. Nor are they in any sense whatever actual but separated from us by time, as Kilimanjaro is actual but separated from us by space."[37] The paradox articulated by Mink is perhaps most apparent when examining our historical pursuit of the past; but insofar as it is a problem concerning the principle of noncontradiction, it is not a paradox restricted to the past, and it is in this sense that I want to explore the "spacing of time that makes it impossible for anything to be in itself."

For Aristotle the principle of noncontradiction entails that "the same attribute cannot at the same time belong and not belong to the same subject" (*Metaphysics* 1005b). Derrida sees this as a consummate assertion of the metaphysical logic of identity. A key aspect of this statement is the insertion of the phrase "at the same time," for it is temporality that allows one to account for change over time. One can think of this as the transition from an object in motion to one at rest or the transition from pleasure to pain as articulated by Socrates in *The Phaedo* (a monster). But this logic is strained when Aristotle addresses the issue of time in book 4 of the *Physics*. Derrida addresses this in "Ousia and Grammē," where he argues, "In *Physics* IV Aristotle begins by proposing a conundrum, an *aporia*. He does so in the form of an exoteric argument. . . . First it is asked if time belongs to beings or nonbeings; and then what its nature, its *physis* might be."[38] One can see the problem in the phrasing of the question, for if time were a being, it could not account for change, and if it were nonbeing, one could not address what its nature might be. Aristotle claims that there would be no time if there were only one single now (*Physics* 219a); thus, "time" cannot adhere to the principle of noncontradiction because "in one sense it has been and is no longer, and in another sense it will be and is not yet" (*Physics* 217b). To recall Dilthey's formulation, strictly speaking, the present never is.

Derrida asks us to consider the sequence of "nows" that make up this temporal construction: "The preceding now, it is said, must be destroyed by the following now. But, Aristotle then points out, it cannot be destroyed 'in itself,' that is, at the moment when it is (now, in act). No more can it be destroyed in an other now: for then it would not be destroyed as now, itself; and, as a now which has been, it is (remains) inaccessible to the following now (see 218a)."[39] The key for us is that despite this internal instability, it is time that holds the philosophical logic of identity as fixed and stable. It is what "defines and not what is defined (218b)."[40] It is the God's-eye snapshot of the past that solves the radical instability of change. To quote Hägglund: "The presence of the present is thus the principle of identity from which all modifications of time are derived. The past is understood as what has been present, and the future as what will be present."[41] This is a privileging of the present that defines the past as change over time while ignoring the problematic coordinates used to make the assertion. What's more, Derrida tells us, "what is criticized, thereby, is not the relationship of time to movement, nor the numbered or numerable Being of time, but rather time's *analogy* with a certain structure of the grammē."[42]

For the writing of history, that certain structure, style, and form of writing is the ontological realist analog ceiling. It is the obsession with the fixity of identity that leads us to posit a definitive, knowable, and stable past—one that is in fact presented as ontologically stable in ways that the present never is.

If I may modify a passage from Derrida's "Freud and the Scene of Writing," this analogy is dangerous, "not because it refers to writing, but because it presupposes [that the past exists as] a text which would be already there, immobile: the serene presence of a statue, of a written stone or archive whose significant content might be harmlessly transported into the milieu of a different language."[43] The danger lies in the assumption that there is an unerasable and indelible trace left in the past by which the ontological reality of the past can be determined. But "an unerasable trace is not a trace, it is a full presence, an immobile and incorruptible substance, a son of God, a sign of parousia and not a seed, that is, a mortal germ."[44] The stability afforded to identity is not the property of a mortal being who exists in and through the indeterminacy of time; such a fixed, immutable quality belongs to a God, or to the dead, and here I think we gain purchase on the force and seduction of ontological realism. For what is put into question by a deconstructive or hauntological approach to history is "precisely the quest for a rightful beginning, an absolute point of departure, a principle responsibility."[45] What is denied is a place to rest in peace. The fiction of a stable past is the fiction of a stable present, and the analog ceiling has served to reinforce that fiction. Indeed, I would say that it is the meaning we don't or can't find in the present that ontological realists construct in the past. This can have pernicious consequences when the surety of temporal comprehension stimulates a "moralistic stance in which the past is charged with the worst of all evil while the present becomes morally discharged by simple comparison."[46] That is, the focus on determining the ontological reality of atrocities committed in the past exonerates us from the critical acknowledgment of contemporary responsibilities. Here, the assumed surety about the nature of evils past can lead to the "wishful thought that evil is past."[47]

But like the institutional and confessional religions in Fasolt's argument, ontological realism has lost its ability to charm and comfort as its presentation of history has become increasingly disconnected from the ways we think about the past leaving its proponents to vacillate between weakly accepting the claims of historical theorists while rejecting or ignoring them in practice. This is because the past has a dual indeterminacy that cannot be ignored. There is the problem of the gaps in the Great Wall that is the past and the possibility of recounting the properties of an "original" that never actually existed. But there is also the problem of the indeterminate status of identity that haunts the present. And these two relentless indeterminacies are entangled and entrapped in the historical tellings of the past. This is all to say that we have reached the point when the very restraints of the analog form have now become the primary justification for the continued use of ontological realism. But recent technological innovations have severed the structural link between analog publishing and ontological realism, leaving only "a few precepts that have been drilled into people's minds for [the last] century."[48]

The discipline of history is facing a paradigm shift, and historians whose mind-sets were formed and constrained by print must now confront the changes that digital media makes in every aspect of their discipline. This is true of the tools we use to research, write, and read history but also in terms of changing human attitudes toward, and relations with, these media. In *How We Think*, N. Katherine Hayles argues that we are witnessing a generational shift in cognitive modes of processing information. Hayles employs the term *technogenesis* to account for the epigenetic phenomenon wherein the tools we use result in significant neurological consequences. According to this argument, our interaction with tools has a strong impact on the way our brains develop and consequently on how we come to understand the world.[49] Following this line of thought, Hayles describes the growing rift between an older generation raised on analog media and a younger generation raised on digital media. "Empirical studies such as the 'Generation M' report in 2005 by the Kaiser Family

Foundation indicate that young people (ages eight to eighteen in their survey) spend, on average, an astonishing six hours per day consuming some form of media, and often multiple forms at once (surfing the web while listening to an iPod, for example, or texting their friends). . . . Going along with this shift is a general increase in information intensity, with more and more information available with less and less effort."[50] This is a generation that engages with and processes information in a radically different manner from those that preceded it. Hayles refers to the older model as deep attention, in which the intense and careful engagement with one object of inquiry is given priority, and the more recent model as hyper attention, in which multiple tasks and avenues of investigation are undertaken simultaneously. Cultural critics such as Mark Bauerlein and Nicholas Carr have decried this shift as resulting in a cognitive deficit. But Hayles contends that "it is far too simplistic to say that hyper attention represents a decline in cognitive ability among young people. On the contrary, hyper attention can be seen as a positive adaptation that makes young people better suited to live in the information-intensive environments that are becoming ever more pervasive."[51] Bauerlein's criticisms smack of nostalgia, but the skills of deep close reading are valuable ones and essential to the life of the mind as we have known it. But Hayles is also right to point to the positive nature of the possibilities opened by shifting our attention from one to many.

The proliferation of screens and windows are altering the way we think, and while such a multinodal process may sacrifice homogeneous depth, it avails itself to heterogeneous breadth. This is to say there may be a connection between an epistemological logic that privileges the singular truth of totalizing answers associated with "realism" and the model of deep attention. It is in many ways a contentious and combative logic that disallows compromise and in this sense coincides with the logic of the modern nation-state. In the same light, I point to the possible connection between a heterogeneous logic of multiplicity and hyper attention. This is a polysemic logic of alterity that embraces and accepts difference. The singular logic of deep attention correlates to the ontological realist approach to history, whereas the polysemic logic of hyper attention correlates to the deconstructive one. This is not to advocate for the current trends in digital humanities such as "surface," "distant," or statistically based reading, which I believe ultimately adhere to the totalizing logic associated with ontological realism. What's more, and as we have seen, deconstruction appeared in an initially agonistic, playful, and challenging relation to analog practices of writing that emphasized attention to detail and close reading.[52] Nevertheless, anxiety about digital media leading to cognitive decline, lack of attention, or constant distraction can be seen as akin to anxieties about deconstruction leading historians to a morass of total relativism, at least insofar as in each case the arguments against innovation are conflicting and evasive, relying more on fear about what might happen than on serious engagement or investigation. The evasion is coupled with a deep nostalgia for the "real" and "realism," dismissing the digital as virtual or ephemeral, while deconstruction is derided as advocating a world without truth. The nostalgia for a "better time" is not surprising given that both analog publishing and ontological realism came of age at the same moment as the formation of the discipline of history. Thus, the logic of ontological realism and analog technology appear "natural" because that is how nature was understood at that moment.[53] But just as Henri Bergson's "machine brain" has given way to Catherine Malabou's "brain as network," we, too, must rethink the coordinates of how we do and write history. Rather than wallow in nostalgia for the way things used to be, we should be encouraging students to imagine new ways of thinking and writing history, and here I want to return to Findlen's admonition that historians, departments, and administrators open their minds to the changes afoot "lest we fall back on a conservative ethos that fails to capture the sense, indeed the possibilities, of where and how intellectual conversations occur."

The forms available to us have changed, as can be seen in multimedia novels such as Steve Tomasula's multimodal digital novel *TOC*, which presents a multiplicity of interfaces (text, textual fragments, video, audio, graphics), each with its own temporal scheme; the "live cinema" of Jay Scheib, where live actors performing onstage, videography of those actors, and previously recorded scenes are projected onto multiple screens in front of a live audience; or the online academic platform of *Arcade*, where academic articles, videos, artworks, and hybrids are offered as an entangled complement of arguments and ideas. Walter Alvarez's *Chronozoom* works on a 13.7 billion year scale in an attempt to make time relations between different studies of history legible rather than assumed. Each of these embodies in its own way an alternative strategy to that of print media enabled by advances in technology that resist the presentation of a monolithic temporal narrative. In each of these models time is, or can be, out of joint. In this way the new forms align with a hauntological narrative reconstruction focused on nonsimultaneity, divergent historical paths, and the instability of time to "shake as a whole, to make tremble in entirety" the domination of ontological realism and analog practices.[54] These new modes "mark the theoretical inadequacy of the *current concept of context* (linguistic or nonlinguistic), as it is accepted in numerous domains of research," paramount among which is the discipline of history, and enact a "displacement of the concept of writing."[55] Here we are talking about the multiply heterogeneous iterations of a narrative form that does not unfold in a strict linear fashion but is threaded through itself in a nonlinear polysemic topology that defies the smooth continuous strategies of ontological realism but coincides much more closely with what we know about space and time and how we should think of the hauntology of the past.[56]

Such a narrative accommodates an understanding of the past as something that is, as present *and* absent at the same time, as something *and* nothing entangled in a seemingly impossible way, where the iterative position of the historian is woven into the past and the present such that it also presses on the future. And here I think that recent work on Reinhart Koselleck's theory of multiple temporalities is particularly instructive. Helge Jordheim presents Koselleck as offering a "radically different theory of overlapping temporal structures and layers, synchronicities and non-synchronicities."[57] Jordheim emphasizes the issue of periodization in Koselleck, but I want to focus on the overlapping temporal structures and the friction between these structures that exposes what Koselleck calls *Ungleichzeitigkeiten*, noncontemporaneity or nonsynchronicity.[58] The phenomenon of *Ungleichzeitigkeiten* occurs at moments when elements of a later time are introduced as contemporaneous with the event depicted or represented.[59] What is fascinating is that for Koselleck this moment of disjuncture, where time is out of joint, points to the coincidence and noncoincidence of the historical telling with the past event. This grinding of gears when multiple temporalities overlap exposes the way that historical accounts tend to "freeze" the events depicted even as the event is continuously reworked and altered by the telling itself. Koselleck presents this specifically in relation to his methodology of *Begriffsgeschichte* or Concept History and the ways that "the sociohistorical relevance of (historical) results increases precisely because attention is directed in a rigorously diachronic manner to the persistence or change of a concept."[60]

By focusing on the concept (and especially the ways that concepts are re-occupied, *Umbesetzung*), one steps in and out of the present and unsettles the assumptions inherent in the historical investigation. In this way "the method of *Begriffsgeschichte* breaks free of the naive circular movement from word to thing and back."[61] But I think that Koselleck's notion of reoccupation can be pushed further if we think of it as a means to understand what Derrida refers to as "inhabiting a tradition." What's more, one could align the disjunction of nonsimultaneity with the Derridean *aporia* to negotiate the constitutive dissymmetry of a past that is. This is *hauntology* as a theory of multiple temporalities and multiple pasts that all converge, or at least could converge, on the present.

I recognize that the development and enactment of these new forms are likely beyond the reach of my generation and will require the imagination and innovation of those scholars for whom hyper attention is their primary mode of media engagement. Indeed, Jonathan Sterne is right to caution that "the real intellectual transformations occasioned by all the digital gear may well come up more sneakily, with more subtlety, and with less fanfare than the millennial rhetoric of the digital humanities might suggest."[62] This is because it is not the tools that will lead to a change but ideas and imagination. Thus, the gatekeepers of "history" need to imagine themselves as the bridge between our ingrained analog practices and the emerging digital future of the discipline. And just as the logic of ontological realism was attuned to analog modes of production, a logic of deconstruction and *différance* is attuned to our current digital moment. This is a moment of heterogeneity, entanglement, polysemy, and drifting context, but it is also one that coincides with serious concerns about the historian's relation to the past that have been at play since the days of Chladenius. We should not go forward with the extinguisher cap of ontological realism pushed firmly over the past, restricting what is now possible for historical research. Instead, we should strive to invent, imagining in the name of *différance* new ways to let the light of the past stream out in all its uncanny glory.

§ 5   The Past That I̶s̶

In this final chapter we will revisit the ghosts that have haunted history throughout this book, but I want to begin with a story from old New England: Washington Irving's *The Legend of Sleepy Hollow*, sometimes known as the tale of the headless horseman.[1] In some ways it is a simple story about a simple schoolteacher, Ichabod Crane, who gets caught up in a series of misadventures until one night he is, so the legend goes, run down by the headless horseman of Sleepy Hollow and never heard from again. It is true that Ichabod has some unusual attributes: despite his meager, skinny frame he had a prodigious appetite for food with the "dilatory powers of an anaconda," and despite his learned calling he had an equally prodigious appetite for tales of the supernatural, as evidenced by his well-worn copy of "Cotton Mather's *History of New England Witchcraft*." But all in all, this legend seems to be less than legendary. Ichabod wants to marry the comely Katrina van Tassel for all the obvious reasons: she's a beauty; her father is a substantial farmer; and the farm itself is a veritable paradise of fecundity. But Ichabod's amorous overtures draw the ire of Katrina's other suitor, Brom van Brunt, who from his "Herculean frame and great powers of limb had received the nickname Brom Bones."[2] Brom is a legendary horseman and a notorious prankster who in retaliation for Ichabod's courtship of Katrina breaks into his schoolhouse "and turned everything topsy-turvy, so that the poor schoolmaster began to think all the witches in the county held their meetings there."[3] In short, Irving provides us with all the clues to deduce that Brom Bones is in fact the headless horseman and that there is nothing supernatural or ghostly about this legend at all: Brom has a motive, and there is ample evidence of his past tricks. Thus, it comes as something of a surprise when at the end of the story, after Ichabod Crane is chased down by the headless horseman while despondently riding home, having been dismissed by Katrina at her father's party, our narrator, a certain Diedrich Knickerbocker, refuses to draw this conclusion. This, even after offering the testimony of an "old farmer who had been down to New York on a visit several years after, and from whom this account of the ghostly adventure was received, brought home the intelligence that Ichabod Crane was still alive."[4] That is, the very person who recounted the legend to the narrator also dismisses it as false. So where does all the ambiguity at the end of the tale come from? Don't we know that Brom Bones is the headless horseman? And if so, is there any legend of Sleepy Hollow at all? This is all to ask what haunts Sleepy Hollow?

Our narrator describes Ichabod as "an odd mixture of small shrewdness and simple credulity," whose "appetite for the marvelous, and powers of digesting it, were equally extraordinary; and both had been increased by his residence in this spell-bound region," until "no tale was too gross or monstrous for his capacious swallow."[5] Indeed, we are told at the beginning that a "drowsy, dreamy influence seems to hang over the land, and to pervade the very atmosphere. Some say it was bewitched by a High German doctor, during the early days of settlement; others that an Indian chief, the prophet or wizard of his tribe, held his powwows there before the country was discovered. . . . Certain it is, the place still continues under the sway of some witching power, that holds a spell over the good people. The whole neighborhood abounds with local tales, haunted spots, and twilight superstitions," but as we know, "the dominant spirit . . . that haunts this enchanted region, is the apparition of a figure on horseback without a head. It is said to be the ghost of a Hessian trooper, whose head had been carried away by a cannon-ball, in some nameless battle during the Revolutionary War."[6]

So what haunts Sleepy Hollow? On my reading it is the past that haunts history—a past of American Indian dispossession, of the Revolutionary War, of the unspoken atrocity that took place at Major Andre's tree, and countless other events great and small. Sleepy Hollow is laden with the ghosts of a past half remembered if remembered at all.[7] This is the latent past beneath the ghosts that haunt the inhabitants. What's more, and, we are told, quite remarkably, this haunting "is not confined to the native inhabitants of the valley, but is unconsciously imbibed by every one who resides there for a time."[8] It is a past that we cannot touch but that nonetheless touches us. The histories, the tales, the haunted spots are all partial reconfigurations, like a headless horseman. Now, the past, like a ghost, is by definition absent and thus has no ontological properties per se, or perhaps more accurately, it has a latent ontology. History is the presence of absence, and what we do have of it is that which presents itself to us or that we force on it. But like the head of the long-departed Hessian soldier, crucial aspects of the past are missing. They lie hidden, buried, forgotten, or lost: latent possibles that we might encounter while searching for something else or that could at any moment break loose and come hurtling at us seemingly out of nowhere as did the horseman's head, striking Ichabod Crane. To push this further, I want to note that Ichabod's future is decidedly altered by this visitor from the past, whether it sent him to New York or to join the other spooks and specters that haunt Sleepy Hollow. Either way, Ichabod, too, becomes a source of legend, for with his departure "the schoolhouse soon fell to decay, and was reported to be haunted by the ghost of the unfortunate pedagogue."[9]

But if we are to consider the past as akin to the ghost and history as a hauntological endeavor (or as holding a latent ontology, for readers who are squeamish), then it is worth asking what it is that troubles us about the ghost? In *Specters of Marx* Derrida asks "*What* is the ghost? What is the *effectivity* or the *presence* of the specter, that is, of what seems to remain as ineffective, virtual, insubstantial as a simulacrum?"[10] The ghost or specter is troubling precisely because it is the past come again but emptied of its physical properties and disobedient to the rules of time and space. "One cannot control its comings and goings because it *begins by coming back*."[11] Thus, unlike the ontological realist narrative, we are not witnessing an orderly and necessary, if forced, return but are instead in the presence of something that has passed and as such should not be present. In contrast to the search for origins and continuities, Derrida embraces the perturbations that the past returned convokes. In speaking of the specters of Marx and Marxism he asks: "How would it be valid for all times? In other words, how can it come back and present itself again, anew, as the new? How can it be there, again, when it is no longer?"[12]

For Derrida the porous and disturbing nature of the past that haunts us provokes us to question the historical ground on which we stand and the borders by which we divide past, present, and future. On this reading, what Derrida calls the specters of Marx and Marxism are not an origin or foundation to which we can return but instead inspire us as disturbing remains that "no longer take the form of a party or of a workers' international, but rather of a kind of counter-conjuration, in the (theoretical and practical) critique of the state of international law, the concepts of State and nation, and so forth: in order to renew this critique, and especially to radicalize it."[13] Derrida calls on us to confront the way we are haunted by the past and to recognize the ways we inscribe ourselves in the present. Thus, for Derrida the legacy of Marx extends to a current and ongoing analysis of laws of capital but also to "modes of representation and suffrage, the determining content of human rights, women's and children's rights, the current concepts of equality, liberty, especially fraternity" in Marxist and non-Marxist countries alike.[14] Thus, Derrida enables a reading of the past focused on the gaps, the places of absence where origins are situated in the present but that as such are unstable haunted grounds.

On these grounds the ghost or specter *begins by coming back*, as did the ghost of Hamlet. "Looks it not like the king?" asks Bernardo, to which Horatio replies, "Most like it: it harrows me with fear and wonder" (1.1). Indeed, Derrida might characterize the inhabitants of Sleepy Hollow as "attempting to ontologize remains, to make them present, in the first place by *identifying* the bodily remains and by *localizing* the dead" in an effort to tame the haunting past.[15] This is, in any event, what I think most conventional historians do, ontologize the remains of the past to make them present by assigning them to a specific location in space and time that is, in principle, observable and, as such, fixed and immutable. No ghosts here. No dead fathers on the ramparts or headless horsemen. No hauntology or latent ontology: just the facts. On such a reading—and as we have seen, this is the conventional historian's reading—time is never out of joint, and assuming one has the right methodological tools, one can master the past and recount it in the form of a realist narrative.

But such a narrative cannot account for the latent ontology of the past or the ways that past possibles condition our possible pasts. What I mean by this is that our knowledge of the past is conditioned by what presents itself to us both in terms of its remains and in terms of our reception. The limits of what we are willing to accept as "past possibles" conditions what we are willing to accept as possible pasts. That which lies beyond this realm appears to us as simply impossible, like a ghost. But the ghost is only impossible insofar as it is a remainder of a different time and place, and its untimely presence disturbs us. The latent past is not the impos-

sible; it was possible, and it did happen, though perhaps it has been rendered inconceivable or unimaginable and thus exiled beyond the realm of
what now appears possible. And when what lies latent appears, returns,
history is haunted, and we are confronted with the possibility that our
understanding of the past is polysemic and contradictory. It is not what
we tell it to be. Any partial past may be one possible past to be sure but
one that does not account or budget for a host of past possibles that have
been suppressed, effaced, lost, or forgotten, and these are the ghosts and
specters that haunt us in the present. The history of Sleepy Hollow is not
only that of charming rustic settlers prone to tales of the supernatural
but also, and importantly, of a violent dispossession of Native Americans.
When what is latent of the past becomes manifest, it opens new historical
possibilities. Of course, these remnants of the past are only "new" in the
sense that they can now appear within the realm of the possible as a possible past, thus altering history itself.

The relationship between the porous nature of the boundaries or borders constructed to separate past, present, future, and the *poros* or pathway that historians construct to cross these borders and take us back to
where we've never been is a tangled and seemingly aporetic one. "In one
case, the nonpassage resembles an impermeability; it would stem from
the opaque existence of an uncrossable border: a door that does not open
or that only opens according to an unlocatable condition, according to
the inaccessible secret of some shibboleth."[16] Here the past is a distinct
and foreign country, a door that does not open or one that opens only
for the historian who can usher us through it and across the border. But
in another case "the nonpassage, the impasse or aporia, stems from the
fact that there is no limit. There is not yet or there is no longer a border
to cross, no opposition between two sides: the limit is too porous, per-
meable, and indeterminate."[17] Here, just as the historian in the present
trespasses on the past, the past itself trespasses on the present, blurring
the boundaries of the path charted by the historian. Derrida offers a third
among his multiple figures of aporia that haunt one another: "the impossible, the antinomy, or the contradiction, is a nonpassage because its
elementary milieu does not allow for something that could be called passage. . . . There is no more path."[18] This could be the limits of representation or the limits of what is allowed to appear.

For Sarah Kofman, "one speaks of a *poros* (path) when it is a matter of
blazing a trail where no trail exists or could exist properly speaking, of

crossing what is impassable . . . an *apeiron* which it is impossible to cross from end to end."[19] The poros and aporia are necessarily linked, and this is the nature of the trail that the historian seeks to forge from a position in the present to the event in the past. But Kofman also reminds us that the term "*poros* should not be confused with *odos*, which is a general term that designates any sort of road or path. *Poros* refers solely to a sea or river route, to a passage that is opened across a chaotic expanse and which transforms it into an ordered and qualified space by introducing differentiated routes, making visible the various directions of space, providing orientation in an expanse previously devoid of any landmarks."[20] I see this as a particularly apt metaphor both for the past and the endeavor of the historian who aspires to chart a route or passage over an unruly and at times indistinguishable expanse that churns beneath his or her endeavors. Indeed, most of the past recedes into the ocean, leaving no discernible trace, like the wake of a passing ship or an item lost overboard. If one comes along in a short enough amount of time, one can follow the wake of the first passing ship or one that came soon after, retracing their route even as evidence of the prior ships dissipates. Then again, at any given moment a sudden surge could bring evidence of past remains to the surface even as it disturbs or destroys the wakes that previously served as marks for orientation. More often, the historian works from a greater temporal distance, relying partly on materials "still immediately present, hailing from times which we are seeking to understand (*Überreste*/Remains), partly whatever ideas human beings have obtained and transmitted to be remembered (*Quellen*/Sources), partly things wherein both these forms of materials are combined (*Denkmäler*/Monuments)."[21] We could think of these as sea charts, buoys, shipwrecks, or reefs that serve as the basis for navigation; though the Sources themselves may very well be the wakes of past ships, "has anyone thought that we have been tracking something down, something other than tracks themselves to be tracked down?"[22]

And as we saw with Dickens's Ghost of Christmas Past, the past itself is the most "mobile, changeable and polymorphous of all spaces, a space where any path that has been traced" can be 'obliterated' and, as such, is analogous to Hesiod's Tartarus (with the image of chaos itself). . . . In this infernal, chaotic confusion, the *poros* is the way out, the last resort of sailors and navigators, the stratagem which allows them to escape the impasse, the aporia, and the anxiety that accompanies it."[23] The chaotic and polymorphous nature of the past provokes anxiety, and in response to such chaos we seek an ordered way out. But here we must pay close attention to the way that the paths historians construct to bring order and intelligibility to the chaotic expanse that is the past can themselves become impasses when a historical narrative precludes other possible voices, vantages, or viewpoints. The pathway forged as an escape itself becomes a trap, restricting one from straying off the straight and narrow ordained route from one point to another. The *poros* becomes an *aporia*, restricting us from accessing other possible pasts and limiting what we can imagine as a past possible just as Scrooge wielded the extinguisher cap in an attempt to restrict the light emanating from the Ghost of Christmas Past. Here again we see the conjuring trick of ontological realism as the conventional historian exerts his or her influence over the past, by restricting its light and all the past possibles that expose other possible pasts that its light reveals. But try as he might, Scrooge could not hide the light as it streamed out from under the cap. The past continues to haunt history.

When E. P. Thompson wrote *The Making of the English Working Class* in 1963, it was not as though the working class had no past prior to this work. Indeed, Thompson states his intention to make explicit "the agency of the working people" and "the degree to which they contributed, by conscious efforts, to the making of history."[24] What's more, Thompson's work took issue with an understanding of history wherein "only the successful (in the sense of those whose aspirations anticipated subsequent evolution) are remembered," and "the blind alleys, the lost causes, and the losers themselves are forgotten."[25] Thompson sought to activate the latent ontology of this forgotten past by actualizing it through the project and writing of history. He cautions that "the working class did not rise like the sun at an appointed time"; nevertheless, the working class had not appeared before as a topic of systematic historical investigation.[26] Whether this was because of the Whigish bias toward political histories of men in power or the paucity of what had been deemed conventional historical sources, the lives and actions of the working class lay beyond that which was imagined as past possibles that could lead to any history worthy of its name. This itself is indicative of the restricted possible pasts available at that time. But the previous historical accounts had been haunted by the making of the English working class all along, as had works of literature and art.

In one way for Thompson, it was precisely the presence of the "owning class" that made the absence of the working one so glaringly visible. The absence of the working class in prior historical accounts haunted those histories. Thompson makes this apparent in his definition of class as a historical relationship that "must be embodied in real people and in a real context. . . . And class happens when some men, as a result of common experiences (inherited or shared), feel and articulate the identity of their interests as between themselves, and as against other men whose interests are different from (and usually opposed to) theirs."[27] This imaginative reconceptualization of past possible actors and events rendered visible evidence in the official records of the ruling class that became a key source for Thompson's own historical account of the working class. Here again, it was not that this evidence did not exist previously, but it lay beyond the realm of what was imagined as a possible past. Once Thompson opened the possibility of a systematic history from the bottom up, a host of past possibles were made available as historical evidence through stories, folk art, or song.

But we must also be aware that while Thompson's achievement represented an imaginative leap that opened up a whole new realm of historical investigation, it was not a theoretical reconsideration of history; thus, it resembles prior historical accounts in terms of method and narrative if not content. The limitations of Thompson's creative imagining are readily apparent when one considers his inability to imagine the possible past of women as historical actors in his account. To be sure, the limits of Thompson's creative imagination were bound by the possibilities open to him in his own time and space, but the theoretical limits of how he conceptualized "history" and the "past" are what allowed the poros he divined that led to a systematic history of the working class to itself become an aporia restricting access to other possible pasts. As this new pathway to the past became increasingly well-traveled, other pathways were neglected, while still other possible pathways were left unexplored. One could argue for similar results in other fields such as women's history, history of gender, African American history, Asian American history, and Latino history. Pioneering historians in each of these fields wrestled free the hidden or repressed and thus latent past to make possible the histories of groups and events that had previously resided as ghosts haunting the dominant historical narrative. Each of these histories presented a new opening, but because they were offered as conventional ontological realist histories, each opening was also a closure. We should think of this closing in the same way that we think of "absolute knowledge as the closure if not the end of history" because "the history of presence is closed, for 'history' has never meant anything but this: presentation of being, production and gathering of the being in presence, as knowledge and mastery."[28] The emphasis on presence and mastery arrests the possibility of a full deconstruction at the moment when what was absent is made present and in doing so locks the historical narrative in a closed system.[29] By contrast, the full or completed strategy of deconstruction "avoids both simply *neutralizing* the binary opposition of metaphysics and simply *residing* within the closed field of these operations, thereby confirming them."[30] The conflict between these competing historical narratives points again to the heterogeneous and chaotic nature of the past that ultimately cannot be mastered. Wrestle with it as we may, we cannot make it do what we want.

So what are historians to do with such an unruly visitor as the past? With a "ghost that offers no visible resistance on its own part" and is "undisturbed by any effort of its adversary" and that yet is all the more resistant and at times adversarial all the same. In a reference to Plato's allegory of the cave, Sarah Kofman provides the template for an answer: "Paradoxically the one thing that can save them is an aporia that renders visible the chains of pleasure and the visible world which bind their souls to their bodies and prevents them from gaining consciousness of the aporetic state into which they were, without knowing, initially plunged."[31] It is the aporia of the past that is that renders visible the chaotic and polysemic conditions of the past. This is to say it is by acknowledging the enigmatic and contradictory nature of the past and the ontological-epistemological entanglement of the historian rather than asserting an extinguisher cap control over it that we can reveal a path forward. These conditions are not visible to the ontological realist conception of history, which casts the past event as a recoverable object and leaves the historian in the position of the captives in the cave, who "do not know they are in chains because they do not know that they know nothing."[32] By contrast, the historian who acknowledges the aporia of history strives to find a route back to where we've never been, to responsibly represent the past without restricting its content and trapping the historian in another aporia of his or her own making or succumbing to Derrida's third iteration of the aporia, where the aporia itself no longer appears possible. This is an uncertain and unsettling position. But like the ghost, the past is a *revenant* brought to the present by the historian. It visits us but does not belong to our time or place, and as such it disturbs us just as there can be no "aporia in the true sense of the word without a transition from a familiar state which affords one every security to a new and therefore harrowing state."[33]

As we have seen, Derrida links the ghost to the trace and to *différance*, thus challenging notions of absolute priority or absolute foundations. So now we must link *différance* to the project of history. Derrida writes, "If the word 'history' did not in and of itself convey the motif of a final repression of difference, one could say that only differences can be 'historical' from the outset and in each of their aspects."[34] History, as conventionally conceived, is precisely the repression of differences in an attempt to generate a singular intelligible narrative that necessarily overwrites those aspects that confuse, confound, or contradict that narrative. Derrida offers *différance* as the counter to this repression, suggesting the "playing moment that 'produces'—by means of something that is not simply an activity—these differences, these effects of difference."[35] Thus, what I am suggesting is that we imagine doing history with *différance* in mind, crafting the playing moment that produces these effects of differences. But in doing so this production of differences should not be taken to be the origin of differences in "a simple and unmodified—in-different—present." Even though this hauntological history would be the "non-full, non-simple, structured and differentiating origin of differences . . . , the name 'origin' no longer suits it."[36] Here we should recall the ways that for Droysen it is ultimately "illusory to search for the origin of something with the belief that it is possible to find the true essence of that from which this development proceeded."[37] When historians assume a definite object or point or event to which they seek to return, even if it is the origin of difference, they engage in the repression of difference by restricting the possibilities of what was possible in the past.

To be sure, the purpose of history is to make the past legible and intelligible, to offer a poros through the chaotic aporia of the past. And insofar as history serves to make the past legible in the present, it should be seen as a writing whose function is to make present what is absent, to render legible that which would otherwise be illegible.[38] But as such it is "a mark that subsists, one which does not exhaust itself in the moment of its inscription and which can give rise to an iteration in the absence and beyond the presence of the empirically determined subject who, in a given context, has emitted or produced it."[39] Thus, even the most methodologically sound and precise historical investigation is not only a necessarily partial investigation bound by the epistemological horizon of the historian's own time and place but also "carries within it a force that breaks with its context, that is with the collectivity of presences organizing the moment of its inscription."[40] This is partly because the historical work is itself haunted by the past it cannot contain (as Scrooge was haunted by the Ghost of Christmas Past) but also because future historians can "perhaps come to recognize other possibilities in [the historical work] by inscribing or grafting it onto other chains."[41] The force of this rupture means that history can never rest in peace. But the rupture can also be seen as an incision that is the emergence of a mark that serves to make visible the various directions of space, providing orientation in an expanse previously devoid of any landmarks. This follows one sense that Derrida ascribes to the verb *différer* as "temporalization and spacing, the becoming-time of space and the becoming-space of time, the 'originary' constitution of time and space."[42] This is a key aspect of the historical endeavor that seeks to situate past events in a specific time and place as best one can, based on the sources and evidence. In doing so, the historian posits the coordinates of time and space through periodization or geographical demarcation. But lest the poros become the aporia, we must recognize that the emergence of this mark "derives from no category of being, whether present or absent . . . , for what is put into question is precisely the quest for a rightful beginning, an absolute point of departure, a principal responsibility."[43] This means that the historian must recognize the play of presence and absence in the historical endeavor, thus permanently destabilizing the poros of a history in relation to the aporia of the past that is no longer.

Here is where I want to modify a passage by Derrida to make the link between *différance* and history explicit. In the project of history one can expose only that of the past that at a certain moment can become present, manifest, that which can be shown, presented as something present, a being-present in its truth, in the truth of a present or the presence of the present. Now if the past is̶ what makes possible the presentation of the being-present of history, it is never presented as such. The past itself is never offered to the present.[44] With acknowledgment to the way this modifies Derrida's argument, but following this move, I see history as linked to *différance* because of the latent ontology of the past. The past as history is̶, crossed out, present and absent. I replace the X/strike-through offered by Derrida with the bar/strike-through to demonstrate the present/absent nature of the past event but also the ways that we are "barred" (barré) from actually having that past event as such in the present. In this way the bar indicates and makes explicit the ontological-epistemological entanglement of history and the historian with the past. The historian is concerned with the traces of the past that we have at hand, but our object of inquiry (if we can call it an object) has no ontological properties of its own in the present and is conjured by the medium of the historian, often entangling the categories of legend and fact. In Tarrytown, New York, there is an official sign that reads "The Headless Horseman Bridge described by Washington Irving in The Legend of Sleepy Hollow formerly spanned this stream in this spot." This is a "historical landmark," marking the site of a now-absent bridge on which a fictional event occurred, but as it turns out even the site of the bridge itself is unknown. The entanglement of "fiction" in fact plays out in different ways, but even when such "fictions" are later accounted for or corrected, this is akin to a judge striking testimony from the record after it has been given and instructing the jury to disregard what they have heard. It isn't actually gone, and it does contribute to the current and future understandings of the past.

A deconstructive approach to history linked to *différance* as the crafting of the playing moment that produces effects of difference unhinges the past from the "as it really happened" of ontological realism problematizing the belief in a fixed and stable past (which is the myth of a fixed and stable present). The emphasis on play is in tension with a conventional approach to history that emphasizes presence because "play is always play of absence and presence, but if it is to be thought radically, play must be conceived of before the alternative of presence and absence."[45] This is an approach that recognizes and embraces both the latent ontology of the past that is and the importance of the imagination required to think radically. It is to begin before the posited coordinates of presence and absence as alternatives and instead allow the project of history to emerge from the generative realm of possibilities: past possibles and possible pasts. To be sure, the historian arrests certain of these possibilities in his or her telling of the story, but this does not negate these possibilities of the past that can return. Indeed, the endeavor of history can be seen as autoimmune in the sense Derrida gives to the word.[46] Because history is charged with the recovery of the past, its rules are intended to protect the past that it represents. In doing so, the writing of history transforms what was alive, changing, and in flux into something dead, fixed, and immutable. But such limitations and restrictions make accounts of the past brittle so that the very act of protection sets up coordinates by which the brittle representation is doomed to fail, to break when new or different aspects of the past come to light leading to revision. To go a step further, deconstruction reveals the moment of decision when the story is structured according to a hierarchical ordering that privileges certain past possibles while rendering others inconceivable, unimaginable, or impossible. In this way deconstruction reveals the legitimizing strategies of the historian while upsetting the authority of any particular telling. This can in turn reveal alternative possible pasts based on the reevaluation of past possibles.

What I propose is a mode of writing history that provides a poros or pathway to the past that activates the latent ontology, making it present but without privileging that presence in the way that the ontological realist narrative does. In doing so this approach inhabits and appropriates the methodological and evidentiary commitments of traditional historical work but in a way that makes evident and legible the limits and barriers of conventional historical method. Thus, fears that a deconstructive approach will inevitably lead to relativism are unwarranted because the very methods of the historical discipline are conserved:

> The movements of deconstruction do not shake up [*solliciter*] structures from the outside. They are not possible and effective; they do not focus their strikes, except by inhabiting these structures. Inhabiting them "in a certain way," because one always inhabits and all the more so when one does not suspect it. Operating necessarily from the inside, borrowing from the old structure the strategic and economic resources of subversion, borrowing them structurally, that is to say without being able to isolate their elements and atoms, the enterprise of deconstruction is always in a certain way swept away by its own work.[47]

Thus, I advocate working from the inside to expose the limitations and restrictions of the historical practice. Such an approach works within the historical tradition to destabilize that tradition and is always cognizant of the past as aporia and actively works to shake the ground it has laid. One way to imagine such an approach is through the techniques and possibilities offered in the previous chapter, but another is through a narrative structure that accommodates the past that is.

This is to be done by what Derrida has called a double gesture (*un double geste*) or double session (*la double séance*) wherein "we must first *overturn* the traditional concept of history, but at the same time mark the *interval*, take care that by virtue of the overturning, and by the simple act of conceptualization, that the interval not be *reappropriated*."[48] Here, the possible past that one recounts cannot preclude other past possibles and thus necessarily remains open to other and alternative possible pasts. "Therefore we must proceed using a double gesture, according to a unity that is both systematic and in and of itself divided, a double writing, that is, a writing that is in and of itself multiple, what I called in '*La double séance*,' a *double science*."[49] A concrete example of deconstruction for the writing of history can be seen in my concurrent book project on Emmanuel Levinas's Talmudic lectures in Paris.[50] In this discrete case study what is at issue are conflicting registers of the immanent and transcendent or secular and religious. The first gesture or session of the project employs a traditional intellectual history of Emmanuel Levinas's Talmudic lectures presented in Paris between 1960 and 1990; the origins of Levinas's turn to the study of the Talmud in the years following World War II; and the reception of Levinas's Talmudic lectures. The thrust of this movement is to dismiss the "myth" of Levinas as a Lithuanian trained Talmudic scholar and explain the ways and reasons that he came to study the Talmud in the aftermath of the Shoah or Holocaust. A key component of this trajectory is also to demonstrate how Levinas has influenced modern Jewish thought by establishing a postrabbinic chain of tradition that allowed him and his successors to reestablish the Talmudic tradition in the wake of the Shoah but devoid of any actual rabbinic authority. At this level the first session is about issues of intellectual legitimacy and the creation of intellectual authority.

But the second gesture or session allows the reader to take stock of the ways that the first adheres to a disciplinary bias that discounts some fundamental aspects of Levinas's thought. By using Levinas's Talmudic readings as contextualized historical documents, the first account dismisses Levinas's own counterhistorical claim that divine and ethical meaning transcends time. Brad Gregory has argued that such rejections of "confessional commitments in the study of religion in favor of social scientific or humanistic theories of religion has produced not unbiased accounts, but reductionist explanations of religious belief and practice with embedded secular biases that preclude the understanding of religious believer-practitioners."[51] Following this line, it is not only possible but also fruitful to imagine an alternative historical account where divine authority, revelation, and election are the key components that allow for critical reflection and ethical judgment (illuminating the tensions and compatibilities between Levinas's "philosophical" and "confessional" writings). Gregory's diagnosis of the hierarchy that privileges secular history is instructive but inadequate because of the way he arrests the hierarchy after overturning it, thus rendering "confessional commitment" the privileged means of understanding the past and reinscribing it in the "traditional mode of history." The deconstructive approach goes further, asking the historian to recognize the ways that particular interpretative approaches serve to close off other possible pasts and write history by means of a double session to destabilize the authority of each possible past, thus leaving the past in a certain sense open. But what is more, and as we saw in Chapter 3, the second tendency is always already at work in the first via the theologico-historical mechanism that is silently employed to "hold" the past and make it accessible in the present. In this light the second reading emerges from and is necessitated by the first. This makes clear the necessity of an interminable analysis wherein the historical investigation turns on itself as the hierarchy is constantly reestablished, each undermining the definitive status of the other.[52] The architecture and presentation of the Levinas book presents a cogent intellectual history of Levinas's Talmudic lectures in the first session that provides a contextual reading of the sources and causes for his turn to the Talmud while simultaneously offering a counterinterpretation in the second session that allows for Levinas's transcendent claims about the past and history to stand in opposition to those of the first. Given our investigation in Chapter 1, it should be apparent that the deconstructive approach is well suited to the practice of intellectual history, with its focus on ideas, text, context, culture, and language. But I want to suggest that the utility of this approach is wider and more far-reaching.

The deconstructive approach is especially warranted when dealing with actors or events traditionally rendered outside the realm of conventional history to make what was absent present and what was illegible legible. Traditional approaches have done this, as we saw in the work of Thompson, but in a way that leaves the field on which the hierarchy was determined intact. Recent attention to "world" or "global" history has shifted the historical gaze to non-European or "non-Western" regions but has done so employing conventional Western epistemological and methodological historical approaches. In this way the Western understanding of "history" is implicitly considered the norm against which all other understandings and logics of history must measure up or be discounted.

The result is a more expansive geographic but an equally restrictive and Eurocentric understanding of the past and history. The deconstructive approach could employ conventional Western historical strategies in one session but place them in tension, and even conflict, with regional understandings of "history" that place the Western approach in question. Here, one could imagine a history of Nepal that looks to Western historiography but also to Nepalese Chronicles (*vamshavali*).[53]

In a more general sense the second session or gesture would serve to undercut the first session by offering an alternative understanding of past possibles, rendering a different possible past, which prevents the traditional understanding of history from imploding. "By means of this double, and precisely stratified, dislodged and dislodging, writing, we must also mark the interval between inversion, which brings low what was high, and the irruptive immergence of a new 'concept,' a concept that can no longer be, and could never be, included in the previous regime."[54] Such a double move shakes the ground on which conventional ontological realist narratives rest. The two sessions pull at each other, creating cracks in any one homogeneous history through which other portions of the heterogeneous and polysemic past that haunts history can rise and be activated. This "concept," the past that is, "marks an irreducible and *generative* multiplicity. The supplement and the turbulence of a certain lack fracture the limit of the text, forbidding an exhaustive reading of it."[55] Far from implying the death or abdication of the author, deconstruction, for the writing of history, requires a strong and careful historian whose rhetorical style guides the reader along the poros that simultaneously introduces and acknowledges the aporia. It is a give-and-take that makes the reader aware of the openings at play and the polysemous nature of the past. To be sure, the latent ontology of the past is bound and constrained by our imagination in the present: by that which we can imagine as having been possible. Nevertheless, the latent and missing portions of the past haunt us, and although conventional historians might seek to press them down like an extinguisher cap on a flame or outrun them as Ichabod Crane tried to outrun the headless horseman, it is folly to think the past is merely what we tell it to be. Instead, historians should strive to enact a historical methodology that is commensurate, if never adequate, to the past that is. For inevitably that which is latent, the missing portions of the past, will come hurtling at us like the severed head of a Hessian horseman.

Notes

Introduction

1. Joyce Appleby, Lynn Hunt, and Margaret Jacob, *Telling the Truth About History* (New York: Norton, 1994), 208, 237.

2. Keith Windschuttle, *The Killing of History: How Literary Critics and Social Theorists Are Murdering Our Past* (New York: Free Press, 1996); Richard J. Evans's *In Defense of History* (New York: Norton, 1997); Georg Iggers, *Historiography in the Twentieth Century: From Scientific Objectivity to the Postmodern Challenge* (Middletown, CT: Wesleyan University Press, 1997); Jerrold Seigel, "Problematizing the Self," in *Beyond the Cultural Turn: New Directions in the Study of Society and Culture*, ed. Victoria E. Bonnell and Lynn Hunt (Berkeley: University of California Press, 1999), 281–314.

3. Joshua Kates, *Essential History: Jacques Derrida and the Development of Deconstruction* (Evanston, IL: Northwestern University Press, 2005), xv.

4. Jane Caplan, "Postmodernism, Poststructuralism, and Deconstruction: Notes for Historians," *Central European History* 22, no. 3/4 (1989): 260–78, 270.

5. Geoffrey Bennington, "Derrida's Archive," *Theory, Culture & Society* 31, no. 7/8 (2014): 111–19; Edward Baring, "Ne me raconte plus d'histoires: Derrida and the Problem of the History of Philosophy," *History and Theory* 53 (May 2014): 175–93; Peter Fenves, "Derrida and History: Some Questions Derrida Pursues in His Early Writings," in *Jacques Derrida and the Humanities: A Critical Reader*, ed. Tom Cohen (Cambridge: Cambridge University Press, 2001), 271–95; Dana Hollander, *Exemplarity and Chosenness: Rosenzweig and Derrida on the Nation of Philosophy* (Stanford: Stanford University Press, 2008); Michael Naas, "Violence and Historicity: Derrida's Early Readings of Heidegger," *Research in Phenomenology* 45, no. 2 (2015): 191–213.

6. Jacques Derrida, introduction to *L'origine de la géométrie*, by Edmund

Husserl, trans. Jacques Derrida (Paris: Presses universitaires de France, 1962); "Violence et métaphysique: Essai sur la pensée d'Emmanuel Levinas," *Revue de métaphysique et de morale*, nos. 3–4 (1964): 425–73; "De la grammatologie," *Critique* 21, no. 223 (1965): 1016–42; "De la grammatologie (II)," *Critique* 22, no. 224 (1966): 23–53; "Cogito et histoire de la folie," in *L'écriture et la différence* (Paris: Seuil, 1967): 51–97.

7. Jacques Derrida, "Histoire et vérité," Irvine Special Collections and Archives, Jacques Derrida papers (MS-C001) (hereafter JDP); Jacques Derrida, *Heidegger: The Question of Being and History*, trans. Geoffrey Bennington (Chicago: University of Chicago Press, 2016).

8. Derrida, "Histoire et vérité," JDP, Box 8, Folder 10, sheets 3–4. For a full analysis of these lectures see Baring, "Ne me raconte plus d'histoires." I want to thank Ed Baring for sharing with me his transcription of the lecture notes.

9. Derrida, *Heidegger*, 80.

10. Ibid., 94.

11. Ibid.

12. Ibid., 95.

13. Derrida, "Histoire et vérité," JDP, Box 8, Folder 9, sheet 22.

14. Fenves, "Derrida and History," 296.

15. Jacques Derrida, *Positions*, trans. Alan Bass, 2nd ed. (New York: Continuum, 2002), 57; originally published as *Positions* (Paris: Minuit, 1972). Page citations refer to the English translation.

16. Bennington, "Derrida's Archive," 111–12.

17. Ibid., 112.

18. See Baring, "Ne me raconte plus d'histoires," 191.

19. Jacques Derrida, *Aporias*, trans. Thomas Dutoit (Stanford: Stanford University Press, 1993); Philippe Ariès, *Western Attitudes Towards Death: From the Middle Ages to the Present* (Baltimore: Johns Hopkins University Press, 1974).

20. Derrida, *Aporias*, 25.

21. Jacques Derrida, *Archive Fever: A Freudian Impression*, trans. Eric Prenowitz (Chicago: University of Chicago Press, 1996); originally published as *Mal d'archive* (Paris: Galilée, 1995). Page citations refer to the English translation.

22. Yosef Hayim Yerushalmi, *Freud's Moses: Judaism Terminable and Interminable* (New Haven, CT: Yale University Press, 1991).

23. Derrida, *Archive Fever*, 38.

24. Ibid., 39.

25. Ibid., 39–40.

26. Ibid., 41.

27. Ibid., 51.

28. Ibid., 64. The original reads: "how does one prove in general an absence of archive, if not relying on classical norms (presence/absence of literal and explicit

reference to this or to that, to a this or a that which one supposes to be identical to themselves, and simply absent, *actually* absent, if they are not simply present, *actually* present, how can one not, and why not, take into account *unconscious*, and more generally *virtual* archives)?"

29. Derrida, *Archive Fever*, 52.

30. Ibid., 84.

31. Ibid., 60.

32. Ibid., 59.

33. Ibid., 85.

Chapter 1

An earlier version of this chapter was published in *History and Theory* 46, no. 4 (2007): 113–43.

1. Michael Roth, "Ebb Tide," review of *Sublime Historical Experience*, by Frank Ankersmit, *History and Theory* 46, no. 1 (2007): 66–73; Nancy Partner, "Narrative Persistence," in *Re-figuring Hayden White*, ed. Frank Ankersmit, Ewa Domańska, and Hans Kellner (Stanford: Stanford University Press, 2009), 81–104.

2. Hayden White, *Tropics of Discourse: Essays in Cultural Criticism* (Baltimore: Johns Hopkins University Press, 1978), 281. White's admonition was first published as "The Absurdist Moment in Contemporary Literary Theory," *Contemporary Literature* 7, no. 3 (1976): 378–403.

3. White, *Tropics of Discourse*, 282.

4. Ibid., 52.

5. Ibid.

6. Ibid.

7. Lloyd S. Kramer asks this same question in relation to White and LaCapra in his "Literature, Criticism, and Historical Imagination: The Literary Challenge of Hayden White and Dominick LaCapra," in *The New Cultural History*, ed. Lynn Hunt (Berkeley: University of California Press, 1989), 97–130, 111.

8. Dominick LaCapra, *Rethinking Intellectual History: Texts, Contexts, Language* (Ithaca, NY: Cornell University Press, 1983), 78. LaCapra's essay was first published as "A Poetics of Historiography: Hayden White's *Tropics of Discourse*," *Modern Language Notes* 93, no. 5 (1978): 1037–43 . LaCapra goes so far as to say that "the things Derrida discusses *are* inside White," and his assessment turned out be prescient as White would come to suffer this same criticism over the issue of emplotment most notably on multiple tellings of the Holocaust at the now famous conference organized by Saul Friedländer published as *Probing the Limits of Representation* (Cambridge, MA: Harvard University Press, 1992). See also the more recent volume that revisits the issues at play in the conference: Claudio

Fogu, Wulf Kansteiner, and Todd Presner, eds., *Probing the Ethics of Holocaust Culture* (Cambridge, MA: Harvard University Press, 2016).

9. Sigmund Freud, "The 'Uncanny,'" in *The Standard Edition of the Complete Psychological Works of Sigmund Freud*, trans. and ed. James Strachey, 24 vols. (London: Hogarth, 1955), 17:248n1.

10. Ibid.

11. See Natalie Davis, *The Return of Martin Guerre* (Cambridge, MA: Harvard University Press, 1983); the review by Robert Finlay, "The Refashioning of Martin Guerre," *AHR* 93, no. 3 (1988): 553–71; and Davis's response, "On the Lame," *AHR* 93, no. 3 (1988): 572–603.

12. Freud, "The 'Uncanny,'" 244.

13. The article was published again in LaCapra, *Rethinking Intellectual History* and also contained the review of Hayden White.

14. Dominick LaCapra and Steven L. Kaplan, eds., *Modern European Intellectual History: Reappraisals and New Perspectives* (Ithaca, NY: Cornell University Press, 1982), 8–9.

15. Ibid., 7.

16. Martin Jay, "Should Intellectual History Take a Linguistic Turn?" in *Modern European Intellectual History: Reappraisals and New Perspectives*, ed. Dominick LaCapra and Steven L. Kaplan (Ithaca, NY: Cornell University Press, 1982), 86–110, 87.

17. Ibid., 109.

18. Ibid., 87.

19. Jacques Derrida, *Positions*, trans. Alan Bass, 2nd ed. (New York: Continuum, 2002); originally published as *Positions* (Paris: Minuit, 1972). Page citations refer to the English translation.

20. Jean Pierre Faye, "Le camarade Mallarmé," *L'Humanité*, Sept. 12, 1969.

21. See Christopher Norris's introduction (xvii–xviii) and Alan Bass's translator's note (103n28) in the second edition of Bass's English translation of *Positions*. See also François Hourmant, "*Tel Quel* es ses volte-face politiques (1968–1978)," *Vingtième Siècle: Revue d'histoire*, no. 51 (July 1996); and Jason Powell, *Jacques Derrida: A Biography* (New York: Continuum, 2006), 103–6.

22. Derrida, *Positions*, 62.

23. Derrida presented this as a lecture in two sessions on April 22 and 23, 1993, at the University of California, Riverside. It was later published in book form as *Spectres de Marx* (Paris: Galilée, 1993).

24. Derrida, *Positions*, 56.

25. Ibid., 57.

26. Ibid., 51.

27. Ibid., 57.

28. Ibid., 51.

29. Ibid., 57.

30. These can be seen in the historical profession's obsession with facts, archives, and the compulsion to get the story "right."

31. Lynn Hunt, "Introduction: History, Culture, and Text," in *The New Cultural History*, ed. Lynn Hunt (Berkeley: University of California Press, 1989), 1. See also Robert Darnton, "Intellectual and Cultural History," in *The Past Before Us: Contemporary Historical Writing in the United States*, ed. Michael Kammen (Ithaca, NY: Cornell University Press, 1980).

32. LaCapra and Kaplan, *Modern European Intellectual History*, 8. LaCapra and Kaplan cite the article by Robert Darnton, "Intellectual and Cultural History," to substantiate the relative stability of intellectual history, but it is also of note that Darnton's analysis reveals that the number of American doctoral dissertations in social history quadrupled between 1958 and 1978.

33. Dominick LaCapra, "Rethinking Intellectual History," in *Modern European Intellectual History: Reappraisals and New Perspectives*, ed. Dominick LaCapra and Steven L. Kaplan (Ithaca, NY: Cornell University Press, 1982), 47.

34. Ibid., 48.

35. LaCapra is careful both to announce the ways that his essay follows a "territorial imperative" (48) and the limitations of alternatives to conventional approaches—deconstruction, for instance (84).

36. See Catherine Gallagher and Stephen Greenblatt, *Practicing New Historicism* (Chicago: University of Chicago Press, 2000).

37. LaCapra offers his criticism of New Historicism in *Soundings in Critical Theory* (Ithaca, NY: Cornell University Press, 1989), 190–96.

38. The *Intellectual History Newsletter* was an annual publication available through the History Department at Boston University. In its initial format it included articles, conference reports, book reviews, and syllabi. It had recently contracted with Cambridge University Press to publish the journal *Modern Intellectual History*. See vols. 2 (1980), 7 (1985), and 8 (1986) of the *Modern Intellectual History Newsletter*.

39. LaCapra also discusses this in relation to the article by Pocock in "Intellectual History and Critical Theory," in *Soundings in Critical Theory* (Ithaca, NY: Cornell University Press, 1989), 182–210.

40. *Intellectual History Newsletter* 8 (1986): 8–9; also cited in LaCapra, "Intellectual History and Critical Theory," 200–201.

41. *Intellectual History Newsletter* 8 (1986): 8; also cited in LaCapra, "Intellectual History and Critical Theory," 201.

42. *Intellectual History Newsletter* 8 (1986): 8; also cited in LaCapra, "Intellectual History and Critical Theory," 201–202.

43. See John Toews, "Intellectual History After the Linguistic Turn: The Autonomy of Meaning and the Irreducibility of Experience," *American Historical Review* 92, no. 4 (1987): 879–907.

44. See Judith Surkis, "When Was the Linguistic Turn? A Genealogy," *American Historical Review* 117, no. 3 (2012): 700–722.

45. The books reviewed were Jean Christophe Agnew, *Worlds Apart: The Market and the Theater in Anglo-American Thought, 1550–1750* (Cambridge: Cambridge University Press, 1986); David A. Hollinger, *In the American Province: Studies in the History and Historiography of Ideas* (Bloomington: Indiana University Press, 1985); Martin Jay, *Marxism and Totality: The Adventures of a Concept from Lukács to Habermas* (Berkeley: University of California Press, 1984); Peter Jelavich, *Munich and Theatrical Modernism: Politics, Playwriting and Performance, 1890–1914* (Cambridge, MA: Harvard University Press, 1985); LaCapra and Kaplan, *Modern European Intellectual History*; LaCapra, *Rethinking Intellectual History*; Dominick LaCapra, *History and Criticism* (Ithaca, NY: Cornell University Press, 1985); Allan Megill, *Prophets of Extremity: Nietzsche, Heidegger, Foucault, Derrida* (Berkeley: University of California Press, 1985); J. G. A. Pocock, *Virtue, Commerce and History: Essays on Political Thought and History, Chiefly in the Eighteenth Century* (Cambridge: Cambridge University Press, 1985); Mark Poster, *Foucault, Marxism, and History: Mode of Production Versus Mode of Information* (Cambridge: Blackwell, 1984); Richard Rorty, J. B. Schneewind, and Quentin Skinner, eds., *Philosophy in History* (Cambridge: Cambridge University Press, 1984); Quentin Skinner, ed., *The Return of Grand Theory in the Human Sciences* (Cambridge: Cambridge University Press, 1985).

46. Toews, "Intellectual History After the Linguistic Turn," 881.

47. Ibid., 899. Here Toews cites LaCapra, *Rethinking Intellectual History*, 15.

48. Toews, "Intellectual History After the Linguistic Turn," 884. Here Toews is referring to Roger Chartier, "Intellectual History or Sociocultural History? The French Trajectories," in *Modern European Intellectual History: Reappraisals and New Perspectives*, ed. Dominick LaCapra and Steven L. Kaplan (Ithaca, NY: Cornell University Press, 1982), 37–38.

49. Toews, "Intellectual History After the Linguistic Turn," 884.

50. Ibid., 906.

51. Ibid., 881. Toews cites William J. Bowsma, "Intellectual History in the 1980s: From History of Ideas to History of Meaning," *Journal of Interdisciplinary History* 12 (Autumn 1981): 290.

52. Lynn Hunt, ed., *The New Cultural History* (Berkeley: University of California Press, 1989), ix.

53. Kramer, "Literature, Criticism, and Historical Imagination."

54. Hunt, "Introduction," 16.

55. Ibid., 10.

56. Patricia O'Brien, "Michel Foucault's History of Culture," in *The New Cultural History*, ed. Lynn Hunt (Berkeley: University of California Press, 1989), 25–46, 9, 46.

57. Kramer, "Literature, Criticism, and Historical Imagination," 100. A cursory glance at the title of Allan Megill's *Prophets of Extremity: Nietzsche, Heidegger, Foucault, Derrida* might also give one the same impression.

58. See Michel Foucault, *Discipline and Punish* (New York: Vintage, 1995).

59. Hunt, "Introduction," 14.

60. Ibid., 15.

61. Ibid., 18.

62. Ibid., 18–19.

63. Jane Caplan, "Postmodernism, Poststructuralism, and Deconstruction: Notes for Historians," *Central European History* 22, no. 3/4 (1989): 260–78, 267.

64. Ibid., 270.

65. Caplan certainly recognizes the ways that deconstruction indicts the project of history, and she echoes the anxieties of earlier thinkers: "There remains, however, a basic anxiety for historians in the face of deconstruction: namely that, in making the text ultimately undecidable, it abolishes the ground for privileging any one interpretation, and therefore makes the writing of conventional history impossible. . . . It may be that here we have to concede deconstruction's ability to discern the paralogies or guilty secrets on which our own practices depend. A deconstructive critique of the historian's practice would point out that it represses what it has in common with its ostensible object, in order to create the illusion of its difference both from literary writing and the real" ("Postmodernism, Poststructuralism, and Deconstruction," 272). Caplan cites White and LaCapra to make this claim.

66. Partner, "Narrative Persistence," 87.

67. See Carl Schmitt, *The Concept of the Political,* trans. George Schwab (Chicago: University of Chicago Press, 1996).

68. In this same year, 1989, Derrida's work turned overtly toward the political in his talk "Force of Law: The 'Mystical Foundations of Authority,'" presented at the Cardozo Law School. In response to Fukuyama's conjuring of the ghost of Kojève, Derrida conjured the specter of Marx in his most "historical" work presented as a lecture at UC Riverside in 1993 and then published as *Spectres de Marx* in 1993. For an investigation into Derrida's move into the "political" see David Bates, "Crisis Between the Wars: Derrida and the Origins of Undecidability," *Representations* 90, no. 1 (2005): 1–27.

69. See Joan Scott, *Gender and the Politics of History* (New York: Columbia University Press, 1988), 6–7.

70. John M. Ellis, *Against Deconstruction* (Princeton, NJ: Princeton University Press, 1989); the Cook Lectures are included in G. R. Elton, *Return to Essentials: Some Reflections on the Present State of Historical Study* (Cambridge: Cambridge University Press, 1991).

71. Joan Scott, "The Evidence of Experience," repr. in *Practicing History: New*

Directions in Historical Writing After the Linguistic Turn, ed. Gabrielle M. Spiegel (New York: Routledge, 2005), 199–216, 201; originally published in *Critical Inquiry* 17, no. 4 (1991): 773–97.

72. Ibid., 201.

73. Ibid., 202.

74. Ibid., 203, 205; see also Derrida, *Positions*, 51, 57.

75. Scott, "The Evidence of Experience," 205 (my emphasis).

76. Joyce Appleby, Lynn Hunt, and Margaret Jacob, *Telling the Truth About History* (New York: Norton, 1994), 205.

77. Ibid., 207.

78. Ibid.

79. Ibid., 208.

80. Ibid., 210.

81. In 1987 it was revealed that one of the chief proponents of deconstruction in the United States, Paul de Man, had written for the collaborationist press in Belgium between 1941 and 1942. See Alan B. Spitzer, *Historical Truth and Lies About the Past* (Chapel Hill: University of North Carolina Press, 1996), 62. Derrida's own problematic defense of de Man also brought back the argument presented by Faye about the ways that Derrida and deconstruction were tainted by the influence of Heidegger and National Socialism. The Paul de Man affair was soon followed by the English translation of Victor Farías's *Heidegger and Nazism* (Philadelphia: Temple University Press, 1989), which brought the issue to an incendiary level.

82. Appleby, Hunt, Jacob, *Telling the Truth About History*, 237.

83. This is annunciated in Keith Windschuttle, *The Killing of History: How Literary Critics and Social Theorists Are Murdering Our Past* (New York: Free Press, 1996); Richard J. Evans's *In Defense of History* (New York: Norton, 1997); and Georg Iggers, *Historiography in the Twentieth Century: From Scientific Objectivity to the Postmodern Challenge* (Middletown, CT: Wesleyan University Press, 1997).

84. Victoria E. Bonnell and Lynn Hunt, eds., *Beyond the Cultural Turn: New Directions in the Study of Society and Culture* (Berkeley: University of California Press, 1999), 5.

85. Ibid., 4.

86. Ibid., 3.

87. Jerrold Seigel, "Problematizing the Self," in *Beyond the Cultural Turn: New Directions in the Study of Society and Culture*, ed. Victoria E. Bonnell and Lynn Hunt (Berkeley: University of California Press, 1999), 281–314, 284.

88. Hayden White, "Afterword," in *Beyond the Cultural Turn: New Directions in the Study of Society and Culture*, ed. Victoria E. Bonnell and Lynn Hunt (Berkeley: University of California Press, 1999), 315.

89. Ibid., 316.

90. These issues were discussed in *Rethinking History* 8, no. 4 (2004).

91. David Gary Shaw, "Happy in Our Chains? Agency and Language in the Postmodern Age," in "Agency After Postmodernism," theme issue, *History and Theory* 40, no. 4 (2001): 1–9, 2.

92. Ibid., 4.

93. Ibid., 7. One interesting aspect of the theme issue is the way many of the authors rely on the volumes by Hunt, *Telling the Truth About History*, and the review article by Toews.

94. Jacques Derrida, *Archive Fever: A Freudian Impression*, trans. Eric Prenowitz (Chicago: University of Chicago Press, 1996); originally published as *Mal d'archive* (Paris: Galilée, 1995). Page citations refer to the English translation.

95. Carolyn Steedman, "Something She Called a Fever: Michelet, Derrida, and Dust," *American Historical Review* 106, no. 4 (2001): 1159–80, 1164.

96. Ibid., 1159.

97. Yosef Hayim Yerushalmi, *Freud's Moses: Judaism Terminable and Interminable* (New Haven, CT: Yale University Press, 1991).

98. Steedman, "Something She Called a Fever," 1160, 1162.

99. We will explore these past possibles and possible pasts in Chapter 5.

100. Steedman, "Something She Called a Fever," 1164.

101. Ibid., 1168.

102. See LaCapra, *History in Transit: Experience, Identity, Critical Theory* (Ithaca, NY: Cornell University Press, 2004), 32–33n18.

103. Steedman, "Something She Called a Fever," 1176.

104. Bruno Latour, "Why Has Critique Run Out of Steam? From Matters of Fact to Matters of Concern," *Critical Inquiry* 30, no. 2 (2004): 225–48, 225.

105. Ibid., 227.

106. Ibid., 228.

107. Ibid., 228–29.

108. Ibid., 230.

109. Ibid., 240.

110. Ibid., 232.

111. Ibid., 243.

112. Ibid., 243.

113. Ibid., 246.

114. White, *Tropics of Discourse*, 282.

115. Scott, "The Evidence of Experience," 201.

116. Derrida, *Positions*, 41–42.

117. See Derrida, *Archive Fever*, 67.

118. See Ernst Breisach, *On the Future of History: The Postmodern Challenge and Its Aftermath* (Chicago: University of Chicago Press, 2003); Martin Jay, *Songs of Experience* (Berkeley: University of California Press, 2005); Jerrold Sei-

gel, *The Idea of the Self: Thought and Experience in Western Europe Since the Seventeenth Century* (Cambridge: Cambridge University Press, 2005). On the last point see Dominick LaCapra, *History in Transit: Experience, Identity, Critical Theory* (Ithaca, NY: Cornell University Press, 2004), 2–8.

119. See Frank Ankersmit, *Sublime Historical Experience* (Stanford: Stanford University Press, 2005); Hans Gumbrecht, *Production of Presence* (Stanford: Stanford University Press, 2004); Eelco Runia, "Presence," *History and Theory* 45, no. 1 (2006): 1–29; and "On Presence," forum edited by Runia and Elizabeth J. Brouwer, *History and Theory* 45, no. 3 (2006): 305–74.

120. Benoît Peeters, *Derrida* (Paris: Flammarion, 2010); Edward Baring, *The Young Derrida and French Philosophy, 1945–1968* (Cambridge: Cambridge University Press, 2011). One could also look to François Cusset's *French Theory: How Foucault, Derrida, Deleuze, and Co. Transformed the Intellectual Life of the United States,* trans. Jeff Fort (Minneapolis: University of Minnesota Press, 2003); and Andrew Dunstall, "Adventure, Schema, Supplement: Jacques Derrida and the Philosophy of History" (PhD diss., Macquarie University, 2011).

121. Edward Baring, "Ne me raconte plus d'histoires: Derrida and the Problem of the History of Philosophy," *History and Theory* 53 (May 2014): 175–93.

122. Ibid., 178.

123. Gabrielle Spiegel, "The Task of the Historian," *American Historical Review* 114, no. 1 (2009): 1–15.

124. Ibid., 5–6. See also Gabrielle M. Spiegel, "Revising the Past/Revisiting the Present: How Change Happens in Historiography," in "Revision in History," theme issue, *History and Theory* 46, no. 4 (2007): 1–19.

125. Spiegel, "The Task of the Historian," 4. Spiegel quotes from Walter Benjamin's *Gesammelte Schriften,* ed. Rolf Tiedemann and Hermann Schweppenhäuser, 7 vols. (Frankfurt am Main: Suhrkamp, 1972–89), 1: pt. 3, 1238; but also from Daniel Heller-Roazen's introduction to Giorgio Agamben, *Potentialities,* ed. and trans. Daniel Heller-Roazen (Stanford: Stanford University Press, 1999), 1. The Hofmannsthal quote is from *Der Tor und der Tod* (1893).

126. Spiegel, "The Task of the Historian," 3.

127. Roth, "Ebb Tide," 66.

128. Partner, "Narrative Persistence," 82.

129. Schelling quoted by Freud in "The 'Uncanny,'" 224.

130. Freud, "The 'Uncanny,'" 245.

Chapter 2

1. Charles Dickens, *"A Christmas Carol" and Other Stories* (New York: Modern Library, 1995), 5.

2. Ibid., 33. We will return to this cap presently.

3. Ibid., 80.

4. Ibid., 53.

5. Hans Gumbrecht, *Production of Presence: What Meaning Cannot Convey* (Stanford: Stanford University Press, 2004), xv.

6. Eelco Runia, "Presence," *History and Theory* 45, no. 1 (2006): 1–29, 5.

7. See Eelco Runia, "Spots of Time," *History and Theory* 45, no. 3 (2006): 305–16, 306.

8. See Ewa Domanska, "The Material Presence of the Past," *History and Theory* 45, no. 3 (2006): 337–48; Gumbrecht, *Production of Presence*, xiii; Frank Ankersmit, *Sublime Historical Experience* (Stanford: Stanford University Press, 2005), 116.

9. Runia, "Presence," 5.

10. Gumbrecht, *Production of Presence*, 137.

11. This emphasis on linguistics also came at the expense of the speculative philosophy of history. See Runia, "Presence," 2–3.

12. Hans Gumbrecht, "Presence Achieved in Language," *History and Theory* 45, no. 3 (2006): 318.

13. Gumbrecht, *Production of Presence*, 7.

14. Runia, "Presence," 2.

15. Ankersmit, *Sublime Historical Experience*, 1.

16. Ibid., 10, 2.

17. Gumbrecht, *Production of Presence*, 106.

18. Domanska, "The Material Presence of the Past," 337.

19. Nancy Partner, "Narrative Persistence," in *Re-figuring Hayden White*, ed. Frank Ankersmit, Ewa Domańska, and Hans Kellner (Stanford: Stanford University Press, 2009), 82.

20. Michel Foucault has largely been absolved of this charge; the most recent accounts present his "latest" works as a return to agency and localized political engagement.

21. Ethan Kleinberg, "New Gods Swelling the Future Ocean," *History and Theory* 46, no. 3 (2007): 446–57, 457.

22. Runia, "Presence," 8; Runia, "Spots of Time," 307.

23. Ankersmit, *Sublime Historical Experience*, 77. Here, too, the argument is presented in language that evokes an era of anxiety over the ability to determine friend from foe or right from wrong as Ankersmit continues: "One could argue that in the days of logical positivism it was at least clear who was friend or foe. And we lost even this with Rorty, Derrida, and Gadamer" (77).

24. Runia, "Presence," 1; see also Gumbrecht, *Production of Presence*, 47–49; and Ankersmit, *Sublime Historical Experience*, 77–80.

25. Runia, "Presence," 4–5.

26. Ibid.; see also Gumbrecht, *Production of Presence*, 107–11.

27. Runia, "Spots of Time," 306.

28. Runia, "Presence," 6. For a substantive investigation into the use of and problems with the trope of metonymy, see Anita Kasabova, "Memory, Memorials and Commemoration," *History and Theory* 47, no. 3 (2008): 331–50.

29. Runia, "Presence," 8.

30. Ibid., 8–9. This investigation into the surface seems akin to Foucault's archaeological methodology best embodied in *Les mots et les choses* but as modified in service of his genealogical project to present a "history of the present" in *Discipline and Punishment.* This is certainly the case in Gumbrecht's presentation of presence; see Gumbrecht, *Production of Presence*, 38–39.

31. Runia, "Presence," 9 (my emphasis).

32. Ibid., 20.

33. Ibid., 13.

34. F. R. Ankersmit, "'Presence' and Myth," *History and Theory* 45, no. 3 (2006): 328–36, 329.

35. Eelco Runia, "'Forget About It': 'Parallel Processing' in the Srebrenica Report," *History and Theory* 43, no. 3 (2004): 295–320.

36. The term *presence* does appear in the article but in terms of the Dutch mandate to its battalions to "deter by acts of presence" (315–19). It would be equally interesting to explore the relation of Runia's book *Waterloo, Verdun, Auschwitz: Deliqidatie van hat verleden* (Amsterdam: Meulenhoff, 1999) in relation to the evolution of "presence" as a historical category. It is also of note that Ankersmit employs aspects of this work in his *Sublime Historical Experience*. See Ankersmit, *Sublime Historical Experience*, 143–44, 165–66.

37. Runia, "'Forget About It,'" 295.

38. LaCapra, cited in Runia, "'Forget About It,'" 297; originally found in Dominick LaCapra, *Writing History, Writing Trauma* (Baltimore: Johns Hopkins University Press, 2001), 142. It is also worth noting Runia's indictment of "trauma studies" as the "busiest and liveliest speak-easy" of speculative philosophy of history (Runia, "Presence," 4).

39. H. K. Gediman and F. Wolkenfeld, "The Parallelism Phenomenon in Psychoanalysis and Supervision: Its Reconsideration as a Triadic System," *Psychoanalytic Quarterly* 49, no. 2 (1980): 234–55, 234. Runia cites this article.

40. Runia, "'Forget About It,'" 299–300.

41. Ibid., 310.

42. Ethan Kleinberg, "Freud and Levinas: Talmud and Psychoanalysis Before the Letter," in *The Jewish World of Sigmund Freud* (Jefferson, NC: McFarland, 2010), 112–25.

43. Sigmund Freud, *Moses and Monotheism*, trans. Katherine Jones (New York: Vintage, 1967), 113; Richard J. Bernstein, *Freud and the Legacy of Moses* (Cambridge: Cambridge University Press, 1998), 40–41. Bernstein uses the Strachey translation: "Fate had brought the great deed and misdeed of primeval days, the

killing of the father, closer to the Jewish people by causing them to repeat it on the person of Moses, an outstanding father figure."

44. Kleinberg, "Freud and Levinas"; see also Brad S. Gregory, "The Other Confessional History: On Secular Bias in the Study of Religion," in "Religion and History," theme issue, *History and Theory* 45, no. 4 (2006): 132–49. I will address the relation of religion and history in Chapter 4.

45. On this point see Gumbrecht's discussion of "real presence" and transubstantiation in Gumbrecht, *Production of Presence*, 145; and Ankersmit's discussion of the "aura" in Ankersmit, *Sublime Historical Experience*, 115–16.

46. On this point see Jacques Derrida, "*Ousia* and *Grammē*: Note on a Note from *Being and Time*," in Jacques Derrida, *Margins of Philosophy*, trans. Alan Bass (Chicago: University of Chicago Press, 1982); for a discussion of Derrida in relation to "presence" see Berber Bevernage, "Time, Presence, and Historical Injustice," *History and Theory* 47, no. 2 (2008): 149–67.

47. Sigmund Freud, "A Note upon the 'Mystic Writing Pad,'" in *The Standard Edition of the Complete Psychological Works of Sigmund Freud*, trans. and ed. James Strachey, 24 vols. (London: Hogarth, 1953–74), 19:227–34.

48. Ibid., 228–29.

49. Ibid., 229.

50. Ibid., 228.

51. Ibid., 230.

52. Ibid., 231 (my emphasis).

53. Sigmund Freud, "Beyond the Pleasure Principle," in *The Standard Edition of the Complete Psychological Works of Sigmund Freud*, trans. and ed. James Strachey, 24 vols. (London: Hogarth, 1953–74), 18:28.

54. Jacques Derrida, "Freud and the Scene of Writing," in *Writing and Difference*, trans. Alan Bass (Chicago: University of Chicago Press, 1978), 215; originally published as "Freud et la scène de l'écriture," in *L'écriture et la différence* (Paris: Seuil, 1967).

55. See Martin Hägglund, *Radical Atheism: Derrida and the Time of Life* (Stanford: Stanford University Press, 2008), 3.

56. In response to this paper Dominick LaCapra suggests that what is common to Freud, Heidegger, and Derrida is the notion that past, present, and future mark one another and are mutually implicated. Thus, it might make sense to relate the uncanny to the return of the repressed, whereby the past returns to haunt the present without being reducible to a pure presence (although Heidegger does not have an explicit, worked-out notion of the unconscious). Furthermore, for Derrida space itself is not opposed to time but mutually implicated with it in the very process of spacing, which takes time.

57. It strikes me that this is probable, given that Runia suggests that all of the

past is literally accessible in the "storehouse of presence." On this point see Kasabova, "Memory, Memorials and Commemoration."

58. Runia, "Presence," 9 (my emphasis).

59. And where one finds the uncanny, the ghost is not far behind. See Gediman and Wolkenfeld, "The Parallelism Phenomenon in Psychoanalysis and Supervision," 234–35.

60. Ibid., 237 (my emphasis).

61. Ankersmit, *Sublime Historical Experience*, 115.

62. Runia, "Spots of Time," 308.

63. Dickens, *"A Christmas Carol" and Other Stories*, 77.

64. Ibid., 78.

65. Runia, "Presence," 19.

66. Dickens, *"A Christmas Carol" and Other Stories*, 6.

67. Except for the perverse notion that the only reason Hamlet's father would do such a thing is "literally to astonish his son's weak mind" (i.e., to drive him mad).

68. Emmanuel Levinas, *Existence and Existents*, trans. Alphonso Lingis (Pittsburgh: Duquesne University Press, 1988), 56; see also Ethan Kleinberg, *Generation Existential: Heidegger's Philosophy in France, 1927–1961* (Ithaca, NY: Cornell University Press, 2005), 245–58.

69. Levinas, *Existence and Existents*, 71.

70. Ibid., 80–81.

71. Gumbrecht, *Production of Presence*, 117.

72. Here one might consider that the appropriate model for Ankersmit's "historical kiss" (125) is not Romeo and Juliet but the Grand Inquisitor and Jesus in Fyodor Dostoevsky's *The Brothers Karamazov* because of the incommunicable nature of the gesture. See Ankersmit, *Sublime Historical Experience*, 115–16, 121–28; see also Roth, "Ebb Tide," 66–73.

Chapter 3

1. Franz Kafka, *Selected Short Stories of Franz Kafka* (New York: Modern Library, 1952), 129–30.

2. Dominick LaCapra, *History and Its Limits: Human, Animal, Violence* (Ithaca, NY: Cornell University Press, 2009), 30.

3. See ibid., 28.

4. Reinhart Koselleck, *Futures Past: On the Semantics of Historical Time*, trans. Keith Tribe (New York: Columbia University Press, 2004), 134–35; Reinhart Koselleck, *Vergangene Zukunft: Zur Semantik geschichtlicher Zeiten* (Frankfurt am Main: Suhrkamp, 1979), 184–86.

5. Chladenius, *Einleitung zur richtigen Auslegung vernünfftiger Reden und Schriften* (Leipzig: Friedrich Landischens Erben, 1742), §307. My translations of

Chladenius are for the most part in keeping with those of Kurt Mueller-Vollmer, Martha Woodmansee, and Frederick C. Beiser.

6. Ibid., §308.

7. Koselleck, *Futures Past*, 128; *Vergangene Zukunft*, 176.

8. Koselleck, *Futures Past*, 128; *Vergangene Zukunft*, 176.

9. Chladenius, *Einleitung*, §309.

10. Ibid., §313.

11. Ibid., §318. See also Frederick C. Beiser, *The German Historicist Tradition* (Oxford: Oxford University Press, 2011), 48.

12. Chladenius, *Allgemeine Geschichtswissenschaft* (Leipzig: Friedrich Landischens Erben, 1752), chap. 1, §§4, 13.

13. Ibid., §17.

14. See Beiser, *The German Historicist Tradition*, 20.

15. Chladenius, *Einleitung*, §§318–19.

16. Chladenius, *Allgemeine Geschichtswissenschaft*, chap. 6, §1.

17. Beiser, *The German Historicist Tradition*, 50.

18. Chladenius, *Einleitung*, §156.

19. See Beiser, *The German Historicist Tradition*, 52.

20. Chladenius, *Einleitung*, §156.

21. Ibid., §§155, 176.

22. Horst Walter Blanke, Dirk Fleischer, and Jörn Rüsen, "Theory of History in Historical Lectures: The German Tradition of *Historik*, 1750–1900," *History and Theory* 23, no. 3 (1984): 331–56, 340. See also Peter Hans Reill, *The German Enlightenment and the Rise of Historicism* (Berkeley: University of California Press, 1975), 43, 105.

23. Chladenius, *Allgemeine Geschichtswissenschaft*, 20.

24. Peter Szondi, *Introduction to Literary Hermeneutics*, trans. Martha Woodmansee (Cambridge: Cambridge University Press, 1995), 55–56.

25. Beiser, *The German Historicist Tradition*, 42.

26. Chladenius, *Einleitung*, §179.

27. Szondi, *Introduction to Literary Hermeneutics*, 25.

28. Jacques Derrida, *Voice and Phenomenon*, trans. Leonard Lawlor (Evanston, IL: Northwestern University Press, 2011), 20 (translation modified); originally published as *La voix et le phénomène* (Paris: Presses universitaires de France, 1967). Page citations refer to the English translation.

29. Chladenius, *Einleitung*, §674.

30. Ibid., §675.

31. Ibid., §677.

32. Ibid.

33. Ibid., §690.

34. Szondi, *Introduction to Literary Hermeneutics*, 34.

35. Chladenius, *Einleitung*, §675.

36. Szondi, *Introduction to Literary Hermeneutics*, 31.

37. Chladenius, *Einleitung*, §690.

38. Ibid., §691.

39. Ibid.

40. Szondi, *Introduction to Literary Hermeneutics*, 33.

41. Jacques Derrida, "Signature Event Context," in *Limited Inc*, trans. Samuel Weber and Jeffrey Mehlman (Evanston, IL: Northwestern University Press, 1988), 1–23, 15; originally published as "Signature Événement Contexte," in *Marges de la philosophie* (Paris: Minuit, 1972).

42. See Szondi, *Introduction to Literary Hermeneutics*, 32.

43. Jacques Derrida, "Différance," in *Margins of Philosophy*, trans. Alan Bass (Chicago: University of Chicago Press, 1982), 1–27, 9; originally published as "Différance," in *Marges de la philosophie* (Paris: Minuit, 1972). Page citations refer to the English translation.

44. Derrida, "Différance," 9.

45. Chladenius, *Einleitung*, §707.

46. Ibid., §324.

47. Kerwin Lee Klein, *From History to Theory* (Berkeley: University of California Press, 2011), 22–25.

48. Peter Novick, *That Noble Dream: The "Objectivity Question" and the American Historical Profession* (Cambridge: Cambridge University Press, 1988), 30.

49. Klein, *From History to Theory*, 22; Novick, *That Noble Dream*, 31; Hayden White, "Review of *Historik*, by Johann Gustav Droysen," *History and Theory* 19, no. 1 (1980): 73–93, 90.

50. Johann Gustav Droysen, *Historik: Vorlesungen über Enzyklopädie und Methodologie der Geschichte*, ed. Rudolph Hübner (Munich: R. Oldenbourg, 1957), 287.

51. Droysen, *Historik*, ed. Peter Leyh (Stuttgart: Fromann-Holzboog, 1977), 236. In the Leyh version the passage in question reads: "*Die objective Unparteilichkeit . . . ist unmenschlich. Menschlich ist es viehlmehr, parteiisch zu sein.*"

52. See, e.g., Droysen, *Historik*, 18, 28, 35. See also Felix Gilbert, "The New Edition of Johann Gustav Droysen's *Historik*," *Journal of the History of Ideas* 44, no. 2 (1983): 327–36, 332–33; and Beiser, *The German Historicist Tradition*, 303.

53. White, "Review of *Historik*," 80–81.

54. Droysen, *Historik*, 325, §5; Johann Gustav Droysen, *Outlines of the Principles of History*, trans. E. Benjamin Andrews (Boston: Ginn, 1893), 11, §5.

55. Droysen, *Historik*, 332, §19.

56. See Beiser, *The German Historicist Tradition*, 302.

57. The passage from Droysen reads: "Nach den Objecten und nach der Natur des menschlichen Denkens sind die drei möglichen wissenschaftlichen

Methoden: Die philosophisch oder theologisch spekulativ, die physickalische (mathematisch-physickalische), die historische. Ihr Wesen ist: zu erkennen, zu erklären, zu verstehen." Droysen, *Historik*, 330, §14.

58. Ibid., 328, §8.

59. Ibid., 326, §6; Droysen, *Outlines of the Principles of History*, 11, §6.

60. Droysen, *Historik*, 287, §91.

61. White, "Review of *Historik*," 84.

62. Droysen, *Historik*, 332–33, §21; Droysen, *Outlines of the Principles of History*, 18, §21.

63. Droysen, *Historik*, 334, §25; Droysen, *Outlines of the Principles of History*, 20, §25.

64. See Beiser, *The German Historicist Tradition*, 311. Droysen, *Historik*, 144, §35.

65. Droysen, *Historik*, 336–37, §§30, 31, 32; Droysen, *Outlines of the Principles of History*, 22–23, §§30, 31, 32.

66. Beiser, *The German Historicist Tradition*, 309.

67. Droysen, *Historik*, 153, §38; see also Kurt Mueller-Vollmer, ed., *The Hermeneutics Reader* (New York: Continuum, 1985), 127.

68. Droysen, *Historik*, 154, §38; Mueller-Vollmer, *The Hermeneutics Reader*, 127.

69. Droysen, *Historik*, 335, §28; Droysen, *Outlines of the Principles of History*, 21–22, §28.

70. Droysen, *Historik*, 154, §38; Mueller-Vollmer, *The Hermeneutics Reader*, 127.

71. Droysen, *Historik*, 155–56, §38; Mueller-Vollmer, *The Hermeneutics Reader*, 129.

72. Droysen, *Historik*, 156, §38; Mueller-Vollmer, *The Hermeneutics Reader*, 129.

73. White, "Review of *Historik*," 80.

74. Ibid., 79.

75. Droysen, *Historik*, 327, §6; Droysen, *Outlines of the Principles of History*, 11, §6.

76. It should be noted that while Derrida appropriates the German term *Spur* for "trace," Droysen actually uses the German word *Scheine* that Andrews translated as "trace." The connection works if one thinks of *scheinen* as slightly unsure of the appearance it purportedly represents or as emitting a "light" that is representative but not actually the object itself as in banknotes or train tickets.

77. Droysen, *Historik*, 330–31, §15; Droysen, *Outlines of the Principles of History*, 15–16, §15.

78. This is a variation on the position held by Hegel. See G. W. F. Hegel, *Grundlinien der Philosophie des Rechts*, "Die Sittlichkeit," §§144–47, *Werkausgabe* 7:293–96. See also Beiser, *The German Historicist Tradition*, 303.

79. Droysen, *Historik*, 357, §83; Droysen, *Outlines of the Principles of History*, 48, §83.

80. Droysen, *Historik*, 356, §80; Droysen, *Outlines of the Principles of History*, 46–47, §80.

81. Droysen, *Historik*, 356, §81; Droysen, *Outlines of the Principles of History*, 47, §81.

82. Droysen, *Historik*, 346, §48; Droysen, *Outlines of the Principles of History*, 34, §48.

83. Gilbert, "The New Edition of Johann Gustav Droysen's *Historik*," 335.

84. White, "Review of *Historik*," 92.

85. Gilbert, "The New Edition of Johann Gustav Droysen's *Historik*," 336; Blanke, Fleischer, and Rüsen, "Theory of History in Historical Lectures," 350. See also Allan Megill, "Jörn Rüsen's Theory of Historiography Between Modernism and Rhetoric of Inquiry," *History and Theory* 33, no. 1 (1994): 39–60, esp. 44, 52. It is important to note that Rüsen substitutes the Kuhnian notion of paradigm change for the Hegelian notion of historical progress. Thus, he conserves the essential notion of transformation but releases the teleological necessity. The rationality of social science replaces the theological trajectory of spirit or mind. Megill relates this to Habermas's notion of the public sphere as the site of rational discourse (52). For Rüsen it is historical universals that hold rather than the "moral world." But here the progressive notion does not actually account for the "empirical" or definite presentation of the past but only our current condition of historical understanding. Less-sophisticated variants of ontological realism continue to stand on this ground.

86. See Friedrich Jaeger, *Bürgerliche Modernisierungskrise und historische Sinnbildung: Kulturgeschichte bei Droysen, Burckhardt und Max Weber* (Göttingen: Vandenhoeck and Ruprecht, 1994), 11. In Georg Iggers's review of Jaeger in *American Historical Review* 100, no. 3 (1995): 915–16, Iggers points out that Jaeger's sympathetic study of how Droysen was modernized contains "elements of a devastating critique" of recent appropriations of Droysen. "A good deal of the recent literature has uncritically portrayed Droysen as the mastermind who placed modern historical scholarship on a firm theoretical basis." Jaeger stresses the extent to which Droysen uncritically accepted the complacent worldview of his time.

87. White, "Review of *Historik*," 92.

88. Droysen, *Historik*, 326, §6; Droysen, *Outlines of the Principles of History*, 11, §6.

89. Derrida, "Différance," 5–6.

90. Ibid., 6, 3, 7.

91. Ibid., 7.

92. See Chapter 1, 51–52.

93. Droysen, *Historik*, 358, §88; Droysen, *Outlines of the Principles of History*, 50, §88.

94. Droysen, *Historik*, 358, §88; Droysen, *Outlines of the Principles of History*,

50, §88. We will take up the issue of our understanding of the "present" in relation to the "past" in the following chapter.

95. Droysen, *Historik*, 149, §37; Mueller-Vollmer, *The Hermeneutics Reader*, 124; Derrida, "Différance," 6.

96. Droysen, *Historik*, 149, §37; Mueller-Vollmer, *The Hermeneutics Reader*, 124.

97. Droysen, *Historik*, 149, §37; Mueller-Vollmer, *The Hermeneutics Reader*, 124.

98. Droysen, *Historik*, 150, §37; Mueller-Vollmer, *The Hermeneutics Reader*, 125.

99. In Derrida the passage reads: "Now if différance is (and I also cross out the 'is') what makes possible the presentation of the being-present, it is never presented as such. It is never offered to the present." Derrida, "Différance," 6.

100. Ibid., 15.

101. The language of retention and protention is Husserlian and well described by Maurice Merleau-Ponty in his *Phenomenology of Perception*:

Husserl uses the terms protentions and retentions for the intentionalities which anchor me to an environment. They do not run from a central I, but from my perceptual field itself, so to speak, which draws along in its wake its own horizon of retentions, and bites into the future with its protentions. I do not pass through a series of instances of now, the images of which I preserve and which, placed end to end, make a line. With the arrival of every moment, its predecessor undergoes a change: I still have it in hand and it is still there, but already it is sinking away below the level of presents; in order to retain it, I need to reach through a thin layer of time. It is still the preceding moment, and I have the power to rejoin it as it was just now; I am not cut off from it, but still it would not belong to the past unless something had altered, unless it were beginning to outline itself against, or project itself upon, my present, whereas a moment ago it was my present. When a third moment arrives, the second undergoes a new modification; from being a retention it becomes the retention of a retention, and the layer of time between it and me thickens. (Maurice Merleau-Ponty, *Phenomenology of Perception*, trans. Colin Smith [New York: Routledge Classics, 2002], 483–84; originally published as *Phénoménologie de la perception* [Paris: Gallimard, 1945], 476)

102. Derrida, "Différance," 16.

103. Derrida, *Limited Inc*, 5.

104. Droysen, *Historik*, 151, 332, §19; Mueller-Vollmer, *The Hermeneutics Reader*, 125; Droysen, *Outlines of the Principles of History*, 17, §19.

105. Droysen, *Historik*, 151, §37; Mueller-Vollmer, *The Hermeneutics Reader*, 125.

106. Derrida, "Différance," 7.

107. Derrida, *Limited Inc*, 9.

108. Derrida, *Limited Inc*, 9. Derrida is referring to "writing," but because he

states that even an unknown or nonlinguistic code constituted in its mark by its iterability can be considered "writing," I take this to be applicable to Droysen's categories for historical research (sources/ *Quellen*, remains/ *Überreste*, monuments/ *Denkmäler*).

109. Ibid.

110. Droysen, *Historik*, 141, §34; Droysen, *Outlines of the Principles of History*, 24, §34.

111. Derrida, *Limited Inc*, 9.

112. Derrida, "Différance," 7.

113. Derrida, *Limited Inc*, 12.

114. Derrida, *Limited Inc*, 12.

115. Derrida, *Margins of Philosophy*, 24.

116. David Harlan, "Intellectual History and the Return of Literature," *American Historical Review* 94, no. 3 (1989): 581–609, 581.

117. David A. Hollinger, "The Return of the Prodigal: The Persistence of Historical Knowing," *American Historical Review* 94, no. 3 (1989): 610–21, 613.

118. David Harlan, "Reply to David Hollinger," *American Historical Review* 94, no. 3 (1989): 622–26, 625.

119. See my introduction, 1–2.

120. Martin Heidegger, *Being and Time*, trans. John Macquarrie and Edward Robinson (New York: Harper and Row, 1962), 449–50.

121. Michael Ermarth, *Wilhelm Dilthey: The Critique of Historical Reason* (Chicago: University of Chicago Press, 1978), 342. Dilthey's quote is on page 217 of vol. 16 of his *Gesammelte Schriften* (hereafter *GS*), 26 vols. (Göttingen:Vandenhock, 1923–2005).

122. Wilhelm Dilthey, *The Formation of the Historical World in the Human Sciences*, vol. 3 of *Selected Works*, ed. Rudolf A. Makkreel and Frithjof Rodi (Princeton, NJ: Princeton University Press, 2002), 297.

123. Dilthey, *Formation of the Historical World*, 215; Dilthey, *GS* 7:192–93.

124. Dilthey, *Formation of the Historical World*, 215; Dilthey, *GS* 7:193.

125. Dilthey, *Formation of the Historical World*, 215; Dilthey, *GS* 7:193.

126. Dilthey, *Formation of the Historical World*, 215–16; Dilthey, *GS* 7:193–194.

127. Wilhelm Dilthey, *Introduction to the Human Sciences*, vol. 1 of *Selected Works*, ed. Rudolf A. Makkreel and Frithjof Rodi (Princeton, NJ: Princeton University Press, 1991), 50; Dilthey, *GS* 1:xviii.

128. Dilthey, *Introduction to the Human Sciences*, 51; Dilthey, *GS* 1:xviii.

129. Dilthey, *Introduction to the Human Sciences*, 48; Dilthey, *GS* 1:xvi.

130. Wilhelm Dilthey, *Gesammelte Schriften* (Leipzig: Teubner, 1924), 5:281. See Charles Bambach, *Heidegger, Dilthey, and the Crisis of Historicism* (Ithaca, NY: Cornell University Press, 1995), 140.

131. Dilthey, *Introduction to the Human Sciences*, 500–501.

132. Hans-Georg Gadamer, *Kleine Schriften*, vol. 1 (Tübingen: Mohr, 1967), 4 (my translation).

133. Wilhelm Dilthey, *Pattern and Meaning in History: Thoughts on History and Society* (New York: Harper Torchbooks, 1962), 120; Dilthey, *GS* 7:208.

134. Jacques Derrida, *Voice and Phenomenon*, 46.

135. Martin Heidegger, *The Concept of Time*, trans. Ingo Farin (London: Continuum, 2011), 79–80.

136. Ermarth, *Wilhelm Dilthey*, 245.

137. Wilhelm Dilthey, *Hermeneutics and the Study of History*, vol. 4 of *Selected Works*, ed. Rudolf A. Makkreel and Frithjof Rodi (Princeton, NJ: Princeton University Press, 1996), 238; Dilthey, *GS* 5:329.

138. Dilthey, *Hermeneutics and the Study of History*, 250; Dilthey, *GS* 5:331.

139. See Bambach, *Heidegger, Dilthey, and the Crisis of Historicism*, 179.

140. Hans-Georg Gadamer, "The Problem of Historical Consciousness," *Graduate Faculty Philosophy Journal* 5, no. 1 (1975): 8–52, 30.

141. See Dilthey, *Formation of the Historical World*, 232; *GS* 7:211.

142. Dilthey, *Hermeneutics and the Study of History*, 389; *GS* 5:9.

143. Dilthey, *Formation of the Historical World*, 235; *GS* 7:215.

144. Dilthey, *Formation of the Historical World*, 217; *GS* 7:195.

145. Derrida, *Limited Inc*, 5.

146. Ibid., 6.

147. Dilthey, *Formation of the Historical World*, 235; *GS* 7:214.

148. Dilthey, *Formation of the Historical World*, 236–37; *GS* 7:215–16.

149. See Beiser, *The German Historicist Tradition*, 215–16.

150. See White, "Review of *Historik*," 80.

151. If Hegel remains in Dilthey's model, it is only in terms of a developing historical consciousness and not a teleology of progress.

152. Dilthey, *Hermeneutics and the Study of History*, 389; *GS* 5:9.

153. Ibid. (translation modified).

154. Yorck is here cited by Heidegger in *Being and Time*, 453–54; also in *The Concept of Time*, 9.

155. Derrida, *Archive Fever*, 67.

156. Derrida, *Limited Inc*, 9.

Chapter 4

1. Franz Kafka, *The Complete Stories* (New York: Schocken, 1971), 244–45.

2. I want to thank Adam Tooze for articulating this at the Yale "Philosophy of History" colloquium in March 2013.

3. Hayden White, *Tropics of Discourse: Essays in Cultural Criticism* (Baltimore: Johns Hopkins University Press, 1978), 122.

4. Paul Roth, "History and the Manifest Image: Hayden White as a Philosopher of History," *History and Theory* 52, no. 1 (2013): 130–43, 138.

5. See Alun Munslow, *The Routledge Companion to Historical Studies* (London: Routledge, 2000), 194–97.

6. Kafka, *The Complete Stories*, 242.

7. See my "Just the Facts: The Fantasy of a Historical Science," *History of the Present* 6, no. 1 (2016): 87–103.

8. Paula Findlen, "What Counts: On Books, Articles, and Productivity," *Perspectives on History*, Sept. 2013, www.historians.org/publications-and-directories/perspectives-on-history/september-2013/what-counts-on-books-articles-and-productivity.

9. Jonathan Sterne, "The Example: Some Historical Considerations," in *Between Humanities and the Digital*, ed. Patrik Svensson and David Theo Goldberg (Cambridge, MA: MIT Press, 2015), 17–33, 28.

10. Jacques Derrida, *Writing and Difference*, trans. Alan Bass (Chicago: University of Chicago Press, 1978), 278; originally published as *L'écriture et la différence* (Paris: Seuil, 1967).

11. Louis O. Mink, *Historical Understanding*, ed. Brian Fay, Eugene O. Golob, and Richard T. Vann (Ithaca, NY: Cornell University Press, 1987), 93.

12. Ibid.

13. Ibid., 56.

14. Ibid., 57.

15. Constantin Fasolt, "History and Religion in the Modern Age," *History and Theory* 45, no. 4 (2006): 10–26, 11.

16. Ibid., 15.

17. Ibid., 21.

18. Ibid., 24.

19. Reinhart Koselleck, *Futures Past: On the Semantics of Historical Time*, trans. Keith Tribe (New York: Columbia University Press, 2004), 21; Reinhart Koselleck, *Vergangene Zukunft: Zur Semantik geschichtlicher Zeiten* (Frankfurt am Main: Suhrkamp, 1979), 33.

20. David N. Myers, *Resisting History: Historicism and Its Discontents in German-Jewish Thought* (Princeton, NJ: Princeton University Press, 2003), 17.

21. Friedrich Kittler, *Gramophone, Film, Typewriter* (Stanford: Stanford University Press, 1999), 4.

22. See Hayden White, "The Fictions of Factual Representations," in *Tropics of Discourse: Essays in Cultural Criticism* (Baltimore: Johns Hopkins University Press, 1978), 121–34.

23. Gordon S. Wood, *The Purpose of the Past: Reflections on the Uses of History* (New York: Penguin, 2008), 60. To be fair, Wood does say that he regrets this sentence but only after telling us that most working historians "sensibly ignored

the business" of writing narrative history stirred up by the influence of Hayden White's *Metahistory*—that is, after assessing that the "peril" had passed. On this see Chapter 1.

24. Ibid.

25. Charles Dickens, *"A Christmas Carol" and Other Stories* (New York: Modern Library, 1995), 39.

26. Sigmund Freud, "The 'Uncanny,'" in *The Standard Edition of the Complete Psychological Works of Sigmund Freud*, trans. and ed. James Strachey, 24 vols. (London: Hogarth, 1955), 17:225.

27. Dickens, *"A Christmas Carol" and Other Stories*, 62.

28. Ibid., 63.

29. Martin Hägglund, *Radical Atheism: Derrida and the Time of Life* (Stanford: Stanford University Press, 2008), 3.

30. See Chapter 3, 104–6.

31. Jacques Derrida, "Différance," in *Margins of Philosophy*, trans. Alan Bass (Chicago: University of Chicago Press, 1982), 3; originally published as "Différance," in *Marges de la philosophie* (Paris: Minuit, 1972). Page citations refer to the English translation.

32. After stating that *Of Grammatology* and *Writing and Difference* might be seen as two facets of the same "work," each inscribed within the other, Derrida noted that "things cannot be reconstituted so easily, as you may well imagine." Jacques Derrida, *Positions*, trans. Alan Bass, 2nd ed. (New York: Continuum, 2002), 4; originally published as *Positions* (Paris: Minuit, 1972).

33. See Sterne, "The Example," 29.

34. Hägglund, *Radical Atheism*, 3.

35. Ibid.

36. Wilhelm Dilthey, *The Formation of the Historical World in the Human Sciences*, vol. 3 of *Selected Works*, ed. Rudolf A. Makkreel and Frithjof Rodi (Princeton, NJ: Princeton University Press, 2002), 215; *GS* 7:193.

37. Mink, *Historical Understanding*, 93.

38. Jacques Derrida, *Margins of Philosophy*, trans. Alan Bass (Chicago: University of Chicago Press, 1982), 39; originally published as *Marges de la philosophie* (Paris: Minuit, 1972). Page citations refer to the English translation.

39. Derrida, *Margins of Philosophy*, 57.

40. Ibid., 58.

41. Hägglund, *Radical Atheism*, 15.

42. Derrida, *Margins of Philosophy*, 59.

43. Jacques Derrida, "Freud and the Scene of Writing," in *Writing and Difference*, trans. Alan Bass (Chicago: University of Chicago Press, 1978), 211; originally published as "Freud et la scène de l'écriture," in *L'écriture et la différence* (Paris: Seuil, 1967).

44. Derrida, *Writing and Difference*, 230.

45. Derrida, *Margins of Philosophy*, 6.

46. Berber Bevernage, "The Past Is Evil/Evil Is the Past," *History and Theory* 54, no. 3 (2015): 333–52, 337.

47. Ibid.

48. Kafka, *The Complete Stories*, 242.

49. N. Katherine Hayles, *How We Think: Digital Media and Contemporary Technogenesis* (Chicago: University of Chicago Press, 2012), 1, 55–83.

50. Ibid., 99.

51. Ibid. See also Mark Bauerlein, *The Dumbest Generation: How the Digital Age Stupefies Americans* (New York: Penguin, 2008); and Nicholas Carr, *The Shallows: What the Internet Is Doing to Our Brains* (New York: Norton, 2010).

52. One might also reflect on the ways that the digital relies almost exclusively on binary oppositions.

53. Henri Bergson, *Matière et mémoire* (Paris: PUF, 1965); Catherine Malabou, *Que faire de notre cerveau* (Paris: Bayard, 2004).

54. Derrida, *Margins of Philosophy*, 21.

55. Jacques Derrida, "Signature Event Context," in *Limited Inc*, trans. Samuel Weber and Jeffrey Mehlman (Evanston, IL: Northwestern University Press, 1988), 3; originally published as "Signature Événement Contexte," in *Marges de la philosophie* (Paris: Minuit, 1972). Page citations refer to the English translation.

56. On this see Karen Barad, "Quantum Entanglements and Hauntological Relations of Inheritance: Dis/continuities, SpaceTime Enfoldings, and Justice-to-Come," *Derrida Today* 3, no. 2 (2010): 240–68.

57. Helge Jordheim, "Against Periodization: Koselleck's Theory of Multiple Temporalities," *History and Theory* 51, no. 2 (2012): 151–71.

58. See "Modernity and the Planes of Historicity," in Reinhart Koselleck, *Futures Past: On the Semantics of Historical Time*, trans. Keith Tribe (New York: Columbia University Press, 2004), 9–25; "Vergangene Zukunft der frühen Neuzeit," in Reinhart Koselleck, *Vergangene Zukunft: Zur Semantik geschichtlicher Zeiten* (Frankfurt am Main: Suhrkamp, 1979), 17–37.

59. Jordheim, "Against Periodization," 159.

60. Koselleck, *Futures Past*, 82; Koselleck, *Vergangene Zukunft*, 116.

61. Koselleck, *Futures Past*, 86; Koselleck, *Vergangene Zukunft*, 121.

62. Sterne, "The Example," 29.

Chapter 5

1. I want to thank my daughter Lili Kleinberg for leading me to this story.

2. Washington Irving, *The Legend of Sleepy Hollow* (New York: G. P. Putnam's Sons, 1899), 71.

3. Ibid., 89.

4. Ibid., 181–83.

5. Ibid., 37.

6. Ibid., 7–11.

7. Matthew Garret helped me think through this part of the text and come to this formulation.

8. Irving, *The Legend of Sleepy Hollow*, 13.

9. Ibid., 185–87.

10. Jacques Derrida, *Specters of Marx: The State of the Debt, the Work of Mourning and the New International*, trans. Peggy Kamuf (New York: Routledge, 2006), 10; originally published as *Spectres de Marx* (Paris: Galilée, 1993). Page citations refer to the English translation.

11. Ibid., 11.

12. Ibid., 61.

13. Ibid., 107.

14. Ibid., 110.

15. Ibid., 9.

16. Jacques Derrida, *Aporias: Dying—awaiting (one another at) the "limits of truth,"* trans. Thomas Dutoit (Stanford: Stanford University Press, 1993), 20; originally published as *Apories: Mourir—s'attendre aux "limites de la vérité"* (Paris: Galilée, 1996). Page citations refer to the English translation.

17. Derrida, *Aporias*, 20.

18. Ibid., 21.

19. Sarah Kofman, *Comment s'en sortir?* (Paris: Galilée, 1983), 18 (my translation).

20. Ibid.

21. Johann Gustav Droysen, *Historik: Vorlesungen über Enzyklopädie und Methodologie der Geschichte*, ed. Rudolph Hübner (Munich: R. Oldenbourg, 1957), 332–33, §21; Johann Gustav Droysen, *Outlines of the Principles of History*, trans. E. Benjamin Andrews (Boston: Ginn, 1893), 18, §21.

22. Jacques Derrida, "Différance," in *Margins of Philosophy*, trans. Alan Bass (Chicago: University of Chicago Press, 1982), 25; originally published as "Différance," in *Marges de la philosophie* (Paris: Minuit, 1972). Page citations refer to the English translation.

23. Kofman, *Comment s'en sortir?* 19–20.

24. E. P. Thompson, *The Making of the English Working Class* (New York: Vintage, 1966), 12.

25. Ibid.

26. Ibid., 9.

27. Ibid.

28. Jacques Derrida, *Voice and Phenomenon*, trans. Leonard Lawlor (Evanston,

IL: Northwestern University Press, 2011), 87–88; originally published as *La voix et le phénomène* (Paris: Presses universitaires de France, 1967).

29. As we saw in Chapter 1, one of the impetuses for the introduction of deconstruction into the field of history was the sense that social history itself had closed off other possible modes of investigation and that the field of intellectual history had to find a new path. See Chapter 1, 18–30; and Dominick LaCapra and Steven L. Kaplan, eds., *Modern European Intellectual History: Reappraisals and New Perspectives* (Ithaca, NY: Cornell University Press, 1982), 8.

30. Jacques Derrida, *Positions*, trans. Alan Bass, 2nd ed. (New York: Continuum, 2002), 41; originally published as *Positions* (Paris: Minuit, 1972). Page citations refer to the English translation.

31. Kofman, *Comment s'en sortir?* 49.

32. Ibid., 47–48.

33. Ibid., 49.

34. Derrida, "Différance," 11.

35. Ibid.

36. Ibid.

37. Droysen, *Historik*, 149; Kurt Mueller-Vollmer, ed., *The Hermeneutics Reader* (New York: Continuum, 1985), 124; Derrida, "Différance," 6.

38. I break slightly with Derrida because I see this as applicable to all "histories," be they written or oral, whereas Derrida draws a distinction between "written" and "oral" communication. I see the making present of the past via transmission as a form of "writing" and thus different from what Derrida describes as "oral communication." See Haun Saussy, *The Ethnography of Rhythm: Orality and Its Technologies* (New York: Fordham University Press, 2016).

39. Jacques Derrida, "Signature Event Context," in *Limited Inc*, trans. Samuel Weber and Jeffrey Mehlman (Evanston, IL: Northwestern University Press, 1988), 9; originally published as "Signature Événement Contexte," in *Marges de la philosophie* (Paris: Minuit, 1972). Page citations refer to the English translation.

40. Ibid.

41. Ibid.

42. Derrida, "Différance," 8.

43. Ibid., 6.

44. In Derrida the passage reads: "One can expose only that which at a certain moment can become *present*, manifest, that which can be shown, presented as something present, a being-present in its truth, in the truth of a present or the presence of the present. Now if *différance* is (and I also cross out the 'is') what makes possible the presentation of the being-present, it is never presented as such. It is never offered to the present." Derrida, "Différance," 6.

45. Jacques Derrida, *Writing and Difference*, trans. Alan Bass (Chicago: Uni-

versity of Chicago Press, 1978), 292; originally published as *L'écriture et la différence* (Paris: Seuil, 1967).

46. See Jacques Derrida, *Rogues: Two Essays on Reason*, trans. Pascale-Anne Brault and Michael Naas (Stanford: Stanford University Press, 2005), 35–36, 150, 152; originally published as *Voyous: Deux essais sur la raison* (Paris: Galilée, 2003).

47. Jacques Derrida, *Of Grammatology*, trans. Gayatri Chakravorty Spivak (Baltimore: Johns Hopkins University Press, 1997), 24 (translation modified); originally published as *De la grammatologie* (Paris: Minuit, 1967).

48. Derrida, *Positions*, 59.

49. Ibid., 41.

50. In a different format or mode one could imagine this work and the one on Levinas as parts of the same project. The Levinas book could be a part of this book to be included in or after this chapter. Likewise, this book, or parts of it, could serve as an introduction to the one on Levinas.

51. Brad Gregory, "The Other Confessional History: On Secular Bias in the Study of Religion," in "Religion and History," theme issue, *History and Theory* 45, no. 4 (2006): 132–49, 132.

52. Derrida, *Positions*, 42.

53. See Velcheru Narayana Rao, David Shulman, and Sanjay Subrahmanyam, *Textures of Time: Writing History in South India, 1600–1800* (New Delhi: Permanent Black, 2001); see also the forum about the book in *History and Theory* 46, no. 3 (2007). For a discussion of Nepalese chronicles see Axel Michaels, Manik Bajracharya, Niels Gutschow, Madeleine Herren, Bernd Schneidmüller, Gerald Schwedler, and Astrid Zotter, "Nepalese History in a European Experience: A Case Study in Transcultural Historiography," *History and Theory* 55, no. 2 (2016): 210–32.

54. Derrida, *Positions*, 42.

55. Ibid., 45.

Index

MERIDIAN

Crossing Aesthetics

Elizabeth Rottenberg, *Inheriting the Future: Legacies of Kant, Freud, and Flaubert*

David Michael Kleinberg-Levin, *Gestures of Ethical Life*

Jacques Derrida, *On Touching—Jean-Luc Nancy*

Jacques Derrida, *Rogues: Two Essays on Reason*

Peggy Kamuf, *Book of Addresses*

Giorgio Agamben, *The Time that Remains: A Commentary on the Letter to the Romans*

Jean-Luc Nancy, *Multiple Arts: The Muses II*

Alain Badiou, *Handbook of Inaesthetics*

Jacques Derrida, *Eyes of the University: Right to Philosophy 2*

Maurice Blanchot, *Lautréamont and Sade*

Giorgio Agamben, *The Open: Man and Animal*

Jean Genet, *The Declared Enemy*

Shosana Felman, *Writing and Madness: (Literature/Philosophy/Psychoanalysis)*

Jean Genet, *Fragments of the Artwork*

Shoshana Felman, *The Scandal of the Speaking Body: Don Juan with J. L. Austin, or Seduction in Two Languages*

Peter Szondi, *Celan Studies*

Neil Hertz, *George Eliot's Pulse*

Maurice Blanchot, *The Book to Come*

Susannah Young-ah Gottlieb, *Regions of Sorrow: Anxiety and Messianism in Hannah Arendt and W. H. Auden*

Jacques Derrida, *Without Alibi*, edited by Peggy Kamuf

Cornelius Castoriadis, *On Plato's 'Statesman'*

Jacques Derrida, *Who's Afraid of Philosophy? Right to Philosophy 1*

Peter Szondi, *An Essay on the Tragic*

Peter Fenves, *Arresting Language: From Leibniz to Benjamin*

Jill Robbins, ed. *Is It Righteous to Be?: Interviews with Emmanuel Levinas*

Louis Marin, *Of Representation*

Daniel Payot, *The Architect and the Philosopher*

J. Hillis Miller, *Speech Acts in Literature*

Maurice Blanchot, *Faux pas*

Jean-Luc Nancy, *Being Singular Plural*

Maurice Blanchot / Jacques Derrida, *The Instant of My Death / Demeure: Fiction and Testimony*

Niklas Luhmann, *Art as a Social System*

Emmanual Levinas, *God, Death, and Time*

Ernst Bloch, *The Spirit of Utopia*

Giorgio Agamben, *Potentialities: Collected Essays in Philosophy*

Ellen S. Burt, *Poetry's Appeal: French Nineteenth-Century Lyric and the Political Space*

Jacques Derrida, *Adieu to Emmanuel Levinas*

Werner Hamacher, *Premises: Essays on Philosophy and Literature from Kant to Celan*

Aris Fioretos, *The Gray Book*

Deborah Esch, *In the Event: Reading Journalism, Reading Theory*

Winfried Menninghaus, *In Praise of Nonsense: Kant and Bluebeard*

Giorgio Agamben, *The Man Without Content*

Giorgio Agamben, *The End of the Poem: Studies in Poetics*

Theodor W. Adorno, *Sound Figures*

Louis Marin, *Sublime Poussin*

Philippe Lacoue-Labarthe, *Poetry as Experience*

Ernst Bloch, *Literary Essays*

Jacques Derrida, *Resistances of Psychoanalysis*

Marc Froment-Meurice, *That Is to Say: Heidegger's Poetics*

Francis Ponge, *Soap*

Philippe Lacoue-Labarthe, *Typography: Mimesis, Philosophy, Politics*

Giorgio Agamben, *Homo Sacer: Sovereign Power and Bare Life*

Emmanuel Levinas, *Of God Who Comes to Mind*

Bernard Stiegler, *Technics and Time, 1: The Fault of Epimetheus*

Werner Hamacher, *pleroma—Reading in Hegel*

Serge Leclaire, *Psychoanalyzing: On the Order of the Unconscious and the Practice of the Letter*

Serge Leclaire, *A Child Is Being Killed: On Primary Narcissism and the Death Drive*

Sigmund Freud, *Writings on Art and Literature*

Cornelius Castoriadis, *World in Fragments: Writings on Politics, Society, Psychoanalysis, and the Imagination*

Thomas Keenan, *Fables of Responsibility: Aberrations and Predicaments in Ethics and Politics*

Emmanuel Levinas, *Proper Names*

Alexander García Düttmann, *At Odds with AIDS: Thinking and Talking About a Virus*

Maurice Blanchot, *Friendship*

Jean-Luc Nancy, *The Muses*

Massimo Cacciari, *Posthumous People: Vienna at the Turning Point*

David E. Wellbery, *The Specular Moment: Goethe's Early Lyric and the Beginnings of Romanticism*

Edmond Jabès, *The Little Book of Unsuspected Subversion*

Hans-Jost Frey, *Studies in Poetic Discourse: Mallarmé, Baudelaire, Rimbaud, Hölderlin*

Pierre Bourdieu, *The Rules of Art: Genesis and Structure of the Literary Field*

Nicolas Abraham, *Rhythms: On the Work, Translation, and Psychoanalysis*

Jacques Derrida, *On the Name*

David Wills, *Prosthesis*

Maurice Blanchot, *The Work of Fire*

Jacques Derrida, *Points . . . : Interviews, 1974–1994*

J. Hillis Miller, *Topographies*

Philippe Lacoue-Labarthe, *Musica Ficta (Figures of Wagner)*

Jacques Derrida, *Aporias*

Emmanuel Levinas, *Outside the Subject*

Jean-François Lyotard, *Lessons on the Analytic of the Sublime*

Peter Fenves, *"Chatter": Language and History in Kierkegaard*

Jean-Luc Nancy, *The Experience of Freedom*

Jean-Joseph Goux, *Oedipus, Philosopher*

Haun Saussy, *The Problem of a Chinese Aesthetic*

Jean-Luc Nancy, *The Birth to Presence*

Made in the USA
San Bernardino, CA
02 September 2017